Becoming Wild

Caitlin Press Inc.
8100 Alderwood Road,
Halfmoon Bay, BC V0N 1Y1
www.caitlin-press.com

Text and cover design by Vici Johnstone
Edited by Audrey McLellan
Copyedit by Kathleen Fraser
Cover photo copyright Vici Johnstone
Printed in Canada

Caitlin Press Inc. acknowledges financial support from the Government of Canada through the Canada Book Fund and the Canada Council for the Arts, and from the Province of British Columbia through the British Columbia Arts Council and the Book Publisher's Tax Credit.

Canada Council   Conseil des Arts
for the Arts   du Canada

BRITISH COLUMBIA
ARTS COUNCIL
We acknowledge the support of the Province of British Columbia
through the British Columbia Arts Council

Library and Archives Canada Cataloguing in Publication

Van Schyndel, Nikki, 1973-, author
       Becoming wild : living the primitive life on a west coast island
/ Nikki van Schyndel.

ISBN 978-1-927575-39-0 (bound)

       1. Van Schyndel, Nikki, 1973-. 2. Wilderness survival—British Columbia—Broughton Archipelago. 3. Women adventurers—British Columbia—Biography. I. Title.

GV191.52.V36A3 2014   796.5092   C2013-908454-1

BECOMING WILD

LIVING THE PRIMITIVE LIFE ON A WEST COAST ISLAND

NIKKI VAN SCHYNDEL

CAITLIN PRESS

For my mother. My guardian angel on Earth.

CONTENTS

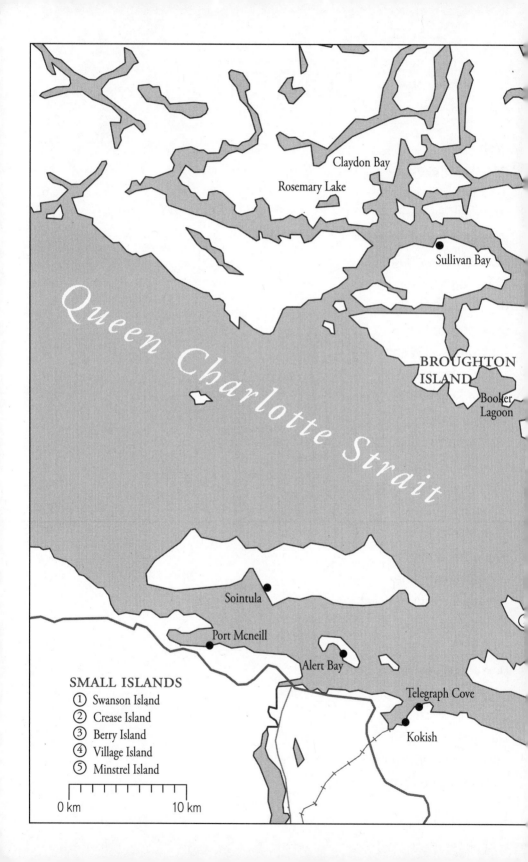

Claydon Bay

Rosemary Lake

Sullivan Bay

Queen Charlotte Strait

BROUGHTON
ISLAND

Booker
Lagoon

Sointula

Port Mcneill

Alert Bay

Telegraph Cove

Kokish

SMALL ISLANDS
① Swanson Island
② Crease Island
③ Berry Island
④ Village Island
⑤ Minstrel Island

0 km   10 km

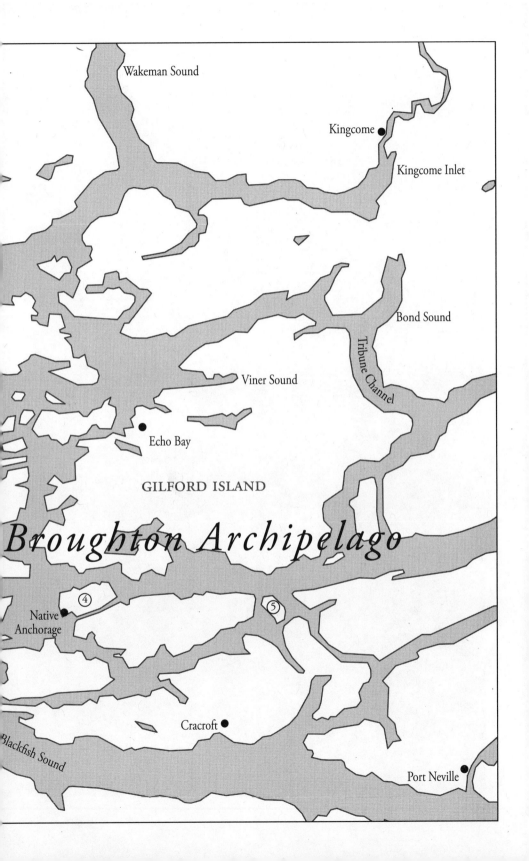

Wakeman Sound

Kingcome

Kingcome Inlet

Bond Sound

Tribune Channel

Viner Sound

Echo Bay

GILFORD ISLAND

Broughton Archipelago

④

⑤

Native
Anchorage

Blackfish Sound

Cracroft

Port Neville

MAYDAY DREAMS

It is only when we follow our dreams that we discover the magic within ourselves.

—Unknown

Journal Entry, Day 71
Here I am in the middle of nowhere, cross-legged in front of a fire, gnawing on bear ribs and sipping dandelion coffee—testing my skills of survival. Lately I've been asking myself, "What the heck am I doing out here?" But tonight, I gotta say, "Thank you, Sam Gribley."

Sam Gribley is the main character in the book *My Side of the Mountain*, by Jean Craighead George. Sam runs away from home to survive in the wilderness with a knife, flint and steel kit, ball of twine, and pet raccoon. By the time I had eight candles on my birthday cake, Sam was my hero.

After school I would sneak off to my secret place to practise "living off the land." I spent hours bending branches for bows, picking berries, capturing grasshoppers, aging perfume I had made from flower petals, and camouflaging my face with pollen, always daydreaming various survival scenarios.

"MAYDAY, MAYDAY! We're going down. This is flight SA341. Do you copy, traffic control?"

No response to the pilot's SOS, not even a garbled voice blurred by static.

Cindy, the flight attendant in charge of me, leans over and touches my arm. "Now, Nikki, don't be afraid. I know you're alone, but everything is going to be all right."

I know she's lying. I'm already picturing the survival tree house I will build. I tighten the seatbelt around my teddy. Giggling, I say, "Oh, don't worry about me. I'll survive."

From somewhere in the back of the plane I hear, "Nikki. Nikki. Where are you?"

I always jolted back to reality when I heard my mother calling me in for supper.

I daydreamed about zipping down the yellow inflatable slide shown on in-flight safety cards, then bobbing around in the ocean until currents swept me onto a deserted island. Anything to get me to the wilderness.

After my ninth birthday, soon after I rode my first pony, Sam Gribley went from being the kid I aspired to be to the kid I never thought of again.

My life veered in the opposite direction. I no longer envisioned my wardrobe full of smoke-stained deerskin clothing. My fashion sense turned to Polo Ralph Lauren. Braces came off my teeth; my short tomboy hairstyle grew into long, wavy locks; and I started hanging out with popular kids at high school. I replaced the pictures of wild animals on my bedroom walls with magazine images of Guess models and favourite TV celebrities. I lived for show-jumping horses and wearing expensive clothes. Thunderbird Equestrian Centre in Langley, BC, became my second home, and its owners my extended family. I dreamed of riding in the Olympics, just like my new hero, Laura, one of my trainers.

At 18, my riding life took a dramatic turn. My trainer and I had just found my dream horse, an undiscovered jumper, the one I believed would start my career as a world-class Grand Prix rider.

I nearly burst with excitement the day my mom drove to the barn to buy her. When she returned, I greeted her at the door. Fighting tears of joy, I exclaimed, "So, did we get her?"

Mom's eyes dropped to the floor. "Well, I got a flat tire on the way to the barn."

Slightly concerned, I replied, "Oh no, is everything okay?"

"Yes, the tow truck came and helped, but I took it as a sign from God. I decided not to buy Ivy. And I think it's time you got a job."

I was devastated. In disbelief I asked, "Are you serious? A sign from God? Are we religious now? I can't believe this. What do you mean, a job? I have to buy Ivy myself?"

In a motherly tone she told me, "I'm just tired of spending so much money on horses, Nikki. I've done my best. I'm sorry. It's just time."

Crushed, but not deterred, I asked for a job at the barn, and for the first time I started feeding the horses and mucking out stalls. After two weeks I received my first paycheque. I read the small amount in the corner with disgust. I knew there was no way I was going to save enough money to buy Ivy. I felt as if a horrible joke had been played on me. I quit a few weeks later and let my Olympic dreams vanish. I had not yet learned the power of determination and hard work.

I heard my childhood dream whisper a few times as I bumbled around in college, trying to decide what I wanted to be when I grew up, but it never yelled loud enough for me to hear it until I was 29. While browsing my survival teacher's bookshelf, I spotted a copy of *My Side of the Mountain*. With book in hand I stood frozen as memories of tree forts and wilderness adventures flashed through my mind. *Bam!* The thought hit me: I could become Sam Gribley.

I didn't have to wait for a plane to crash. I opted for Plan B: Pay someone to abandon me in the wilds.

On February 25, 2004, I stepped into my childhood dream, crunching ashore on a deserted, white-shell beach with a feral cat, a tiny rowboat, and a stranger I now call my best friend. I abandoned a life of pedicured toes, Thai restaurants, and diamond rings for dirty nails, roasted mice, and bear-claw necklaces. I rubbed sticks together to create fire, hunted game, harvested wild salads, and cured injuries with plants. I had become Sam Gribley.

PART ONE
A WHOLE NEW WORLD

THE WHISPERING TREE

The most beautiful thing we can experience is the mysterious. It is the source of all true art and science.

—Albert Einstein, physicist

Crrrrhhh! I awoke to the sound of a coffee grinder; another workday for Mom. When I visited my mother, her early mornings always started with the crackling of coffee beans, followed by the groaning moans of an "I don't do mornings" daughter.

Not ready to face the day, I snuggled back into a freshly fluffed pillow. "Just five more minutes," I grumbled. After my third five-more-minutes routine, I heard the front door open and close. Mom had left for work. I shoved back the blankets and rolled out of bed. Eyes still half-closed, I shuffled to the kitchen for my usual peanut butter toast, anticipating the thoughtful note my mother usually leaves.

My eyes caught a flash of movement through the sliding glass door. Ignoring my stomach's gurgling, I tiptoed to the door, trying not to frighten the black-capped chickadees hanging on the bird feeder. Rays of sunshine peeking through dense foliage illuminated a beautiful flowering tree.

Spooked, the chickadees flew off as I slid the door open and stepped out onto the balcony. Although I had seen the tree thousands of times, I couldn't remember ever noticing it before. This morning I admired the details of its ladderlike array of leaves, its shiny grey bark, and clusters of small, creamy white flowers, like a lady's dainty parasol. The tree captivated me.

I didn't grow up hugging trees. I was a 23-year-old sponsored snowboarder, whose motto was Live Fast—Die Young. In the summer, while waiting for snow, I rode a bored-out Honda XR 200 dirt bike. I partied with friends, played hours of video games, and visited the equestrian centre only a few times a year. I thoughtlessly picked leaves off bushes, cursed weeds without wondering their names, and trampled plants wherever I walked.

Why am I awestruck by a tree? I thought now. This is crazy.

An unfamiliar deep voice startled me. "Do you know my name?"

My head swivelled as I looked for a reasonable explanation of the voice, but no human was passing by. "Okay, this really is crazy." I faked a laugh and assured myself that trees don't talk.

Two major problems existed for my logical mind. First, the voice I heard was not my own; second, I heard it again. I stood rooted to the balcony, mouth agape, in a state of shock and disbelief. My worldview stretched like a gigantic balloon. The only thing I could think to do was answer the question. Shaking my head, I whispered, "No, I don't know who you are."

Embarrassed, I realized how little I knew of the natural world, the world I had loved as a child. I couldn't name most of the plants I saw, not even the ones I passed every day.

Running inside to find some clothes, I tugged on a pair of jeans, rummaged for socks, and pulled them on while hopping up and down to the table searching for keys. With a sweatshirt still covering my head, one arm in and one arm out, I slipped on shoes and turned off the light: it was a new out-the-door record for this sleeper-inner. I drove to the nearest bookstore to buy my first field guide, *Plants of Coastal British Columbia* by Jim Pojar and Andy MacKinnon. I sped home, rushed to the mystery tree, and turned page after page until I found it. *Sorbus aucuparia*, the mountain ash. It read:

> *The Haida sometimes ate the berries raw. The berries are now used occasionally to make a tart jelly, which is served with game. The Nuxalk rubbed the berries on the scalp to combat lice and dandruff.*

Flipping through the pages of my soon-to-be bible, I saw that nearly every wild or backyard plant had a beneficial use, even that scourge of a perfect green lawn, the dandelion. The mountain ash, once called the "Whispering Tree," had kindled a fire in my head to learn all I could of the green world. I obsessed, studying and experimenting with the edible, medicinal, cosmetic, and utilitarian properties of each plant I met, researching the history and legends surrounding it. I began with my new favourite tree. This was the moment I took my first unconscious step toward surviving in the wilderness.

MIRACULOUS MEETINGS

Once in a while you find yourself in an odd situation. You get into it by degrees and in the most natural way, but when you are right in the midst of it, you are suddenly astonished and ask yourself how in the world it all came about.
— Thor Heyerdahl, *The Kon-Tiki Expedition*

Hearing a tree talk did not compel me to run away into the wilderness, but it did open a doorway to the forgotten world of nature and spirit. Stepping across this threshold, I met a stinging plant I could make rope from and an otherworldly raven, two encounters that set me on a path to eating mice in the wilderness with a feral cat and Micah Fay.

Although I read that making rope from stinging nettle was easy, finding someone in 1999 who could teach me this skill almost required a time machine. Many of the ancient arts and skills had been lost to "progress"; the few keepers of knowledge were tucked away in obscure corners of the country. Miraculously, I found one by browsing through a newspaper. The ad read:

BIRDING—EDIBLE PLANTS—TRACKING
Learn skills of the naturalist, survivalist and tracker
with WOLF School of Natural Science. Call (360) 778-3654

At the time I associated nature studies with bearded hippies wearing drab hemp clothing. "Survival" meant militia organizations, sporting camouflage clothing, and guarding bunkers of supplies for looming end-of-the-world scenarios or threatening conspiracy theories. I saw the ad three times before I puffed up the courage to call.

"Hello, WOLF School of Natural Science."

"Hi, I saw your ad in the paper. I was wondering if you knew how to make stinging-nettle rope?"

I felt an uncomfortable pause, positive the guy was thinking, Okay, we got a whack-job here. But he answered with a confident, "Sure I do."

With an enthusiasm he had probably never heard before, I exclaimed, "No way, really? That's rad. When can I sign up?"

Based on our ensuing conversation, Chris Chisholm pegged me for a flake and figured I'd never show up the following Tuesday. But right on time I knocked on his door.

He rented a 1930s-style house, hidden by skyscraper-tall poplar trees, with two other roommates in the quaint town of Fairhaven, Washington. His classroom was his backyard. We sat on stumps around a firepit. With his neatly trimmed beard and fire-engine-red flannel shirt, Chris fit my mental image of a survival teacher.

"Have you ever seen a fire started with a bow-drill?" he asked.

"No. I don't even know what a bow-drill is."

He went inside and came back with what looked like a short hunting bow and a handful of carved sticks. Perhaps the faint memory of Sam Gribley sparked my interest in learning survival skills, and maybe a small part of me even related to those good ol' boys wearing camo, but Chris Chisholm's friction fire hooked me into the primitive world. On October 15, 1999, I enrolled in WOLF's Naturalist and Primitive Survival Training program, and Chris became my lifelong mentor.

I didn't fit in. I didn't call myself an environmentalist. I barely knew the word "recycling," and although I had been studying herbal medicine for the past three years, inspired by my meeting with the mountain ash, I didn't have a degree in any scientific field of study. I polluted the air with an obnoxiously loud dirt bike, enjoyed skeet shooting, and drove souped-up cars. I wore tight skater shirts and designer jeans instead of wool sweaters and Birkenstocks. My vocabulary included words like "rad," "sweet," and "stoked," and I wasn't looking to find a new network of friends. I just wanted to learn the secret of natural rope making (and I still have the faded green cordage I made from the outer skin of a stinging nettle).

The school's curriculum required students to do their own field research, following lessons outlined in several workbooks. Based on Native American teachings, the course not only covered survival, tracking, and nature awareness, but also guided the student into deeper spiritual secrets of the natural world through storytelling and ceremony. My first lesson required me to find a secret spot, a place I felt drawn to, where

I could be alone. The workbook suggested that the spot should be easily accessible, preferably near my home. I needed to look for the best example of nature I could find: a forest with a creek running through it, or a meadow with wetlands, or even a tree in the backyard. It needed to be a "transition area," frequented by animals, like the corner of a field next to a forest or a protected trail next to a food source, where I could learn the rhythms of the natural world and develop skills to understand the patterns of how animals and plants co-exist. The book also suggested my secret spot should be between 50 and 100 feet in each direction from a central point.

Fortunately, I lived on the outskirts of a small town. I shared an idyllic life with the man of my dreams, a super-cool guy who was the love of my life. Our cute little country house backed onto state-owned forest land, with trees stretching for miles and only one neighbour along a five-mile rural road. A small creek babbled through the yard under the canopy of big maple trees. It was a perfect location to find my secret place.

On a cloudless autumn morning I awoke to the sound of a raven calling. I looked out the window to see the shadow of a large bird cross the lawn below.

I jumped out of bed, quickly dressed, and darted out the door, pausing on the porch to give thanks for all I might see and find during my search for a secret place. The *whoosh, whoosh* of flapping wings distracted me. Looking up, I saw a raven, his feathers a metallic black, circling over my house. He flew lower and lower until I felt the subtle breeze from his wings upon my face, then landed in an old-growth bigleaf maple at the corner of the driveway, croaking three times.

I decided to see how close I could get to him. When I reached the large, mossy branch he was perched on, off he flew toward the old logging road I had planned to hike up. As I approached the gated road, I saw the bird sitting in a grey-barked alder tree. *Croak, croak, croak,* he called, flying farther up the road. I followed.

At the top of a small hill, I found him sitting on another alder branch. I had a strange feeling the raven had waited for me. When I reached the alder, up he flew, gliding low over the moss-covered road to land on an old Douglas fir tree.

Could the raven be leading me to my secret place? I wondered.

Yeah right, my cynical side whispered back.

I had just finished reading a book about King Arthur in which a raven named Solomon leads young Arthur through the forest to meet Merlin for the first time. In Celtic lore, ravens are believed to be messengers from the spirit world, offering an initiation of sorts, marking a beginning of one thing and the death of another. It sounded exciting. Logically, though, I decided the bird was calling its mate and I, the intruding human, kept scaring it off as I followed.

I stopped thinking and looked up at him.

The sun shone upon his glossy, iridescent plumage. I could see his long, shaggy throat feathers and thick, whiskered beak. He twisted his head to stare down at me. I had never noticed the beauty of a raven before. He glided off into the trees. *Croak, croak, croak.* I kept following.

I bushwhacked through the brush and entered an unfamiliar part of the forest, certain the raven would be gone. To my surprise, he shimmered ahead in a patch of sunlight beaming through the foliage. He called three times in his deep, guttural voice, flying to another low perch in the woods. On he led…

Eventually I found myself at the foot of a steep hill, deep in the forest. His husky calls turned to soft, sweet cooing. The gentle murmurings continued while I scrambled up the hill, grabbing roots and thin branches to pull myself along. When I reached the crest I looked for my spirit guide, but he was gone. I never saw or heard the beat of wings or the movement of tree branches. He had simply vanished. Lowering my gaze I found myself staring at a young mountain ash. I had found my secret spot.

With bare feet and bits of fallen leaves in my hair, I brought home wild edibles to cook, skulls to clean, and flowers to press. I didn't just love *being* in the woods, I wanted to *live* there. I wanted to know what every nick, scrape, and scuff on the ground told me. I wanted to know every plant and every bird call. I had become obsessed. I knew I had lost my modern mind the day I brought home unidentifiable scat—a pleasant word for animal poo—wrapped in maple leaves so I could pull it apart with tweezers to study its content.

I felt foolish sharing my newly acquired knowledge and otherworldly experiences with my friends and loved ones. How could I tell them "I'm not up for a game of Nintendo because I've got some poo to examine"? Of course, my poor communication skills made us drift even farther apart. For reasons I couldn't explain or understand, my secret place compelled me to turn naturalist studies and survival skills into my life's purpose.

I began missing football parties to sit alone under the mountain ash. I wanted to spend every day at my secret spot. Close friends joked, "Hey, where's Nikki? Out bounding like a rabbit somewhere?" They never knew how accurate their jest was.

Shortly after spending my first night sleeping alone in the forest, I asked my boyfriend to take a wander with me in the woods. We stopped to listen to my

favourite bird belting out his long, warbling song.

In adoring tones, I told him, at length, all I had recently learned about the tiny winter wren.

Rolling his eyes he said, "You're, like, in awe or something. It's just a bird."

I felt like an extinguished cigarette butt stomped into the pavement, although a tiny part of me agreed, thinking, I must be going "Thoreauly" mad.

This same part of me considered primitive skills irrelevant to the modern world and wanted to forget the experiences at my secret place so I could continue living my American dream life. I questioned my new passion; wasn't life about having a successful career people admired, working hard for an eventual retirement? How was I going to accomplish that by rubbing sticks together?

However, a larger part of me wanted to run away to the forest, leaving the apathy and greed of the civilized world behind me. I had reached a crossroads. Even though my newly found purpose scared me, my heart compelled me to do what my mind deemed crazy, and I walked away from my old life forever.

I said farewell to dear friends and my cherished loved one, who could not follow my chosen path. I gave up my half of the house, left my truck behind, and hugged our dogs goodbye. I cried myself to sleep for nearly a year, tormented by the grief of hurting those I loved. I knew in my heart I had made the right decision, but it will forever reign as the best and worst time of my life. I miss them still.

With a few belongings boxed up, my teddy bear, Mousey, and I headed down the road to who knows where. I made new human and furry friends and found a naturalist's dream cabin on a small island in the Pacific Northwest. The property had 43 acres of forested land with grassy fields and a small pond that became my study site. I invested all my time and money in becoming the best woodswoman I could be.

I set aside my shoes for town trips only and walked barefoot everywhere I went. I belly-crawled on every animal trail around my new secret spot, studying the plants, insects, animals, and tracks left behind. I slept amongst the ferns, rain or shine. I spent every waking hour studying nature and journalling my discoveries.

I took courses on survival, shivering in makeshift shelters until I built them correctly. I made bow-drill and hand-drill friction fires with combinations of different wood. I took animal and search-and-rescue tracking classes from the best trackers in North America. I practised invisibility, stalking, and camouflage. I learned to make baskets, mats, and bowls with natural materials, such as cedar bark, tule rush, pine needles, cattails, and tree roots. I took courses on hunting and trapping, tanning, and flint-knapping, the ancient art of making stone tools.

After four intense years of training I found *My Side of the Mountain* on Chris Chisholm's bookshelf, and the memories it triggered inspired me to leave for the wilderness as Sam Gribley had done.

Several months later, while instructing at WOLF Camp, I met Micah Fay. He had been living on the US East Coast, learning how to start bow-drill friction fires, wandering the city parks, chewing black birch twigs, dreaming of primitive survival in a wild place. Like me, he felt he was walking this path alone. When he heard about WOLF College, he joined the school's apprenticeship program, even though he was already a skilled primitive survivalist and overqualified for the apprenticeship, which gave him an opportunity to live with the WOLF staff for mentoring in exchange for volunteer work with the summer camp program. When I asked him later why he stayed, he said he just needed a place to live and practise survival skills, and he wanted to hang out with like-minded people.

At the end of camp season I planned a road trip to Idaho to attend the Rabbitstick Rendezvous, the oldest and largest primitive technology gathering of its kind. I intended to ask a lot of questions about my upcoming survival adventure. By the time my friend Krista and I were loading up her Subaru with camping gear, only one person, Micah, was still joining us out of the five who had originally said yes.

We hit the road like a trio of nerdy nature geeks, stopping at all unidentifiable plants, gathering lichen for dyes, and plucking quills from a roadkill porcupine. Rabbitstick itself was like a time warp to the fur-trading era. Hundreds of people with varying knowledge of primitive skills sauntered around teepees, trading tents, and fire circles in buckskin clothing, Hudson's Bay Company jackets, and fur hats. Near the tent offering deep-fried bannock, a message board displayed a long list of lectures and workshops. Given the multitude of questions I wanted to ask about the logistics of living primitively for a long time, and over the winter, I had trouble choosing the classes to attend.

I bumped into Micah at my first three classes. "Are you following me?" I teased.

"No, I think you're following me."

Our interests were identical, and a strong friendship began growing between us. Like kids in a candy shop, we eagerly picked out classes to sample next.

One evening near twilight, waiting for the first star to shine, Micah asked me, "Have you ever read *My Side of the Mountain*? It was my favourite book as a kid."

"Heck, yeah," I laughed. "That book is a big reason why I'm gonna live in the woods."

"Me too," Micah sighed happily.

We talked long into the night about our individual dreams and found it comforting to know someone else walked a similar path.

Others weren't quite so encouraging. At Rabbitstick I was repeatedly told, "Why don't you try surviving for a week or two first, before venturing out for a year? Can you even start a fire without matches? Are you sure you can make an arrowhead good enough to hunt with?"

I was no weekend primitive enthusiast, making crafts to sit on dusty shelves in my comfy home. I had made this my life. But most people had trouble taking me seriously. I didn't fit the image of a hardcore primitive survivalist. I still don't. Pink toenail polish sends the wrong message to bush folk. Most are appalled by it. They also wondered why I wasn't wearing a coyote-skin jacket or my cedar-bark hat every day instead of name-brand, tight-fitting jeans and a Little Miss Sunshine T-shirt. I'm a confusing contradiction: one day a princess Dr. Jekyll, and the next a feral, nature-loving Mr. Hyde. I love smearing charcoal on my face for camouflage, but can't live without painting my toenails.

At Rabbitstick, I came across as a bubbly young girl who probably screamed at tiny spiders, but no one attended the class on butchering a fly-ridden elk leg except Micah and me. Our pockets bulged and dangled with our on-the-go projects, and rotten coyote paws dried atop Krista's hatchback for further study.

To be accepted into the world of primitive living is similar to getting your first big-time corporate job: you have to have the right credentials to be seen as worthy by your peers. But, ultimately, it didn't matter whether people believed in my abilities or not. All the instructors eventually shared their hard-earned knowledge with a kind smile, and ended by wishing me good luck. I had found a group of people who spoke my language and dreamed of surviving in the wilderness. The difference was that Micah and I weren't dreaming: we planned to do it. We were tired of reading about other people's adventures.

The only question that remained was whether to set off separately or together. The more we thought about it, the more it made sense to adventure as a duo.

The problem was I hardly knew the guy. Spending a week travelling together was not the same as living together in the wilds, far from our rainproof homes and ordinary thought processes.

Micah wrote this letter to me from a Montreal bus station, shortly after our trip to Rabbitstick:

Nikki, you and me we gotta make a pact. Whether we do it together or not, we'll never give up on our dreams. People just get tired I think. It can be hard to stand up for the truth against the world. My dad gave me a quote once, I forget the words exactly, but it was something like, when one totally commits oneself on a difficult path and begins to move towards that path, Providence moves too, and all manner of things happen to benefit the traveller that never would otherwise have occurred. There are a few things that have happened to me that I consider Providence inspired. Meeting you is one of them.

I felt the same way about him. Our savings dwindled on long-distance phone calls over the next several months as we talked long into the nights, discussing our dreams of surviving off the land. Our hopes were exactly the same. We envisioned living purely primitively, making functional replicas of the Native tools and crafts we drooled over when we saw them behind glass in anthropology museums. We wanted to see if we could prosper with this technology in the 21st century. We wanted to live as humans once did, in harmony with the Earth, without schedules, clocks, or predictable routines, directed by natural rhythms.

As we talked and planned, our mission became more than just testing our abilities, mastering the primitive skills, and living as close to nature as possible. We had personal and spiritual questions we sought to answer. I believed by simply humbling myself before nature, I would find these answers. Sitting in silence under trees, I came to view the physical world as a tiny part of a larger, invisible world that was hiding just around the corner of our imaginations. This spoke of something Divine. We both wanted to become closer to this divinity, to the spirit that moves through all things. I call it God, but I know a lot of people shy away from that word, and its mention can be uncomfortable for those without a Christian or religious background. I simply believed in a higher power, and I wanted to learn the truths behind it all. I wanted to be as pure as when I was born. I couldn't exactly define what that meant; I only knew I lived without it. I also sought the deeper meaning of goodness. The survival trek turned into a quest for the true heart of all things, and we both felt that living in the wilderness had to be the purest place to find these truths.

We found only one point we didn't agree on. Micah thought perhaps he was meant to live this new lifestyle even after we finished the year. I knew, with great certainty, I would not be a stone-age woman forever. I needed a rose-petal-filled

Micah and Scout became my family and my only companions for almost two years.

bathtub, with the gardenia scent from candles wafting through sparkling bubbles. I needed to seek a balance between the worlds, if it existed.

Even though we agreed on so much, I couldn't understand why I still balked at the thought of Micah joining me. Our meeting was miraculous. It made sense and felt right to expand my tribe, but I couldn't say yes.

In Vancouver, I had dinner with my best friend, Jeff, at a quiet café and asked what he thought about my situation. Always speaking from his heart, Jeff said, "If you truly knew why you wanted to go on this thing, deciding if Micah should come should be a no-brainer."

The blast of truth kicked my ego to the curb. I realized it was ego that had been clinging desperately to the notion "I want to do everything myself" so it could boast, "I succeeded at the ultimate test of survival, and I did it alone."

The next evening I phoned Micah for a late-night talk session. "Well, Micah, a friend of mine made me realize my ego has been trying to make me go on this adventure alone. I'd really like us to go together. You up for it?"

I held my breath through the pause that followed.

"Yeah. Let's do it together." He paused again, then said in a bashful tone, "Well, I have to tell you something."

"Please, don't say it," I jumped in. "I know what you're thinking."

He said, "I have to say it. I have to be honest. I'm startin' to dig you."

I blushed. "You really shouldn't like me, Micah. I'm a heartbreaker. I have a terrible history of it. I would be lying if I said I didn't have feelings for you too, but I don't want to hurt you, and I know in the end I'll break your heart." My frankness startled him.

"I don't care, Nik. I'm willing to take the chance."

I smiled, chuckled, and shook my head. "Okay, but don't say I didn't warn you."

We flew to each other's hometowns to meet the other's family, then rented a tiny floathouse in Lagoon Cove, on the coast of British Columbia, to make sure we could get along in tight quarters. A deep friendship was sealed. We didn't know exactly where our intimacy would go once we reached our wilderness home, but we were certain we would live our dreams of survival together.

Besides, as Sterling Seagrave splendidly wrote in the foreword to *Desperate Journeys, Abandoned Souls,* "It helps to be marooned with somebody else, for you can commiserate, quarrel, and feud like newlyweds, and when things really get difficult, you can always eat him, or vice versa."

THUNDERBIRD'S PREDICTION

I went to the woods because I wished to live deliberately, to front only the essential facts of life, and see if I could not learn what it had to teach, and not, when I came to die, discover that I had not lived.

—Henry David Thoreau, naturalist

Black strands of hair whipped my face as I leaned over the railing of the *Gla'lis* (*glah-lees*) like a dog hanging its head out the car window. This boat, whose name meant "finning whale," was a Ferrari in the world of water taxis and my ride to the unfamiliar wilderness of British Columbia's rugged raincoast.

I closed my eyes, tipped back my head, and took a deep breath of clean, chilly, salty air. My heartbeat thumped in my ears as my body jittered with a jumble of emotions. The *shh-shh-shh* of ocean spray rushing alongside the boat hull drowned out my thoughts while the twin engines roared past desolate bays and steep, rocky shorelines amongst a maze of evergreen islands. The landscape of the Broughton Archipelago appeared untouched, primal, and perfect, painted with a palette of blues and greens. I had heard the mountains stretched all the way to Alaska. This was the wilderness I had dreamed of. Never had I felt more alive.

With a Cheshire cat smile beaming on my face, I stepped back inside the warm crew cab to sit beside the skipper, Tom Sewid. Tom grew up on the waters of the BC coast, first as a commercial fisherman and hunting guide, then as a water-taxi captain and tour operator. He is of the Kwakwaka'wakw (pronounced *kwah-kwahk-ee-wahk*) nations, which early white settlers called Kwakiutl. He had a gift for storytelling.

Tom turned to me. "Welcome to God's country," he said.

Without taking my eyes off the water, my perma-grin preventing me from speaking, I nodded, thinking, It sure is.

Scout, my kitty friend, thought otherwise. White-socked paws pushed out between the bars of her carrier as she yowled her unhappiness with the pounding waves. Micah, my human friend, radiated bliss, as I did.

Charting our way, Tom pointed out a snow-capped double peak in the distance. "That's Thunderbird Mountain." People call it Mount Stephens now, the name it was given in 1792 by Captain Vancouver, but the mountain was originally known as K'we, Thunderbird Mountain, by those who spoke Kwak'wala.

K'we is home to the great Thunderbird, who roamed the heavens with supernatural powers. With the head of an eagle and a huge curving beak, Thunderbird could shoot bolts of lightning from his glowing eyes of fire and send cracks of thunder with one mighty flap of his wings, which were twice as long as a war canoe. He preyed on killer whales, carrying them in giant claws to his home atop K'we.

Our guide spoke in a prophetic tone. "Travellers should take notice the first time they see Thunderbird Mountain before venturing off on any quest, for it is known to foretell the future. Look at the sky—it is blue all around, yet the top of the mountain is covered with clouds. I suspect you will have a tough time ahead, with many hardships, but it will be successful."

Enjoying the legend, but skeptical of the divination, thinking perhaps my Native guide was making up a good story for his white clients, I stared at the mountain. Now that our journey was beginning, I wondered what really awaited me. Fortunately, I had little time to ponder the potential hardships.

Tom was pointing out different places of interest for a survivalist. "In that bay is great crabbing…That's my secret cockle clam beach…There's cod anywhere from 60 to 250 feet off that rock…Beware of the tide and current here…These white-shell beaches are either harvesting sites or village sites of the Kwakwaka'wakw people. They are called middens and testify to just how long my people have lived on this coast." Tom time-warped me back to those early days with stories of bighouses and totem poles, both visible and lost in the forest and sea. He marked on our chart a little-known shrimp hole, called the "teacup," and a place to find halibut. We attempted to memorize all he told us, but to our untrained eyes the landscape blended into one green-blue mass, making it nearly impossible to determine what was an island and what a channel, inlet, or dead end. The information overwhelmed me.

We had never set a prawn trap, rowed a boat, read a tide chart, or seen a halibut. We had never even fished before. For the first time, a nervous twinge crept into my gut. Was I really ready for this, or was I taking a terrible gamble, plunging in over my head?

Thankfully, Tom's voice interrupted my thoughts of Holy crap, I'm screwed!

"There's your home. That's Village Island."

The boat slowed as we approached the small, white-shell beach of Native Anchorage. A haphazard structure stood just above the beach on a grassy bank, with leafless alders growing around it. We didn't have time to take in our surroundings; the tide was ebbing and Tom needed to hurry before the boat ran aground.

We quickly offloaded *Gribley*, the ten-foot rowboat we had bought the night before we left, tossed our gear in, gave Tom our last $480, and carefully lowered ourselves, kitty and all, into the boat atop our wobbly supply bins, animal hides, and traps. Looking up, we spotted several bald eagles circling above us.

Tom called out, "*Gilakas'la, Kwikw (gay-lah-kahs-lah, queek)*. Hello, Eagle! The chiefs have come to say hello." Somehow, the masters of the sky comforted me with their *kleek-keek-eek-eek-eek* call.

As *Gribley* drifted away from the red and silver boat, Tom advised us to visit the ancient village nearby, suggesting we tell the spirits and ancestors of the land what we were doing and how we would respect the area. He spoke of "unrest" in the abandoned villages. While the Native band office had given us permission to live on the island, we agreed to ask the ancestors too.

Gla'lis, with a Kwakwaka'wakw whale design painted on its side, was turning to leave when Tom leaned out the window and pointed to shore. "Hey, Nikki," he called, "that's the tree I haven't been able to identify. Maybe you know what it is?"

My gaze followed his pointing finger to shore. I blinked twice to make sure my eyes weren't fooling me, but even without its leaves, I recognized the shiny silver bark of the mystical mountain ash. "Oh yeah," I replied. "I know that tree. It's a rowan or mountain ash."

Like an old friend, the tree was once again reassuring me I was skipping along my chosen path in life. I don't believe in coincidences, but I laughed and shook my head with a smile, suggesting I knew a secret no one else did. The Celts of long ago called the mountain ash *Li Sula*, meaning "colour of hope." The sight of the tree gave me hope for a safe survival quest. Barely audibly, I recited my favourite poem by Cicely Mary Barker:

They thought me, once, a magic tree
Of wondrous lucky charm,
And at the door they planted me
To keep the house from harm.

❧

Crunch. The scrape of metal on rock snapped me back into the present. Little *Gribley* ground ashore under the arm-power of Micah. Scout leapt off my lap to what she mistakenly assumed was the safety of land before Micah and I had even stepped out of the boat. Standing side by side, we watched our connection to the civilized world become smaller and smaller until *Gla'lis* disappeared from sight. *Poof!*

I gaped at the vastness of the country. I felt like a ladybug set adrift on a leaf in the middle of the Pacific Ocean. For reassurance I glanced over at the mountain ash. It stood as if welcoming me to another new beginning. A tiny, mischievous smile crept onto my face. I felt ready. I scrutinized my companions, while Micah, lost in his own thoughts, gazed at the daunting expanse of solitude.

Standing six foot three, wearing Carhartt work jeans and a lumberman-style flannel jacket, Micah resembled Paul Bunyan. A kind-hearted, strong, sharp-thinking, extremely skilled primitive survivalist, he exuded the air of a classic woodsman. I had also recently witnessed the magnitude of his food-consuming qualities at an all-you-can-eat buffet. It was impressive. I questioned our winter start, knowing it would take a heck of a lot of food to feed him.

I hoped to find super-sized portions of food, but perhaps more importantly, I prayed we'd get along. I didn't want this dream to turn into a *Lord of the Flies* scenario. There was an eerie similarity between the two situations: kids stranded on an island, fighting, turning into cavemen, each trying to gain dominance over their meagre supplies, leading to an epic battle of strength versus stealth. I realized both of us had a breaking point, and I had no idea where mine was.

At five foot seven, I felt dwarfed next to Micah, and in my baggy GUESS jeans and cute V-neck sweater, I'm sure I appeared to be a pretty girl lost in the woods. I considered myself a tough, determined, seasoned survivor, even if I had dared to arrive with magenta toenails.

I didn't need a lot of food. I had experienced enough mini survival sojourns to know I could peck at a few seeds, snack on a palm full of miner's lettuce, or eat a couple of grasshoppers and still have a smile on my face when I returned two weeks later. These crash survival diets always gave me the flat abs of a run-way model and a renewed zest for life. But when I glanced around at the drab winter colours and bare trees of Village Island, I had a sudden mental image of a pale, sunken-cheeked castaway crawling amongst a weathered patch of dandelion leaves. I wondered how big our smiles would stretch after months of eating a paltry winter diet. The zombie image stomped my enthusiasm for a super-skinny body. I turned my attention to the now.

"Where's the cat?" I spotted her black, white-ringed tail slowly flicking back and forth in the safety of the salal brush behind us, a usual sighting of the young, feisty, feral cat who had come into my life unexpectedly as I was preparing for my dream. "Phew, I see you in there, kidder cat."

Scout was the epitome of a wilderness survivor. I would have bet my savings with a Vegas bookie on her skills, but I wasn't sure I wanted to play the odds on Micah and me. One thing I did feel sure of was our determination to live our dreams to the fullest.

BEER-CAN GREETINGS

What would you attempt if you knew you would not fail?
—Robert Schuller, Christian pastor

Slinging on our backpacks, we surveyed our survival supplies. The meagre load of gear stacked on the beach would have scared most city folk, but to a couple of primitive survivalists it looked like cheating. I had never heard my famous tracking teacher, Tom Brown Jr., say, "So I packed an entire boatful of survival gear and headed out for a year." I resented lugging it all around, but the insightful book *Into the Wild*, by Jon Krakauer, a going-away gift from my bow-making teacher, helped me resist the urge to chuck our supplies. Krakauer tells the puzzling story of Chris McCandless, who one day abandoned most of his possessions and set off to "live life to its fullest" alone in the Alaskan wilderness. Chris starved to death 112 days later. Point made.

Through my years of survival training, it was easy for my ego to adopt the philosophy "If you aren't living entirely primitively, it doesn't count." Or put more bluntly, "You suck." Being able to live 100 percent primitively was like reaching enlightenment in the primitive survival world. But I knew leaving our island early because I was unprepared would be worse than feeling I had failed some "primitive creed." We were a tribe of two; perfectly crafted tools would not be passed down to us, and no help was on the way.

We hauled our provisions up the beach, tying our boat to the nearest alder tree, and then climbed up the short hill to check out our new home. Crumpled beer cans greeted us. Broken bottles, rusty nails, and an old spring mattress littered the area. We stood, stunned, in front of a rundown wooden structure built off a dilapidated beige 15-foot travel trailer. The wooden porchlike "add-on" looked as if it could collapse on our heads at any time, the roof leaked, and the wall boards that weren't missing dangled loosely in all directions. This was our living space?

I turned to Micah, "Is this for real? I can't believe Tom dropped us off here. This isn't even close to what he described."

"Yeah, I can't believe this. What was he thinking?"

"I have no idea. What a nightmare."

I recalled my phone conversation with Tom several months earlier.

"Hello, I'm hoping to charter someone to get me to Claydon Bay, near Rosemary Lake. Do you know the area?"

"Oh, Cockle Thrower Bay. Yeah, I know the place. That's in an area we call 'the edge of the world.'"

"Sounds perfect, but what's up with the name Cockle Thrower Bay?"

He chuckled. "Well, you don't want to go there. People have had bad experiences up there."

"Yeah? Like what?" I asked.

"Lots of stories…cockle shells being thrown from the woods at clam diggers, strange noises coming from the bush, some guys so spooked they won't go back. That's why it's called Cockle Thrower Bay. You know, cockles being Sasquatch's favourite food."

"What?" I said with a tinge of apprehension and skepticism.

He said, "Oh yeah, lots of B_akw_as (bahk-kwus) up there!"

I had just spent weeks browsing through file cabinets full of maps covering the area from Oregon to Alaska, road-tripping to examine specific places deemed "survivable" according to our list of requirements, and then mailing Micah maps of the locations I judged worth his scrutinizing. Now it turned out our number-one geographical area was home to the legendary Sasquatch. My "sounds perfect" comment seemed a tad premature.

I didn't know what to think. Essentially, I was being asked if I believed in Bigfoot. I hadn't yet made up my mind about that, but whether or not B_akw_as really does roam the beaches of Claydon Bay, the area's topography and geographical location sounded less inviting as our conversation continued. Claydon Bay was out. This left Booker Lagoon, on Broughton Island off Queen Charlotte Strait.

That's when Tom suggested we move into his small trailer at Native Anchorage on Village Island. He proposed we stay for six months to familiarize ourselves with the terrain, become skilled at fishing—which we had never done before—and prepare for the year-long primitive living experience. He said, "Once you're out there you'll know what you need in an area." It sounded like a good idea. I talked it over with Micah, and we decided to start our adventure in Native Anchorage.

Now, as we stood in front of the vandalized trailer door, my imagination clinging desperately to the vision of a comfy couch and a pine-scented kitchen, Micah stepped up and clicked the door open.

"What a *dump*," I scoffed. "Yeah, like I'm living in here."

Dark, dank, and depressing, oozing a breathtaking stench, the interior epitomized the worst-case scenario of a trashy trailer I had ever imagined. Even the gloom shed by the filth-stained windows couldn't hide the mould, dirt, and garbage scattered everywhere. To our right was a stained, bunk-bed-style couch, the broken windows behind it patched with loosely hung tattered sheets of clear plastic. Rotten scraps of food, mouldy half-opened cans, and dirty dishes were strewn all over the counters and shelves. I didn't dare open the cupboards.

Turning to one another in glassy-eyed disbelief, we wondered aloud how anyone could suggest we move into this squalor.

"I'm not living in here, Micah. Or anywhere near it." Not even a lifetime supply of Breyers vanilla ice cream could entice me to stay one night in that nasty trailer.

"I don't want to sleep in here either, but we need to store our things somewhere. I think we should at least use it for storage."

Disgusted, I reluctantly agreed. "Okay, but we have to clean it up."

Surprisingly, the front portion of the trailer roof hadn't rotted away. We used a handleless broom and a couple of old shirts that were lying around to sweep and wipe down the place.

While I felt positive I was going to contract some disease from the mouse droppings and grime, Micah said, "I'll check out the bathroom."

I quickly responded, "I wouldn't go in there if I was you. It can't be good."

He couldn't control his curiosity, but he opened and closed the door in two seconds. "Yeah you're right, don't go in there." It was the first, but not the last, laugh we shared at the strange start to our adventure.

Never did Tom use the words "trashed," "dump," "pigsty," or "it'll probably need some cleaning up" when he was describing the trailer. Nor did he mention an unflushed, overflowing toilet, which anyone plunked down in the middle of nowhere to live out their childhood dreams would consider important.

Luckily, most of our supplies were in waterproof Rubbermaid bins that could stay outside, so only our backpacks of clothes and a few other precious items stayed in the trailer. However, shelter is number three in the Sacred Order of Survival, which Chris Chisholm taught me during one of my first classes with him. So Micah and I agreed to build a tarp lean-to in the woods until we figured out what to do for a permanent shelter. Then it was on to number four, water.

In 15 minutes we hiked to a small, woodland stream at the head of a muddy, V-shaped bay around the corner from camp. Following the creek upward, we discovered a beautiful little pool surrounded by sword ferns and thick mossy logs, a gnomacious woodland bower. The tracks of a lone wolf along the creek bank shifted us into our remote and wild reality. The comforts of home, the convenience of supermarkets, the supportive voices of family and friends were no longer a car ride away.

We sat down on the spongy, damp bank to inhale our surroundings. I nudged Micah. "Now *this* is the setting I always imagined surviving in. We're finally doing it, Micah."

"I know. I can hardly believe it, Nik."

I knelt down at the water's edge. Cupping my hands, I dipped them into the cool, brownish gold water. With a silent prayer of gratitude I took my first tiny sip of wild water.

The tannic acid from the coniferous trees had leached into the water, turning it the colour of weak Earl Grey tea. From a city dweller's point of view, it looked dirty. We had little concern, however, as tannic acid has astringent qualities and is used as a healing agent in herbal medicines. It just tasted brown.

We filled our pots to the brim with the golden water and began hiking back to camp. I meowed for Scout. She appeared in seconds and trotted along behind us.

The thin wire handles of the pots had etched deep grooves in our hands by the time we reached the small, grassy clearing behind the trailer. With a loud exhaled *phew*, I said, "Wow, that was painful. Hauling water isn't gonna be easy."

"Yeah, we gotta find a better way. I'm thirsty. Let's get a fire going."

Survivalists are taught to boil their water for at least five minutes to kill *Giardia*, a one-celled microscopic parasite that wreaks havoc in the host body when a human or animal drinks contaminated water. Giardiasis, the resulting infection, causes a variety of intestinal symptoms that send the unfortunate victim to the nearest bathroom with a twisting, cramping gut. In the bush, *Giardia* can be a killer.

I offered to make the first friction fire. Rummaging through my gear, I pulled out a beaded buckskin pouch filled with my primitive fire-making kit, the bow-drill. If only bags could talk; this one had been on every painful, gruelling, and enjoyable survival trek I had taken part in. The bow-drill has been a treasured teacher.

Laying out the bow, fireboard, spindle, and handhold in front of me sent shivers up my spine. A friction fire is a combination of magic, science, grace, skill, energy, art, and spirit. It is a gift, and not only for the survivalist. Anyone can toss a bunch of "Boy Scout fluid" on a brush pile to burst it into flames, and we turn knobs on our stoves to create fire without a hint of thankfulness. In the process of trying to master these primitive techniques, I had come to realize the importance

The Sacred Order of Survival

1. Air (Deep breathing reduces panic and keeps you warm.)
2. Laughter (I've added this. Those who can find wonder and humour in life-threatening situations turn from victims to survivors.)
3. Shelter (You can die within hours from exposure to the elements.)
4. Water (Most claim you can live without water for only three days, but some people have survived 15 days without it.)
5. Fire (A gift from the universe.)
6. Food (You can live without food for approximately 30 days.)
7. S'mores (This is also my addition. Any treat is a joyous pick-me-up.)

of the skills of the coastal First Nations. These ways of the past reawaken a lost sense of connection with the natural world and, perhaps, alter our sense of self. The primitive skills bring us a feeling of self-reliance and self-confidence, and a deep appreciation for what modern civilization has given us, which becomes ever more important in our rapidly changing world.

Primitive fire-making is a mystery. Friction causes heat, heat causes dust, dust causes charcoal, and charcoal at about 800 degrees Fahrenheit turns into a small, glowing ember. Scientifically, it should happen every time, but it doesn't. That's why I love my bow-drill. Perhaps we are stealing fire from the gods, or perhaps they are simply taking pity on us.

I fluffed a small bundle of shredded cedar bark into a beautiful bird's-nest shape. I held my arm's-length driftwood bow in hand and couldn't believe how attached I was to a stick. While my modern hands once again remembered the old ways, I bowed my head and silently gave thanks for the miracle I needed. I took off my left shoe so I could hold down the flat, V-notched fireboard with my bare foot, then twisted the dowel-shaped cedar spindle around the string of my bow, holding it in place on the fireboard with the wooden block handhold. I slowly began to move the bow back and forth. Faster and faster I stroked, my left arm burning from my downward pressure on the handhold. A sweet, scented smoke began billowing from beneath. Breathing hard, I stopped when I saw the shape of the smoke change ever so slightly into a wisp of creation. A small, delicate coal glowed inside the carved notch.

All too often this is when someone yells, "Hey, need a lighter?" and, *poof*, the glow disappears for no apparent reason. No lame comment fizzed out our first coal. I knew Micah respected the fire as much as I did. With laboured breath I whispered, "*Gilakas'la*, thank you, fire."

Crouching beside me, Micah stared at the faint red glow smoldering in the tinder bundle. Gently I blew on it, tenderly closing the nest to give more fuel to the coal. White, chalky smoke billowed from my cupped hands. *Whoosh.* The bundle flashed with flames.

Quickly and carefully I placed the handful of burning cedar into the teepee structure of wood Micah had set up. Together we watched the burning sticks crackle and pop—the miracle of fire. Unpacking my leather-bound journal, I wrote, "I don't think getting a fire with my bow-drill ever felt so good."

At twilight, quietly sitting on the beach alongside Micah, sipping hemlock and spruce needle tea, my mind finally relaxed and registered what had happened; I had become Sam Gribley. Scout came to sit by my side and we all gazed at our million-dollar view. (Well, maybe our ten-thousand-dollar view; the trailer behind us definitely brought down the price.)

It takes a lot of practice to create a burning coal from friction using a bow-drill, but it's nearly as fast as a match once you learn the technique and understand the language of wood.

The shiny, speckled, round head of a harbour seal popped up for a curious look, while _Gwa'wina_ (_gwah-wee-nah_), Raven, hoarsely croaked nearby. Laughing, I envisioned people buzzing around the city, sitting in traffic, compulsively shopping, working the grind, surrounded by smells of exhaust and sounds of ticking clocks. No words were exchanged, but Micah laughed too as a bald eagle flew around the point toward us.

"Suckers," he teased. A vision of the trash trailer popped into my head.

"Maybe we're the suckers." I giggled half-heartedly.

What We Took to Village Island

General Supplies
- Box of obsidian for flint-knapping arrows and knives (obsidian is a volcanic glass-like rock from Oregon, not locally available)
- Antler tools for flint-knapping
- Bag of raffia for basketry (we hadn't identified any supplies of sweetgrass in the area)
- Porcupine quills and beads for decorating crafts
- 6 rawhide deer skins and other "roadkill" hides (we weren't willing to hunt more food than we could eat)
- 6 primitively tanned sheep hides for my dream sleeping bag (couldn't find a buffalo hide in time)
- Deer sinew for lashing
- Spool of rope
- Several balls of twine
- Hide glue, rock pigment paint, and coloured clay for camouflage, painting, and facials
- Small point-and-shoot camera and 10 rolls of Fuji film
- Blank journals and two bags of Bic pens
- My personal notes on plants and their uses, compiled from hundreds of studied resources
- Assorted field guides and books, including:
- _Plants of Coastal British Columbia_ by Jim Pojar and Andy MacKinnon
- _Mammal Tracks and Sign_ by Mark Elbroch
- _Tracking and the Art of Seeing_ by Paul Rezendes
- _How to Catch Bottomfish_ by Charlie White
- _All That the Rain Promises and More..._ by David Arora
- _Western Birds_ by Roger Tory Peterson
- _Pacific Coast_ by Audubon Society

- *Exploring the Seashore* by Gloria Snively
- *The Sermon on the Mount* by Emmet Fox
- *Cedar* and *Indian Fishing* by Hilary Stewart
- *Flintknapping* by John C. Whittaker
- *Trapping North American Furbearers* by S. Stanley Hawbaker
- *The Traditional Bowyer's Bible*, Vol. 1, by Steve Allely
- *Camp Life in the Woods and the Tricks of Trapping* by W. Hamilton Gibson
- Tide book
- 2 marine charts of the Broughton Archipelago that Tom Sewid had given us
- Several topographical maps of the area
- Compass

Tools
- Frost knife and sharpening stone
- Axe
- Old crosscut saw
- Drawknife
- Adze
- File
- Handmade hickory bow and 2 ocean spray arrows
- Rowboat and oars
- Tape measure (for tracking)

Cooking Utensils
- 3 stainless steel pots
- Cast-iron fry pan
- Cast-iron Dutch oven
- Several gourds to use as bowls and containers
- Strainer, spoon, flipper

Clothing (for Nikki)
- 3 wool sweaters
- 2 long underwear
- 4 pairs of pants
- 2 jackets (fleece and wool)
- Several pairs of wool socks
- 2 hats
- 2 pairs of mitts
- 2 hoodies
- Hooded rain jacket and pants
- Rubber boots
- Waterproof shoes

Food
- Cooking oil (so we wouldn't have to harvest as many animals for fat)
- Flour and rice (starchy lily bulbs are now rare, and we wanted to experiment with new recipe ideas)
- Baking powder
- Assortment of dried wild plants for starters (stinging nettle, dandelion root, rosehips, and hazelnuts)
- Nettle vinegar
- Rosehip syrup

- Leftovers from my house, including a bag of cat food

Hygiene and Herbal Spa
- Hairbrush and elastics (I refused to cut my long hair)
- Toothbrush and 1 tube of paste
- Towel
- 2 bandanas
- 2 bars of handmade soap
- 1 sea sponge
- Nail polish
- 2 razors (1 for each of us)
- Scissors

Emergency Kit
- 1 down sleeping bag and Micah's 2 cotton bags
- 2 lighters, 1 flashlight, 24 taper candles, 1 bag of tea-light candles
- First-aid kit
- 2 large garbage bags
- 1 bucket
- Whistle
- 2 life jackets
- Crab trap and prawn trap
- Tarp
- 2 emergency blankets
- 6 emergency vitamin C drinking packs
- VHF radio (1 set of batteries)
- 2 waterproof bags
- 2 boxes of Ziploc bags
- Medicinal herbs, chunk of beeswax
- Medicinal tinctures and oils (herbs infused in vodka and oil)
- Tiny woodstove made from two propane tanks welded together (a gift from my godfather)
- Teddy bear

PART TWO
VILLAGE ISLAND

CUDDLING MY FEAR

"This is as far as I am going."
He looked all around and said, "You live here?"
"No," I said, "but I am running away from home, and this is just the kind of
forest I have always dreamed I would run to. I think I'll camp here tonight."
—Sam Gribley in *My Side of the Mountain*

Journal Entry, Day 2
This morning I awoke to a raven calling from a hemlock tree above. It was
time to get up and greet the sun. The scene I awoke to was like a National
Geographic *photo. It was the kind of sunrise a lone person, trekking to the*
edge of the world and back, would see. It was the kind of picture that when
you looked at it you wanted to be there too.

I never knew the ocean could be glassy calm. Not even a slight breeze rippled
the water's surface. Like a mirror it showed a perfect reflection of land and sky.
White-patched bufflehead ducks fed nearby, and our neighbouring eagles called
out to greet the day.

I sat down on a large, flat rock near the water's edge to watch the wildlife
awaken. I felt like the lone survivor of a worldwide disaster. The stillness of the
water and the vastness of my surroundings made me ask the question I didn't
want to think about: Are you afraid?

It took only a second for my mind to flash back to my first forest slumber
party. A few years earlier I had decided it was time to face my fears of the forest.
I was terrified of mountain lions and afraid of the dark, which allowed my child-
like imagination to conjure the cruellest man-eating cat ever to stalk a moonless
night. Alone in the shadows of a midnight forest, I felt most vulnerable, most
inadequate. I knew I no longer held the conquering crown of nature; I became a
mere part of it. To overcome my fears I chose a pitch-black night in November to

sleep out under the stars. And I mean black—it was like the inside of a gumboot.

Before nightfall, I silently fox-walked down the logging road to my secret place with a borrowed sleeping bag under my arm. Never having slept alone in the forest, nor camped without a tent, I didn't know the protocols of making a comfortable bed with ferns, so I took three steps off the main deer trail and crawled into my bag.

Twilight crept over the forest, that in-between time known in the past as "owl-light." I burrowed deeper inside my protective cocoon and waited for the cougar to walk down the trail and eat me. I questioned what I was doing out there, wondering if I really was losing my grasp on modern-day reality.

As if in answer, a barred owl flew over my bag to perch on a branch above me, hooting his familiar *hoohoo-hoohoo-hoohoohoohooaw* call.

In many cultures the owl is a messenger; its hoot can foretell death. Long, razor-sharp cat fangs flashed before my eyes. I took a deep breath to ease the panic shaking me. I thought about the lore that says owls bring wisdom to those with irrational fears.

"Isn't that right, Moonwalker?" I whispered. "You wouldn't be bringing me bad news, would you?"

Moonwalker was my buddy. I had known him for months, ever since I met him the day after I found my first secret spot. He had a quizzical nature, and his round grey head always reminded me of an astronaut's helmet. Now I watched him fluff his feathers as he settled in for a sit, as he had done many times before. In the fading light the camouflaging patterns on those feathers made him almost invisible next to the bark of the hemlock tree. Seeing him was like finally noticing a friend among the horde of wild-eyed people at a massive party I'd arrived at alone.

He looked down on me with his big, dark eyes, cocking his head as if to say, "What the heck are you doing here at this time of night, two-legged girl?"

"I have no idea," I told him. "At one time I thought it would be good to face my fears out here."

He closed his eyes in a long blink, which I translated as "You poor human."

His head bobbed up, down, and sideways to increase his hearing and depth perception, homing in on an unsuspecting mouse. Soon after, he flew off in search of dinner. Owls have the softest feathers of all birds, and their primary flight feathers have serrated edges to help diffuse the rush of air, making their movement silent as a shadow. The slight rustle of a branch was the only sound Moonwalker made as he left.

When he flew off, in flew my fears. I scooched down farther into my bag, as if it would help, and pointed my flashlight at every rustle in the leaves. Flick on. Flick off. Flick on. Flick off. "This is ridiculous. I need to surrender to the dark," I scolded myself. I hid the flashlight and lay awake for a long time until I began to relax on the soft leaves. I tucked my head into the sleeping bag and finally fell asleep.

I awoke to the sound of footsteps, certain I was a goner. I didn't dare move to peek outside the bag. I listened for the walking gait of a deer. Deer have sharp, hard hooves and their steps are staccato, very distinct from the softer, flowing rhythm of a coyote. The footfall I heard was neither. This was a deliberate step, a gentle, slow pad moving toward me.

It walked right up to me, slowly circling the bag.

I held my breath, hoping to create a cloak of invisibility around me. When I felt I was about to burst, I tried exhaling ever so quietly through pursed lips, but I couldn't hold back. My exhale sounded like a whale's loud, misty release of air. *Pfooof.* My mind whispered, "Nice one, Nikki. That'll keep you alive."

Luckily, the animal showed no indication it had heard me. It was too busy performing the classic shuffle-snuffle routine a dog does before it settles down beside you. By the time I was holding another full breath, I heard a purr. A deep, rumbling purr. My fear had snuggled up beside me.

Surprised it hadn't ripped me to pieces, I considered the possibility it was just taking a short catnap first. But as the minutes passed, it became evident the cat was not at all interested in eating me. From my experiments with less intimidating animals, I had seen how wildlife reflected my own feelings, sensing my emotions and thoughts, so I abandoned the "deep breath and hold till you pop" technique and began to enjoy the warmth and gentle trembling of the big cat. I didn't take a peek or try to touch it, but I did want to pinch myself to see if I would wake up, because the whole scenario seemed too unbelievable. There I was, in full consciousness, lying beside what I presumed was a cougar. Its purr lulled me to sleep.

I awoke sometime later, sucked down into my bag as if tucked into a well-made military cot. The cat was hogging the bed. I could hardly breathe.

At home I would lightly nudge my human companion with my foot and turn away, pulling the blanket with me in a tuck-and-roll manoeuvre. I doubted my "Gimme the blanket" technique would work on a mountain lion. I had to try, though. I gave the cat a teeny-weeny nudge, a pathetic attempt. I tried again. I'm not even sure my hands moved the second time.

Should I wake a possibly cranky cat? I asked myself. I reckoned a cranky cat is a cranky cat no matter how much love I directed at it. I went with the safe plan; stay snuggled up to the back of the cougar. Heavy eyelids finally overcame the uncomfortable position and I went back to sleep.

When I next awoke, the sun's soft morning rays beamed through the tree branches, creating a highway to heaven. The cougar was gone, and with it my fear of the dark and the "devil-cat" itself. I questioned the reality of the night over and over, and at that time I decided I would not share my story with anyone but my teacher, Chris. I doubted my friends would believe me, and the story would only fuel their growing concerns for my future.

I sat up in my bag and marvelled at the beauty around me. A hairy wood-pecker, with its undulating flight pattern, glided through the misty light and landed on the trunk of a hemlock tree in front of me. I noticed a small hole above him and wondered if it was his home. In that moment I knew I could never go back to who I once was. I felt at home in the forest. I didn't want to leave. If cuddling a cougar was just the beginning of my reality with nature, I wanted more.

Five years later, as I sat alone on my special flat rock in Native Anchorage, the memory of my devil-cat sleepover proved to me I wasn't scared. I spontaneously waded into the frigid ocean. Most claim a person can only survive in the 50-degree Fahrenheit water for around 20 minutes, but cold water is all about the mind. When you can accept it for what it is, rather than what you want it to be, you can bob around for quite some time.

Migwat (*mee-wot*), the seal, swam in close to shore, beckoning me to join her. I shed my clothes, like the magical selkie or seal maiden, and slowly walked farther into the salty, calm water. It felt wonderful. I swam around, diving and playing with the seal, until I noticed two eagles soaring above. I floated on my back to watch.

For eons, eagles have been revered in many cultures, seen as a symbol for the soul or of new vision and the power to become far more than imagined. They are the messengers of the Creator. Today their feathers are still used in sacred ceremonies, for healing, and even for shape-shifting. I wondered if these eagles had been among the ones who had greeted us on our arrival. They reminded me that it was

The remains of the longhouse at Mamali-lacull̲a on Village Island. The ancient village was originally named Mim'kw̲amlis.

time to talk with the ancestors, as Tom Sewid had asked us to do.

We rowed over to the ancient village site on the island. (We estimated it took 30 minutes to row there from Native Anchorage, but without a watch, time became a guessing game—we lived in "bush time" and relied on the tide, the sun, and our intuition for our clock. Strangely, even though the numbers on a clock did not govern our lives—we ate whenever we could, went to bed when we were tired, and woke up when we felt rested—we always wondered what time of day it was. As I wrote in my journal: "I'm keeping track of days on my castaway notched stick. Doubt I'll keep up with this, but it's fun. Haven't a clue what the day is and not the vaguest idea the time. It's dark, that's all I know. Been that for a while.")

Now called Mamalilaculla (*mah-mah-lil-lah-coolah*), the village's real name is 'Mim'kw̲amlis (*meem-quahm-lees*), meaning "the island with the rocks and islands in front," and there were indeed rocks in the sheltered bay. While we manoeuvred through them to reach shore, we spied a bighouse frame still standing amidst the tangled berry bushes. I was immediately transported back to the days when there were hand-carved bighouses down the length of the beach, smoke billowing from their roofs, and welcome poles with arms outstretched in front.

Walking ashore set my skin tingling, not only from the excitement of exploring an ancient village. I also felt the air was vibrant with history, and with unseen guides leading me on. Micah and I followed different paths, and as I wandered along the grassy trail, past dilapidated 1930s-style houses and old fruit trees, I noticed a hidden totem pole, its wolf eyes and teeth barely visible, which had turned into a nurse log supporting tiny huckleberry bushes and young hemlock trees. I sat down amongst the old stalks of the stinging nettles surrounding it and felt a sense of déjà vu, as if past and future dimensions of time and place were overlapping one another and the present. Since I had never explored the island before, I wondered what had triggered this feeling of remembrance.

The trail beckoned me farther. Emerging from a thicket of thimbleberry, I came upon a small clearing where a fallen pole lay on its back under the canopy of cherry and maple trees. It had to be the mortuary pole for the powerful chief that Tom had told me about. Although the raven, killer whale, and eagle that had originally topped it had broken off and washed away, the pole was still impressive and must have stood at least 40 feet high when first erected.

Totem poles tell a story to those who can read them. Only crests owned by a family, passed down through the generations or obtained by trade or marriage, can be displayed on a pole, and the more crests (and dances and songs) a family possesses in its "box of treasures," the more wealthy and powerful it is. Supernatural beings are the most powerful crests.

With my finger, I traced two faces of *Dzunukwa* (*joo-neh-qwa*), the Wild Woman of the Woods or female Sasquatch, that were carved into the paws of a mighty grizzly bear standing atop the giant head of the chief. Above the two *Dzunukwas* crouched *U'ligan* (*oo-lee-gan*), the wolf, hanging over the bank. Touching and identifying the figures on these poles was magical for me. I felt like I was living among the myths of the old ways and creating a new myth along the way.

Standing next to the pole felt like the perfect place to begin my one-way conversation with the Great Spirit and ancestors of the land. I bowed my head in reverence and spoke aloud, "Hello, ancestors and all beings of Light who watch over me. I've come to live here and follow in your ways of the past. To honour and learn from Nature in the purest way I know how. Please share your wisdom and help guide and protect me along my journey. With all my heart, thank you." I concluded by offering a downy eagle feather to the ancestors in hopes that they would send me a sign my prayers had been heard.

When I lifted my head, through the branches of a cherry tree I saw a large bird flying directly toward me. Within seconds I could hear the flapping of wings and the rustling of branches above me. A young, golden brown bald eagle had settled in the tree I sat under. I knew in three years his dark beak would change to golden yellow, and his blotchy, camouflaging baby colours would transform into the striking white head and tail of his parents. He was magnificent. I felt like that young eagle, learning the ways of survival from an ancient lineage so that I could one day shed a mask of feathers to reveal the divine truth of who I truly was. I knew in my heart all my prayers and dreams had been heard. I hadn't had a one-way conversation after all.

MY WILD REALITY

Solitude and retirement from the world is not such an insufferable state of life as most men imagine…It may likewise instruct us how much a plain and temperate way of living conduces to the health of the body and the vigor of the mind, both [of] which we are apt to destroy by excess and plenty.
—Woodes Rogers, 18th-century privateer

Our workload gave us only brief moments to sit on rocks, pondering nature or our situation. We split everything 50–50, alternating all chores to eliminate arguments about individual workloads. Native Anchorage kicked our butts. We dragged our weary selves around for several weeks, organizing our camp.

The first five nights I lay awake with a chill on my spine. This was followed by five more sleeps of night sweats. We obviously needed to improve our makeshift shelter. It received only dappled sunlight; the result was cold, damp gear and restless nights, with the chill dampness settling into our bones regardless of how many layers we wore. We needed to suck up all the warmth of the sun when it did emerge, so, reluctantly, we moved into the front yard of the decomposing trailer.

I spent an entire day rebuilding our lean-to, cutting new poles to length for the frame and harvesting perfect sheets of bark from fallen trees for roof tiles. For the sidewalls, Micah split boards from cedar logs, as we had seen in Hilary Stewart's book *Cedar*.

We rowed *Gribley* to nearby beaches to collect scraps of washed-up wood, scrounged rusty nails from old boards, patched the lean-to roof as best we could, replaced the broken roof beam, and gathered armloads of bark to use as carpeting. We lined a firepit with shells to reduce the risk of starting an underground fire, and carried clay from the stream to cement stones together in a firewall to more efficiently reflect the heat.

Next, in order of priority, we built a smokehouse and then an outhouse. Technically, our privy would not have qualified as a "house," though we did eventually give it a roof.

Robin's egg blue skies and gorgeous sunsets spoiled us the first week, making us forget we were living on the rain-coast. Then the constant winter drizzle set in. Rain blew into our shelter from all angles, and wind howled through the cracks. I had been naively excited about experiencing raw elements, even in my home, but after four days I finally grumbled, "Micah, you're right. Let's board the place up." Lying night after night in a wet sleeping bag dispelled the notion of "becoming one with the weather." I wrote in my journal, "When

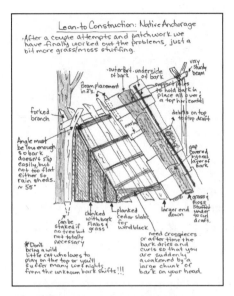

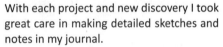

With each project and new discovery I took great care in making detailed sketches and notes in my journal.

it's 38 degrees [Fahrenheit] out and it feels tropical, talk about getting used to the elements. It helps that there's nowhere else to go."

We used our cedar planks to cover as many open areas of the existing structure as we could, building a fortress to protect us from our elemental enemies. We chinked the lean-to with moss and grass, covered it with a layer of forest debris to cut down on drafts, and collected armfuls of evergreen boughs to use as a mattress that would also insulate us from the cold ground.

After we built the essentials, I treated myself to more backbreaking work by constructing the ultimate naturalist's desk, as well as a wobbly chair and a small table where we could prepare food. Journalling at my little desk for the first time, with numb fingers, I sketched a snail I had had for dinner. I felt like the naturalists of the past.

Henry David Thoreau once wrote, "If one advances confidently in the direction of his dreams, and endeavors to live the life which he has imagined, he will meet with a success unexpected in common hours." I prayed for this success.

The place began to look good. Relatively. Each day I felt a bit of shock as I awoke, realizing I was still living with Micah, crammed together in a bark lean-to next to a grunge-pit trailer.

Day 11
Mom, you won't believe what I am living in. It's beyond hillbilly. I'm not even sure what to call it.

Hovel comes to mind, defined as a small, humble, dirty, disorganized dwelling. When we renamed the trailer we lived beside *The Chateau*, I somehow managed to become happy with it. Or happier, at least, trying to ignore it.

Within three days, we stopped boiling water, ready to take our chances with giardiasis. We couldn't cope with the added effort of boiling water every day, and sipping a hot cup of water while sweat dripped off our faces did not provide the needed pick-me-up. I tried to refrain from thinking about the primitive year to come, and the nightmare of boiling water with rocks in steam-bent wooden boxes.

We washed the dishes we'd salvaged from the mess in the Chateau with sand and shell, down at the water's edge, numbing our hands daily. Every field guide states that the silica-rich horsetail plant is an excellent pot scrubber, metal polisher, or sandpaper substitute, but all three uses absolutely eluded me. Fresh horsetail just made a green mess of things. Dried stems worked better, but those required too much patience. Beach sand worked as well as any modern scouring pad. I had grit-ground hands rather than dishpan hands.

The first time I washed our dishes, there was a coating of gooey, nasty scum at the shoreline. I called Micah down to see if he could make sense of it.

"Oo, yuck," he said. "Maybe it's clam poo." Laughing hysterically at how ridiculous that sounded, Micah walked back up the beach, leaving me to figure out how to navigate our dishes through as little ocean barf as possible. I missed lemon-scented, bubbly dish soap.

Micah didn't have city-life hang-ups like I did. He maintained a cheery attitude in any gross situation. Comfortable with himself, he never worried what others thought. He had a beautiful spirit, and it didn't take him long to step into the role of caveman. My previous life of pedicures, plucking eyebrows, and picky eating kept me from embracing the beginning of human evolution when things were gross.

I never did become content with ocean scum on my plate. Calling it jetsam or flotsam didn't make it better. I nearly resorted to Micah's personal dishwashing method after several days of having to wash my dishes in sea puke. When Micah had breakfast duty and the dishes hadn't been washed for two and a half days, he casually picked up a plate and started licking it. I knew he hadn't brushed his teeth in days. With a scrunched-up face I said, "Oo, what are you doing? That's disgusting."

"No it's not. My friends do it all the time. There's nothing wrong with it."

"Yeah, I'm pretty sure there is, Micah. You shouldn't be licking dirty dishes that have been sitting around here, especially mine," I laughed. "We found these in the trailer, remember?" I wrote, "Maybe he has antibacterial slobber. I don't know, but I'll wash mine."

The practice of good hygiene is important for those living in the bush. Whenever I looked down at my hands, I wondered why I didn't follow it. Perhaps exhaustion played a role, or maybe it was simply due to being away from my civilized routines for too long. Whatever the cause, I could not remember to brush my teeth, wash my face, or comb my hair. Dirty fingernails became the norm, and matted hair the style. I hated my lumberjack look. I missed being "pretty."

> *My friend Jeanne would be proud. I haven't worn a bra in weeks; it's too cold to get dressed. It's funny, the things that were once "normal" are not so important when you're just trying to live. Micah wonders how my hair could smell good still. His sure doesn't. It's been forever since I've washed it. 25 days! Two hair rinses, if you can call them that, and a sponge wash. Come on, that's sickening. How long can you go I wonder. It's funny not having a mirror. We have to tell one another if we have junk in our teeth or something smeared on our face. I haven't noticed too much though, because we've been so busy. But I definitely feel scrubby most days.*

Micah's socks topped the stink list. I never believed stinky socks with enough old sweat could stand on their own, but Micah's did. He would only change them when they reached that stage. Gross.

Day 42
I washed my thermal shirt today, just in case you can get something from wearing the same clothes day after day. It's strange how you forget to do things that are totally natural at home, like changing clothes. All the hygiene stuff. At the end of the day, we're so tired after cooking and getting the bed ready that Micah is asleep in two seconds, like an old man on his chair.

I somehow managed to stay up a bit later to journal the day's events every day, even when I could barely keep my eyes open or lift my pen to write. I scribbled, "I'm pretty sure I'll be going blind soon from all the smoke in the eyes! So I got that going for me."

By eliminating the draftiness of the shelter, we had invited in the smoke. Worse, we reeked of it. Everything turned a smoky yellow colour. I often wondered how long it would be until my skin turned yellow too.

The sea air and the dry heat of the fire is enough to make me turn into a raisin.

We had the worst case of nasal drip, too. Micah hardly noticed the slimy drips hanging from his nose. It drove me crazy. Wiping my nose on shirtsleeves became unacceptable when I knew how many days I would wear the same clothes. Distressed, I opted for a bandana, but the thought of blowing into it and then having to hand-wash the snot triggered my weakened gag reflex. I developed a new appreciation for throwaway Kleenex. I sniffled continually until finally breaking down to learn the art of the One-Finger Nostril Blow.

The progression of becoming wild had begun. With my Paleolithic roots emerging, there was no longer a place for the word "glamorous" in my vocabulary.

The lack of glamour definitely extended to toilet paper. This necessity taught me to be specific when I make a wish. If I'm not, the universe will plunk in the small details I've left out. When I dreamed of primitive living, for example, I didn't remember to factor in toilet paper. As a result, a tiny part of every day turned into an "I can't believe I'm resorting to this" experience. The best toilet paper was the soft new leaves of the thimbleberry bush. However, our harvesting rules didn't allow us to pick more than a third of a plant's leaves, which forced us to resort to other things. I kept a list of survival toilet paper in order of preference, along with the modern equivalent.

1. Thimbleberry leaves (tissue paper)
2. Fluffed cedar bark (newspaper)
3. Brown grass (lined stationary)
4. Dead and damp alder leaves (glossy paper)
5. Moss
6. Cedar boughs
7. Hemlock boughs
8. Sticks
9. Spruce bark chunks
10. Rocks
11. Clamshells
12. Sharp, waxy salal leaves

My mother sympathized with my plight, and later, when she was able to send us care packages, she would wrap every item in tissue paper, toilet paper, or paper towel. She always sent a tabloid newspaper from the grocery checkout too, for a bit of city entertainment.

The saddening list of toilet paper continues. I've used sticks and now a People *magazine. Give a bush person a magazine and they'll use it for all kinds of things other than reading.*

I have never been more thankful for a National Enquirer *in all my life. This issue reads, "My boobs are picking up signals from space." One night my evening T.P. read, "Space Alien teens using glaciers for party ice, scientists say it gives them a real buzz!"*

I found no escape from my list of discomforts, not even in sleep. No matter how many times I moved a stone or stick from under me, by the time I crawled back into my sleeping bag, another lump had magically appeared. Even when I achieved comfort, I couldn't close my eyes because the lingering smoke in the lean-to caused our watering eyes to sting when we shut them.

Most mornings I wondered if I had slept at all. We experienced what I call "wolf sleeps"—when a person sleeps for about half an hour, wakes up, turns over onto a pain-free side, waits to fall asleep again, and then wakes up 15 minutes later to relieve that side of the body. This pattern continued until morning.

We considered it a good morning when we woke up dry. Scout loved to play on the lean-to roof, and we never knew how much she had shifted the bark tiles until it rained. Then I would wake up to a repetitive drip on my head, like medieval torture.

One night we decided to bring the cleanest couch cushion from the trailer to sleep on. I looked forward to the nights I had the cushion side of the lean-to, though I'll never understand why. I had the worst sleeps on that cushion. It had a crack down the middle of the foam so it could be folded in half, and I awoke every morning squished into the crack with a good-morning backache. For months I suffered, unwilling to believe I couldn't make the soft cushion work. Micah the Giant, on the other hand, woke from his cushion sleeps as if he had just come back from a massage therapist.

Finally I brought myself to concede. "Micah, the cushion's all yours." I settled for the thinning, needle-dropping hemlock mattress. Darkness always came before I had time to hike around to harvest a fluffy new mattress. For months, the Sacred Order of Survival never expanded past number 6: food. I positioned a new mattress at about number 42.

We rowed, hauled, sawed, chopped, lifted, hiked, explored, harvested, hunted, prepared, cooked, and cleaned. We had never felt more exhausted in our lives. At night, our smoky eyes watering, we'd ask one another, "Does your back hurt?"

"Yup."

"Do your arms ache?"

"Yup."

"Is there any part of you that *doesn't* hurt?"

"Nope."

Pitiful laughter always followed.

But lying back, looking up at cobwebs, knowing a good night's sleep wasn't coming, I also knew the hardships were worth it. I could lie on a log, watching eagles clasp talons and tumble through the air, without a bill to worry about or a schedule to keep. I could awake to the gentle *poofs* of harbour porpoises feeding in the bay instead of being swept up in the manic energy of a city's rush-hour buzz.

I learned I could do anything. No matter how tired, hungry, or sore I felt, I could row those extra miles or lift loads I once thought too heavy. I could do it because I had to. Nothing could be put off until tomorrow, and I loved every minute of it. I loved knowing I had worked my body to its physical limit. I loved the pain, because I no longer felt numbed by conveniences.

I had a dream once of an angel telling me, "If you can love the worst of things, you can love anything." I practised love a lot.

STARVING ON CLAMS

I am reminded of the man who, alone in a vast desert with no hat, no water, and a broken leg, pulled himself up on one bruised and battered elbow and smiled at a bunch of dry grass, saying, "You know, if this keeps up I might get discouraged."

—Larry Dean Olsen, survival expert

Prior to this expedition, three weeks was the longest either of us had spent surviving off the land in one stretch. We could go home after a weekend or two, pig out on our favourite foods, shower till our feet were wrinkled, and lounge around on the couch, watching movies until we felt revived. At Native Anchorage, however, we found ourselves weakening as the weeks passed.

Our leftover town food dwindled quickly, even though we tried to ration it, and our knowledge of seashore survival was minimal. We couldn't catch anything with legs in spite of daily attempts, so we relied on steamed clams for dinner every night. I could barely force myself to swallow the gooey, goopy butter clam, even after a long day of physical labour. Many claim that one cannot starve to death living on the coast, but I sure lost a lot of weight living on clams.

We harvested four kinds: butter clams, horse clams, littlenecks, and cockles. Each preferred a certain type of beach, and all dug distinct houses. Tracking clams is an art, and we slowly began to recognize who lived in the different sizes and shapes of holes along the seashore.

The biggest holes lured me first. I assumed the fattest clams dug the largest homes, but this theory produced nothing but an empty bucket and the deep, bubbling hole of an escaping mud shrimp. We also avoided the home of the gigantic horse clam, which the Kwakwaka'wakw considered "slave food." With a huge, wrinkly, hairy siphon and an enormous brown stomach-pouch, the horse clam appeared extremely unappetizing, even to a hungry survivalist.

Our favourite clam was the heart-shaped cockle. Once only eaten by chieftain families, the cockle has a tender, firm texture without the large, goopy

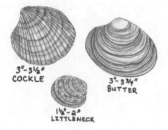

3"-3¼"
COCKLE

3"-3¾"
BUTTER

1½"-2"
LITTLENECK

stomach of other clams. Cockle-hunting became my obsession.

Unlike the sandy golden beaches favoured by butter clams, cockles prefer a muddy grey clam bed and often live directly on the surface. I would scan the beach, searching for the cockle's high, powerful spit. I loved watching clams spit. It transformed the beach into an entertaining water show for a movie-deprived wilderness dweller. On misty mornings, with the sun's soft rays beaming on the steamy beach, I imagined a symphony accompanying the irregular rhythm of the sparkling, jumping water as each spit followed its individual arc.

Since clams were our main source of protein, I was determined to learn how to cook them in such a way that I could get them down without having my throat close up. I became a clam chef. The clam burger, made with butter or cockle clams, wild onions and bladderwrack seaweed pods as binder, and a garnish of dandelion leaves, wall lettuce, or other winter greens, was my favourite delicious discovery. I also made a delicious stir-fry from chewy button clam muscles mixed with leftover clam juice, wild onions, bladderwrack seaweed leaves, cattail shoots, and a handful of mint added at the end.

We spent many gruelling days preserving clams. Each type required specific processing procedures. Tom Sewid, our water-taxi driver, had told us how to prepare *ku'matsi* (*q-maht-see*), or smoked clams. Once they were steamed, barbecued, and smoked we strung them on thin branches, which we then tied into rings. These rings were traditionally used as currency by the Kwakwaka'wakw hundreds of years ago. Heaps of hung *ku'matsi* were regarded as a sign of wealth.

Processing clams is big work. Sitting here all day carving cedar sticks, skewering and barbecuing clams, started me thinking about them a whole bunch. Those lovely, gooey, sloppy guys. Why the hell am I doing so much clamming? There is plenty of summertime food, isn't there? And I can eat all the fresh clams in the world in the winter. I'm on smokehouse duty all night tonight. Hope my eyes don't look as puffy and bloodshot as Micah's did this morning.

Standing over the hundreds of harvested clams in our water-filled rowboat, watching them spit out the sand collected in their bodies, I wondered how wealthy we would have been back in the days of the dugout canoe.

There was only one problem: smoked clams were disgusting. We wouldn't likely be trading them for anything. Micah's empty stomach tolerated the foul stench and the black, rock-hard clams. I spit them out before swallowing. Scout shot me a look of disgust when she sniffed them. I scribbled, "I'd rather eat the inner bark of a hemlock tree and feel like a beaver." We saved them for the dismal day I too would be hungry enough to eat them.

Micah ate a lot more clams than I did. One night he said, "Hey, do you feel a tingling from these clams?"

"No. Do you?"

"Yeah, I think so."

The smoked clams looked appetizing but tasted awful.

Our eyes bulged. We turned away and spit out our mouthfuls of steamed clams.

"Holy crap, are you serious? You could have PSP. You gotta puke that up. You could die!"

"What? How am I supposed to do that?"

"I don't know. Stuff your finger down the back of your throat."

He headed out of the lean-to. I could hear the sound of his gagging over the crunching of shell and rock as he ran down to the beach.

"It's not working," he yelled. "I'm going to try drinking salt water."

"Wow, that's gnarly," I called out as I listened to him retching up the tingling clams. Eight cups of nasty salt water finally emptied his stomach. He was lucky.

Deadly paralytic shellfish poisoning, or PSP, is caused by microscopic single-celled algae called dinoflagellates. When the ocean's conditions are perfect, a bloom of these algae occurs, known as "red tide," even though PSP is rarely associated with a red tinge to the water. Because clams and other shellfish are filter-feeders, they can become infected with PSP. It doesn't affect them, but it can kill humans who eat the infected meat. The first indication of poisoning is a tingling of the lips or tongue. PSP toxins are estimated to be 1,000 times more lethal than cyanide. We always cut off the black tips of the shellfish siphon—the breathing and feeding tube—which retain the largest quantity of toxins, and only dug during the safe months of November to March.

Heaven eventually smiled down on us when we caught our first Dungeness crab, *ku'mis* (*goo-mees*), in our hoop trap. Scout loved this new diet. I thought about eating *her*, however, the night she stole the precious picked crabmeat I had saved for an afternoon treat.

Micah obviously needed a lot more food than I did. He suffered hunger pains. We both began showing signs of malnutrition. We called our daily fatigue *The Fibro*, after fibromyalgia. When we were on the beach, we had to walk up a tiny hill to reach the lean-to. Some days I stood at the bottom with pots full of water in each hand, contemplating how I would force my legs up that hill.

Chronic dehydration and cold contributed to our fatigue. We unconsciously started rationing our water to spare ourselves the burdensome task of gathering it, even though our bodies needed it for energy and warmth. Every common task we did without thinking in the city took great effort in our new surroundings. While midday munchies brought the worst hunger pains, cooking lunch was a luxury we didn't give ourselves. We didn't have enough food for a third meal, nor the energy to find and harvest more. I began to entertain strange ideas, like, "Maybe I won't be so hungry if my stomach shrinks to the size of a pea. It won't take much to fill it then." Often I tried to save a bite of dinner for the next day, to allay the afternoon pain. Micah never could; he needed every mouthful at every meal.

We pushed ourselves harder than we thought possible. We fell asleep as soon as we zipped up our sleeping bags, and it was easy to sleep through the morning singing of the birds.

Jolted awake, I sprang out of bed, banging my head on a pole of the lean-to. I roused Micah. "Hey, you hear that? What's that noise?"

He rubbed the corner of his eye as he awoke. "It sounds like a boat, doesn't it?"

"Yeah, let's get up."

A wooden fishing boat was anchored in the bay, and a little grey skiff was motoring to shore. We walked down the beach to meet the skipper, who introduced himself as Jim Davis. He was 60, born and raised on Berry Island, several miles west of Native Anchorage. He came from a family of boat builders and still fished from the decks of the 38-foot wooden troller *Cedar Isle*, built by his father.

We invited him up to our lean-to for fir-needle tea, but when he sat on the steps of the trailer, he politely declined. The state of the Chateau didn't speak well of the tea blends on offer, especially when they were served in an old mug we had found discarded in the trailer.

Looking around, Jim slowly shook his head. "Pretty grim. Pretty grim scene." He drew out each word.

"Oh, come on, Jim," I replied with a smile. "It isn't that bad."

An uncomfortable silence ensued until the laughing began; it *was* that bad.

Jim told us about the old days, when he had seen the abundance of the sea. He could remember when the herring used to spawn around Native Anchorage, when rockfish flourished, when he wouldn't be thrown in jail for harvesting abalone, and when salmon used to return to our small creek. Up until the late 1960s, he told us, salmon had spawned in many of the creeks near us, but these runs were now extinct, like those of myriad other empty creeks in the area. "Yup, it's a desperate show around here," Jim would say when talking about how things had changed. Even in the wil-

Jim Davis, a local fisherman, was born and raised on Berry Island. His family built wooden fishing boats.

derness, where I least expected it, I sensed I was living in a dying world, surviving with dying skills.

Surprisingly, Jim also told us that when he was young, the Mainland, now known as the Broughton Archipelago, had had a large community of families scattered throughout the islands, living near hand-logging claims and fish-buying camps. In the 1940s, the nearest post office to us was in Freshwater Bay, and there were 45 individuals or families who picked up mail there. The Oien family had homesteaded Native Anchorage until around 1945. They sold strawberries. All that remained of the Oien farm were small grassy patches surrounding our lean-to, a few old fruit trees hidden amongst a salmonberry thicket, and the remnants of a broken-down fence.

Knowing the history of a place is powerful; it made me feel more attached to the land, which ultimately led to my wanting to aid in its preservation. And Jim's short visit was a welcome gift in itself, and a much-needed break from our lives of clam digging.

SHIPWRECKED WISHES

You have the gift of a brilliant internal guardian that stands ready to warn
you of hazards and guides you through risky situations.
—Gavin de Becker, *The Gift of Fear*

It would have taken us half a day to row for help. If neither of us could row, it would have probably taken weeks to flag down a boat. I loved that feeling of isolation, but it immediately made us vigilant about all survival safety protocols— rules we casually ignored back home. One small knife cut could become seriously infected if not treated properly. I felt confident I could heal our wounds and common ailments with herbal medicine, but the hassle of tending injuries took time from imperative chores. When one of us was in trouble, both were in trouble.

During our first two months I had only minor cuts and scrapes, bangs and bruises, and one heck of a sore back. Parts I never thought could ache throbbed all the time, like the backs of my hands and sides of my fingers. One day I wrote, "I noticed how sore my hands were today. The pads on my fingers are swollen, have been sore for days. But otherwise, tip-top shape, I guess."

Micah took a far worse battering than me in the first couple of months. I had graduated from the Dominion Herbal College in 1998, but I hadn't had many willing patients to practise on. Micah gave me the greatest gift anyone could give a budding herbalist: volunteering his body for experimental research. Like a witch apothecary, I had brought various dried herbs specific to each system of the body in my first aid kit, along with several amber-coloured dropper bottles of tinctures, a thermometer, a chunk of beeswax, a tin of homemade coltsfoot cough drops, and a few medicinal oils.

He's fallen apart. He's popped out his shoulder, has a gnarly sore festering on
his hand, nicks and scrapes everywhere. He has shooting pains in his knee.
We've been shucking so many clams; we think the juice is turning a cut into
an infected hole. Something is eating out his flesh.

Micah also contracted a terrible case of diarrhea, which we termed "The Rhea." Neither of us could find a treatment to cure it, nor did we know the cause. Laughter became the only remedy. He never felt sick or tired, nor did he develop any more serious problems from The Rhea. He simply lived with the condition for an entire year, with cedar bark and leaves for toilet paper.

Infection was one of our worst enemies. Sap that oozed from wounds in evergreen trees or woodpecker holes was our best remedy. Memorizing the location of trees with clear, clean, dripping pitch became a necessity.

If a wound was free of dirt, I let it bleed as much as possible to help remove bacteria while I hiked to the nearest pharmacy tree. Carefully, I spun the gooey sap onto a carved stick and transferred it to a littleneck clam shell. Back at the fire I tenderly heated the pitch. When it had melted to the consistency of liquid honey, I slowly poured the warm, golden, anti-bacterial syrup into the wound, sealing it as well as if I'd put on a waterproof bandage. The pitch would stay on until the cut healed perfectly from the inside out.

Serious wounds demanded astringent herbal teas. The tannic acid and oils found in the bark of the Douglas fir, western hemlock, and red alder trees made excellent cleansing washes. I pounded and boiled their inner barks until the water turned a bright reddish orange. Once cooled and strained through a bundle of grass or fern fronds, it was ready to use, like hydrogen peroxide.

Knowing the hidden, healing powers in the lifeblood of a tree, flower, or root made me feel like I was a part of the secret inner workings of nature. After all, members of the animal kingdom have not forgotten how to treat themselves with herbal remedies. Gorillas know how to select and prepare 30 different plants to cleanse their systems of various parasites, while bears eat clay before hibernation. Elephants eat the leaves and roots of a tree in the Boraginaceae family before giving birth, just as Kenyan woman do to help induce overdue babies. Rats and raptor birds weave anti-microbial herbs into their nests to control insect infestations, and chimpanzees use the bitter pith of the mujunso tree to cure diarrhea.

While we both felt comfortable and confident about our knowledge and skills on land, on the ocean we were two city slickers plunked down in an unfamiliar, watery world. We didn't fear it, but we didn't yet respect it. *Gribley* became our teacher.

We had many obvious, first-timer lessons to learn. First we acquainted ourselves with our ship. I had never rowed a boat before. Muscles new to the art of rowing screamed with use, but after several weeks, when my lean body had learned the rhythm, and blisters had turned to calluses, I enjoyed arm-powering our little boat, even when we were going against the tide, with the wind at our back. Hungry wilderness dwellers could not await a favourable tide.

While we were learning the various lessons of How to Properly Tie up a Boat, we spent many days pouring water from our gumboots after rescuing *Gribley*. We learned never to leave the boat in a flat bay with a receding tide. The punishment for this mistake was dragging the boat for several hundred feet through what was locally known as "loon-shit"—gooey, shin-deep mud with a suction grip on our boots. We also learned not to tie our boat below the high-water line when the tide was coming in unless we wanted to swim out to untie it. Once we even failed to tie the boat up at all. It floated away. Luckily, a man from the nearest First Nations village, a few miles away, caught *Gribley* and brought her back for us.

I didn't have to wait long to fulfill my childhood wish of being shipwrecked on a deserted island. Three weeks after our arrival, when the rain ceased and the water became glassy calm, we decided to give fishing another try. We still had not caught a fish. The friendly, rain-free sky enticed us to push off toward the hopeful halibut spot two miles away, which Tom had marked on our chart. Through trial and error, our standard method of learning, we were teaching ourselves how to set a longline. Leaving baited hooks attached to a long piece of rope on the bottom of the ocean sounded like an excellent idea to our growling stomachs. The line would fish for us while we continued with our other life-sustaining tasks on shore.

When we reached the fishing hole, Micah began clipping the hooks on the line and sinking the rope with rocks, while I rowed us farther out in a straight line so as to keep the rope flat on the bottom of the ocean.

After we sank half of our 12 hooks, I felt a gust of wind on my face and noticed Micah's shirt flapping. It came out of nowhere. The unruffled water turned to frenzied, white-capped waves. Rain gushed from the sky.

The squall made it nearly impossible to keep little *Gribley* from spinning sideways into the waves, which would have sunk our ten-foot rowboat instantly. Micah madly began letting out the rope, trying to avoid getting tangled.

"Keep the boat straight into the wind," he yelled, clinging to the sides to keep from flipping out.

I had trouble maintaining control when the big gusts blasted us, and I hollered back, "I'm trying. I'm doing the best I can." In my head, I said, Gimme a break, buddy. On a good day, rowing you around with these Mickey Mouse oars is like having an elephant in the back.

I was digging deep into the water with all my strength when the right oar popped out of its oarlock. Precariously close to falling overboard, I fumbled to get it back in place. I knew that the short, featherweight oars could break under the stress at any second.

Crack. An oarlock bolt broke. Not wanting to add to Micah's stress level, I kept the broken oarlock a secret.

He finished letting out the rope, tossed the log buoy into the water, and crouched down in the back of the boat, holding on to the gunnels.

"Hey, maybe you should row, Micah. You're stronger than me."

"Yeah, okay, get ready to switch when we get a break in these gusts."

As we executed a quick, choreographed pass-by, I warned, "Be careful how hard you crank on the oars. We lost one bolt already."

His head swung down to look and then tilted back up to the sky, as if asking God, What else could possibly go wrong?

The water was soon level with the stern, and smaller waves began pouring over the sides.

That's what else, I thought. I scrambled around Micah to the bow, hoping to keep us from sinking.

The boat spun and rocked. Time slowed as I tasted salt spray on my lips, felt rain dripping down the back of my neck, and watched Micah's deeply furrowed brow. I knew just one bigger wave would swamp little *Gribley*. I expected to be bobbing in the ocean at any moment and attempted to brace myself for my body's automatic shock response. I knew that 20 percent of drowning victims die within two minutes of submersion as a result of their uncontrolled gasping and rapid breathing.

I spotted our lifejackets, which we had a bad habit of using as seats rather than safety gear. Micah reached down and tossed me a dripping jacket from the bottom of the boat before I even uttered a word. I pulled it on, though wearing the bulky gear didn't instill a great feeling of safety.

Our closest refuge was Hail Island. I pictured a shipwrecked sea captain hailing a vessel for rescue and naming the island after his ordeal. If the guy lived to name it, perhaps this is a good sign, I told myself.

The islet began to grow in my field of vision. Trying to surf onto the sharp, rocky beach was another hard lesson about the ocean. I touched Micah's shoulder. "We must get *Gribley* out of these rocks, Micah. She'll be smashed full of holes for sure. Let's try to get to the lee side of the island."

He turned around, his face dripping with water. "I was just thinking the same thing. We'll never land her here."

Bumping and grinding along the shoreline, we finally found a safer place to jump from the boat. We scrambled along the slippery rocks, pulling *Gribley* to safety with only minor dents. About 15 minutes remained before the already dark grey sky would turn out all the lights.

We had entered the second stage of hypothermia, with an increasing loss of motor function, blue lips, and deathly pale digits. We shook uncontrollably. I, luckily, wore a hat, but Micah had left the lean-to wearing only a skimpy amount of winter clothing.

We did a hasty inventory of our supplies. Shivering, I shoved my hands into the pockets of my soaking wet jeans, searching for the survival goodies I should have had. I flashed back to a thought that crossed my mind at the lean-to: "Oh well, Micah has his lighter." We had agreed to carry a lighter that we would use only in the event of a life-threatening emergency. It became a test of willpower, knowing a quick flick of fire hid in our pockets.

However, when we held out our hands now, displaying our offerings, we each held only a knife. No tinder material, no garbage bag, no piece of rope, no lighters, nothing. A deflating silence punctured our shred of gusto.

"Here's our test of survival," I thought.

The hum of a distant motorboat jolted us out of our empty shock. Micah, in his puffy red lifejacket, jumped onto a nearby rock, frantically waving his arms above his head to hail the boat, just like in the movies. I roared with laughter.

"Dude, what are you doing? They can't see you," I teased.

"It's worth a try," he stated emphatically.

"Is it?" I laughed. We could always make fun of each other, knowing our teases came from the heart. He soon sat down and laughed with me.

Bleak as our situation was, we welcomed the challenge. With only a few precious moments of light remaining, we had to get moving. Performing jumping jacks all night, which often works to fend off hypothermia, would not be possible in thick salal brush or on the slippery, algae-covered rocks.

Micah's whole body shivered violently, and we had begun to feel lethargic. Soon we would lose the muscle control needed to start a friction fire.

I said, "I've screwed up enough in the past to know I don't want to relive the same mistakes. A warm bath and a hot cup of cocoa are not waiting for me this time. I want to stick to the Sacred Order of Survival. You agree?"

He nodded. "Yeah, I'll work on fire."

Scrambling among the boulders, I discovered a small, uncomfortable cave for shelter. Micah found all the material necessary for a bow-drill kit in less than ten minutes. He started carving and I started stuffing the cave with leathery salal leaves and evergreen boughs that would serve as insulated bedding.

When our eyes failed to adjust to the darkening sky, we stopped to assess our situation. The lifejackets had proven their worth as warmth providers, and I anticipated using them as spine-protectors against the sharp rocks lining our tiny cave. Micah pulled out his round shoelace as an emergency bow-string, while I fluffed up a tinder nest.

The trees stopped swaying and the rain quit.

"What should we do? Try to row home?"

Micah shrugged. "I know a bow-drill. I don't know the ocean."

I felt exactly the same way.

He added, "You decide. Your intuition is better than mine."

In pitch-darkness, I picked a rock, sat down, cleared my mind, and asked the question: Will we be safe if we leave this island right now?

I listened to how I felt, opening myself to whatever the world offered. I became aware of my breathing, my heart rate. I questioned the feeling in my chest and gut; was it tight, relaxed, or fluttery? What was I drawn to? Was anything out

We learned early on that water conditions can turn quickly. We used the rowboat almost every day, but after our first near-disaster in *Gribley* we never again underestimated the changeable weather on the coast.

of the ordinary happening around me? I breathed deeply, closing my eyes. After paying close attention, I stood up. "Let's go."

We pushed *Gribley* from the safety of land to float on the uncertainty of water. With the sound of slapping oars and the dark, silhouetted form of Hail looming behind us, we took turns rowing home so we could warm up enough to control our shivering and chattering teeth.

As we rowed, the ocean glowed with bright green, fluorescent fireworks that shot off in all directions around the boat. It was like a celebration that brightened the long journey home. I thought of the cave-dwelling glow worms I had seen in New Zealand and wondered if they lived in the ocean. We had never seen or heard of phosphorescence, and it wasn't until I returned to civilization that I discovered it was the same microscopic algae that causes PSP which created the beautiful green sparks we saw that night. (When the algae are disturbed, a chemical reaction takes place within them, producing a bright glow.) At the time, I simply deemed it a gift from the ocean.

Watching the phosphorescence dance gave my mind something to love, distracting it from complaints about being soaking wet and dangerously cold. Studies have shown that possessing a sense of awe and wonder in life-threatening situations can turn victims into survivors.

When we saw the vague shape of our hovel in the darkness, I smiled. For the first time I felt like I was coming home, home to a place I loved. I believed something had been watching out for us—perhaps testing us, too. We made a pact to live by the lessons we learned: to respect the ocean, to carry a survival bag, to bring a rain jacket even in the sun, and to always carry a lighter.

My last, exhausted oar stroke crunched *Gribley* onto our beach. Slumping my shoulders, I mumbled, "I've gotta be careful what I wish for."

THE CRABBY COUGAR

The first rule is: Face reality. Good survivors aren't immune to fear. They know what is happening, and it does "scare the living shit out of them." It's all a question of what you do next.

—Laurence Gonzales, *Deep Survival*

Scout followed me everywhere. She was not your average house cat. I had rescued her nearly two years earlier, when she was a tiny feral kitten abandoned in a blackberry bush by her wild mother, who I often glimpsed near my gnomish, naturalist cabin.

I had meowed for over an hour, trying to entice the little furball out of the brambles. Grabbing her by the scruff of her neck, I dangled her away from my body until she calmed down. I took a good look at her. She had the dark, calico stripes of her mother and a faded raccoonlike tail. I knew her father must have been the property's tomcat because she had his white cheeks, chest, belly, and four perfectly white paws. She had the eyes and temper of a wild cat and survived when all her siblings had perished. I admired her.

Still, I didn't want a kitten. She didn't seem to want me either, even after a bit of milk. I decided to sit her down and tell her face to face what the deal would be. "Look, little kitten, I am going to live for a year alone in the wilderness with very few supplies. If you decide to live with me, you will have to come along. You will have to follow me wherever I go, stay wherever I tell you, hunt your own food, ride in a car, in a boat, and on a plane. You will have to act like a dog. If you want to do all these things, then stay. If you don't, go back to the blackberries and I will leave you a bowl of milk to help you get started."

The moment I took my hands off her, she bolted for the thicket and disappeared. "Phew," I huffed, turning around to leave.

A few seconds later, a small cry came from behind me. I looked over my shoulder and there sat Scout, staring up at me.

❧

After we arrived on Village Island, Scout needed retraining. When she was a kitten, I had taught her special command meows. In the wild, my shrill *mew, meew*, meaning "Get your butt over here," sounded like an injured baby deer. For predators in Native Anchorage, this was like hearing a lunch bell. I had to adapt our language. We switched to whistling like birds.

Scout also needed to make friends with *Gribley*. She dreaded the rowboat. Every time we loaded it up, she would follow us down to the beach, acting like she wanted to come, but when I went to pick her up, the chase was on. With her raccoon-striped tail sticking straight up, she glanced over her shoulder with a bratty "good luck to you" look on her face, and off she bounded.

I would eventually catch her and bundle her onboard, but for the first 15 minutes her piercing, high-pitched *mew* could be heard for miles. I wanted to toss her overboard at the three-minute mark, but no amount of scolding, spraying, or mouth clamping would quiet her, not even a quick dunk in the water. Scout yelled until she felt satisfied. She soon learned that a mass of floating bull kelp would only support the weight of a great blue heron, floating logs were not stable enough to leap onto, and balancing on the rim of the bow when there were boulders near the surface put her at risk of flying, with paws outstretched, into the chilly water. She also quickly figured out that the maximum distance she could leap from a standstill on the boat was 12 feet.

Her wildness kept her alive during the day on her own, but each night in Native Anchorage she curled up inside my sleeping bag. We were inseparable.

Scout became my teacher. First, she taught me to walk like a cat—taking a few quiet steps, then pausing to

Scout proved to be quite adaptable, but it took some time to train her to be comfortable on the little rowboat.

look and listen. A feral cat walks with an awareness most humans only fumble for. It seeks to know everything about its surroundings.

Scout's mind was always focused on the information her body was receiving; she lived in the now and never rushed. In contrast, I noticed my mind was always busy with rambling thoughts of past and future that clouded my awareness of what I was doing in the present. Watching Scout move through the landscape, climb trees, and pause in the shadows was like watching a miniature cougar; her sleek, muscular body was quick and agile. Hiking with my wild kitty helped me understand something I had heard at a survival training program: "When you walk, make sure every step blesses the earth."

🌿

Another cat lived on our island, far bigger than Scout. He too was the epitome of a perfect hunter. His presence was a tracker's dream, or so we thought.

"You'd better get up and check out these tracks!" exclaimed Micah on our 27th day in the wilderness. I jumped out of bed, pulled a sweater over my head, and dashed out of the shelter. Micah crouched on the path a couple of steps from our lean-to. I knelt down, smiling at the perfect fresh tracks of a mountain lion.

Those paw prints were a mystery asking to be solved. We spent the next three hours on our bellies, studying them. Based on the animal's trail width or straddle (distance between the inside heels of its rear feet) and other indicators, we believed the cougar was a young male. His front paws were 3⅛-inch wide by 2⅝-inch long. His rear tracks measured 2⅜-inch wide and 3⅛-inch long. In the early hours of the morning he had passed the lean-to with a quickened walking gait. He chose a relatively unused trail through the salmonberry thicket that led to a grassy clearing, and he continued walking toward the forest beyond.

We found other tracks of various ages near a small pool of water, saw evidence of cat-chewed grass and a scratching post, and found hair samples left on an overhanging salmonberry stalk approximately 2½ feet above the ground. I wanted to follow the tracks until they led me to the cat, but we too had food to hunt. I wanted to see the mountain lion and hear him roar. I was sure I'd feel blessed, since the cougar is one of the most elusive animals of the forest.

Scout and I had developed a morning ritual of sitting on my favourite flat rock, back to back, watching the wildlife. Two days after tracking the big cat, I heard the short *shweet shweet shweet* of a song sparrow and the *chip chip* of a winter wren from the forest behind us.

Their exact words eluded me, but I knew they were neither talking to their mates nor scolding their nearest neighbour. Their alarm calls sounded serious.

Yes, birds talk. They don't sing purely for enjoyment, except perhaps during the dawn chorus when all the birds welcome the day together. Birds are the watchmen of the forest, park, street, or backyard. All animals can understand their language, including humans. It just takes practice and patient observation of their calls and gestures.

Birds have become my closest allies in the forest and city alike. They warn me of danger, alert me to nearby adventures, and somehow touch my soul with their song.

On that day in Native Anchorage, my mind raced through previous experiences, trying to identify the *chip chip* mystery animal they were referring to. I recalled the sound of song sparrows giving away the location of coyotes, and wrens chipping after weasels darting through the brush. I remembered the baby Swainson's thrushes I saved from the belly of a garter snake, and the panic of a mother robin who flew at my study cabin's window so I would help chase off the jays trying to steal her babies again. But my mind couldn't find a connection in this new alert and settled on believing that the *chip chip* was a mink, even though my intuition didn't accept this theory.

When Micah came rowing around the corner after checking the crab trap, my mouth began to water at the thought of a giant pot of crab legs, and I immediately dismissed the birds' alarm calls. I grabbed a small cedar basket filled with dandelion leaves and spinywood fern fiddleheads, and carefully scrambled down the barnacle-encrusted rocks to the beach below. Scout, busy chasing the mouse scurrying in the rocks, decided to stay behind.

I met Micah on the beach and helped him drag the boat to the usual tie-up tree. The big crab dinner I had envisioned unfortunately still lived on the ocean floor. We had caught one seven-inch-wide Dungeness crab. Thankful but dejected, Micah began cleaning our ten precious, skinny legs for dinner on a large flat rock near the boat, while I harvested the tiniest gel-filled fronds of bladderwrack seaweed to steam for our standard low-calorie side dish.

Kneeling down to cut the first fronds, I heard Micah bellow, "Ahhh, get outta here!"

Sounding like a galloping horse, a lean, rusty-coloured cougar thundered toward Micah, missing him by a couple of feet and leaping over the rowboat in pursuit of Scout.

Micah's yell spooked the cougar, giving Scout the split second she needed to get away. Both cats ran toward the lean-to and disappeared into the woods.

We could hear the concentric rings of bird alarms following the mountain lion, b_adi (*bah-dee*), into the forest beyond.

Moments later, Scout dashed out of the brush, heading back to the rocks she had been chased from.

"Come back, Scout! Come here, kidder," I called, trying desperately to convince her to stay with me. She didn't look back until she reached the rocky bank, where she turned to glare at me for a brief second.

I thought I might never see her again as she slunk off into the bush. I hoped she truly did have all the stealth and wild-animal wisdom I saw in her. We called for hours, trying to coax her out of her hiding spot, but she didn't appear. I was devastated, especially when the darkening sky and lurking cougar halted our search. I understood Scout's instinct to distrust her human friends; she needed to rely on her keen awareness, not the small knives we carried for protection.

We cautiously made our way back to the lean-to in the straitjacket grip of terror. While fear can put one's senses on high alert, it is not a desirable survival tool, and too much of it can lead to death.

We built a raging, white-man fire. As soon as the flames blazed, Scout ran into the lean-to with her tail and hair puffed up as if she had been electrified. I was so happy to see her back. She was *u'mista* (*oo-mi-stah*), a Kwak'wala word meaning "the return of something special."

I picked her up, gave her a soft hug, and locked her in the trailer for safety. Micah and I continued to build up the fire, somehow feeling a little safer near it. In every movie we had seen, ferocious animals were scared off by fire. In Hollywood, grabbing a flaming stick from a fire and waving it at fearsome foes drove those foes away. This didn't work in Native Anchorage. Our hopeful torches only smouldered by the time we stood up with them.

I began to think about the warning calls of the birds I had heard earlier that day. The cougar had obviously been lying quietly, watching Scout and me on the rocks, patiently awaiting the chance to catch her. I thought it lucky my cat looked tastier than me.

Just when the sky turned from the dark bluish purple of a woodland violet to nighttime black, we heard the cougar's spine-tingling roar.

Let me just say this: For years I have wanted to see and hear that roar, and today, well frankly, it scared the hell out of me. I'm quite certain it would raise goosebumps on anyone, no matter how comfortable they felt in the forest.

A mountain lion cannot physically roar. The base of its tongue cannot vibrate like that of its African cousin. Instead, it screams. And scream it did, right behind our lean-to made of sticks. This was not a home in which we could feel safe. Continuous erratic jolts of fearful dark energy raced through my nerves and body. I felt like prey, engaged in the fight-or-flight response.

Terrified, Micah and I kept asking each other, "What do you think we should do?"

None of our teachers had taught us about this kind of scenario. I knew never to run from a cat, as their strongest instinct is to chase. I knew that a 150-pound cat could jump 12 feet straight up off the ground and 25 feet forward from a standstill. If he wanted to kill me, I knew he would. If a cougar displayed aggressive behaviour, I knew the standard protocol was to somehow make myself look big, wave my arms, and yell. I didn't like the idea of adding more aggression and fear to the situation, but if he attacked I knew I should try to stay on my feet and fight back. As I finished going over cougar etiquette, the cougar let out another long, demoniacal scream.

Micah and I knew, with absolute certainty, that we were not going to leave the lean-to to try to scare him off. We didn't even stand up to look. Instead, we armed ourselves for battle, expecting the cat to sneak under the trailer, jump off the roof, or smash through the bark walls. We may not have been thinking rationally, but, after all, we did have a raging devil-cat pacing back and forth behind our stick hut, screaming and growling.

"Oh yeah, let's track the cougar," I sarcastically said to Micah as we scrunched closer together. "What fun, now that it's come back to eat us!"

From the darkness came a horrifying low growl. The hairs on the back of my neck stood up like Scout's puffy tail.

Barely breathing, we strained to hear any hint of padding paws sneaking closer. Micah scanned right, while I looked left.

"Hey, are you scared?" I whispered.

He mumbled a reply I could barely understand, then asked, "Are you?"

I answered in much the same way. "Well…I mean…you know…kind of." Two seconds later I came out with the truth. "Okay, I'm nearly peeing my pants over here. I'm totally freaked out."

He broke down too. "This is by far the scariest thing ever."

In the ensuing hours, we continued asking each other, "What are we going to do?" We didn't know what else to say. The rest of the time we huddled in silence, with knives drawn, hoping one of us would figure out what to do next.

The cougar kept snarling its menacing growl, interspersed with bloodcurdling screams, late into the night. We could hear it now and then, slinking around, brushing past the crackly salal leaves, but finally the screams and growls ended. It was as if he had vented all his frustration and given in, much like Scout did in the boat. Micah and I were exhausted.

"How do you feel about sleeping under the lean-to tonight?" I asked. I looked down at my shaking legs, "I've always felt safe out here, but tonight I can't imagine being able to fall asleep. Maybe we should take turns staying up."

Micah mumbled indecisive words, not wanting to be first to chicken out, but his face looked as grim as mine felt.

I caved. "Let's be safe. Let's sleep inside with Scout."

We piled more logs on the fire and sheepishly opened the door to the trailer. Once bedded down, we huddled in our bags, straining to hear the noises we didn't want to hear. I couldn't believe I was lying on that nasty, grungy floor, but we were that frightened.

After a long time staring at the Chateau's ceiling, breathing in the stench, listening for the screams of a mad cat, gripping a knife, and hugging my teddy bear, I finally let myself cry. I didn't want to be the tough bush chick any longer.

That night I felt a galaxy away from my home and family. I couldn't remember ever missing my mom with more emotion. I remembered hugging her goodbye when I left for the wilds. I was bursting with excitement, while she was full of fear.

"I'll be back," I told everyone. But Mom kept saying, "I don't think she will be."

Now, lying on that scummy floor, trembling every time the cougar screamed, I realized how much my family meant to me. I also recognized that missing my family was the only thing that might convince me to leave the wilderness sooner than I had planned. A small smile came to me as I remembered our going-away party.

Micah had already said goodbye to his friends and family, who sent him off with hugs, tears, laughs, and looks of worry under forced smiles. My mother, in turn, had invited 18 of our friends and family members to bid us farewell. An hour before our guests were to arrive, Micah and I charged into my mom's lovely apartment with a dead beaver that we proceeded to slide into the oven.

When my mother arrived home with the cake, she cried out, "What stinks in here?"

Enthusiastically, I replied, "Micah and I found a perfectly good roadkill beaver on the way home. It's super-fresh, Mom. We're cooking it up for the party."

"Get it out," she said, "before it stinks up the whole apartment."

Micah put on the oven mitts and pulled out the baked beaver, its two front paws hanging over the side of the pan. The steaming scent of gamey fat billowed from the stove as Micah high-tailed it to the porch with our surprise entrée.

At the unveiling, there were shocked looks from those who didn't know me well and head-shaking laughs from those who knew me best. There were a lot of leftovers, but few people refused to at least try the tail. It became the party no one could ever forget.

Everyone had a different perspective on my primitive living adventure. Some couldn't understand my reasons for needing to leave, some wished they could follow along, and a few thought I was plain crazy, but after they all realized I was fulfilling a dream, they smiled and wished me luck and success in finding what I was searching for.

I left the modern world with the hope I'd come home with a true understanding of love. I believed the casual and often poisonous use of the word had somehow veiled its original, divine meaning from me. I wanted to return with a genuine, universal depth of love, not only for nature but also for people, a love that would take me well beyond society's niceties and protocols. The cougar brought me a step closer to this understanding.

The devil-cat also brought me love for Micah, replacing frustration and doubt with the deep knowledge that I was indeed blessed by his companionship. There were many days when I struggled living with Micah, annoyed by his presence and wishing to experience this challenge alone as I had always dreamed of doing. The cougar brought us closer together. We were no longer two strangers living separate dreams, but two allies sharing one dream together.

> I'm embarrassed to say it is the first time I have thought just how glad I am that we are out here together. It's this family feeling. This feeling of making sure everyone is safe, especially Micah. I think it has helped me accept us being here together.

The cougar made me realize I was willing to do anything to keep Micah safe—and, by extension, that someone else's life meant more to me than my own. It wasn't because Micah seemed incapable of taking care of himself; he certainly could. I simply realized how much I cared for him. In that moment, I knew I wouldn't have hesitated to give up my own life for his. And I sensed he'd do the same for me.

So that first night with the cougar, thoughts of loved ones finally lulled me to sleep. And I was glad I had included my 30-year-old stuffed teddy, flattened beyond recognition, in my emergency kit.

❦

The next morning we woke with an eerie, lingering fear. Scout did little to reassure us, as she refused to leave the trailer for days. However, even with the unpredictable cougar lurking around, we eagerly left the trailer as soon as the early morning rays illuminated its filthy windows. I built Scout a steep wooden ramp from a broken window, giving her a little cat door for quick bathroom breaks.

Micah and I stood guard for each other at the outhouse.

During the day we stayed close together, always watching each other's back and looking up into the trees wherever we went. Up is a blind spot. Mountain lions know it, and we didn't want to fall into the trap.

An average human's awareness is pathetic. Most of us are in a perpetual rut, trapped in basic patterns of tunnel vision, which make our surroundings and things in them appear as vague blurs. My training and wild lifestyle forced me to use my owl eyes at all times, and this wide-angle vision gave me an enormous range of view.

The cougar is all I think about, almost every second. It's the same for Micah. When I am in the trailer I feel cut off from knowing what's going on and I don't know if that makes me feel more scared or not.

The cougar, who was obviously sick or starving, came back two more nights. We booby-trapped our place as best we could, with a bow-and-arrow-type trap and snares. We sat by the fire each night, knives unsheathed beside us. And we always agreed to sleep on the Chateau's floor when he was around.

It's quite ironic that the cougar is the one who made me unafraid of the dark and the one who has taken it away. Micah's scared too, but we just laugh and pee right out the front door, sometimes even on the fire.

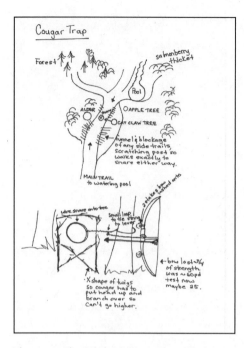

The cougar's nightly visits made us feel quite powerless so we decided to set primitive traps to catch him. I sketched our plans and added adjustments each time they failed.

I was also afraid because I didn't trust my senses. I had spent years developing and expanding a keen sense of awareness, so it surprised me when I didn't believe in myself. I could sense danger before it happened, understand the birds, catch important scents on breezes, read the stories left in tracks, and use my powerful intuition to locate critical items or find my way home after being lost. I decided to have faith in my abilities. Whenever I began to give in to fear, I reminded myself of my training and skill. This gave me courage and a willingness to face my fear in a new way. I appreciated the lessons my fear taught me.

As trackers, we were taught always to ask the sacred questions: What am I feeling? What is this teaching me? We both thought about dying. We talked about facing death. After all, wasn't the fear that we would die the reason we were terrified? Accepting death would give us the courage we needed to survive any life-threatening situation. This is what makes a hero.

In the midst of this ordeal, Tom Sewid swung into the bay to check up on us during a water-taxi run, his first visit since he'd dropped us off. We rowed out to see him, and when we told him about the cougar, he said, "You've got to harvest that cat. That's a dangerous animal to have around." He opened a hatch in the floor of the boat and pulled out a shotgun, reaching over to give it to me.

I held up my hands, saying, "Tom, we totally appreciate the offer, but you know we don't want to have a gun with us out here. We've set some primitive traps and hopefully we'll catch him."

With a stern tone Tom replied, "Look, Nikki, this is the bush and you're playing by different rules right now, whether you like it or not. You have to take this cat out in whatever way you can."

Reluctantly we accepted the shotgun and a handful of shells. It looked old and beat-up, nothing like the 12-gauge Mossberg I had used on so many skeet-shooting weekends. It felt odd to hold a gun again. We told Tom that we'd return it to him the next time we saw him.

We didn't get a shot at the cougar. We never saw him during daylight and couldn't see well enough in the dark to take aim when he was around. And after three nights the cat moved on. I couldn't decide what was worse: knowing he was around or waiting for his return. Life was on edge.

A week later he returned for another four nights of wet-your-pants terror, always evading our traps and snares. He then left for good. We never saw his tracks or heard his banshee screams again. We stowed the gun safely in the trailer and forgot about it.

Rebecca L. Grambo wrote in her book *Mountain Lion,* "Whether we venerate them as gods or damn them as evil killers, mountain lions are merely doing what they have evolved to do, living in the only way they know. It is up to us to understand this [and] appreciate the role they play in the world. For, as our own lives grow increasingly crowded and stressful, there is a quiet peace in knowing that somewhere mountain lions continue to walk alone—silent, elegant, and elusive."

I had only had what I would call "beautiful" interactions with cougars before this. I didn't want to fear them again, as I did when I first began my naturalist schooling, so to feel safe again I tried to distinguish between fear and caution in unhealthy situations. I studied how I reacted when I felt the tingle of fear rise inside me and compared it to the calm, centred feeling of caution. Fear immobilized me. I felt it as a cold armour that insulated me from divine possibilities and often caused me to miss the wondrous experiences nature bestowed on me, like swimming under a moonlit winter sky, following the dancing, V-shaped water lines made by a mink; shadow-walking within arm's reach of a grazing doe nibbling secret salad buffets; and sitting next to a mama thrush incubating her blue and brown speckled eggs. Fear changed my loving interaction with nature into domination, human vs. animal. I wanted the magic, not the fear-based illusions. So whenever I realized I was seeing cougars as evil killers rather than simply as fellow animals, I remembered to let go of constricting fears and reclaim my divine power.

IN THE SHADOWS OF TOTEMS

Grandson, when you can feel the same pain and suffering for a blade of grass ripped from the Earth as you do for that deer, you will truly be one with all things.

—Stalking Wolf
(From *Tom Brown's Guide to Wild Edible and Medicinal Plants*)

I watched the sunrise today. It is the first day of spring, I think. The salmonberry flowers are so lovely and taste beautifully sweet. I feel like a hummingbird.

Another week passed before Scout and I ventured back out to sit on our rock. My whole being smiled again. High above I heard the *shoooo* of a jet fighter. Looking up, expecting to see a grey military plane, I instead saw a bald eagle diving headfirst, with wings held slightly outward, into a group of scoter ducks feeding in the bay. I didn't know wings could create the sound of a rocket blazing through the sky. With talons stretched at the final seconds, she missed. I didn't know if I should feel happy for the scoter or disappointed for the eagle, who was only hunting food in anticipation of nesting season.

With the arrival of spring, our eagle neighbours busily carried evergreen branches and specially selected sticks to repair their already gigantic nest behind our lean-to. Winter resident ducks began their journeys to northern nesting grounds, while summertime birds squabbled over new territory.

Spring also enticed us to explore. We had to investigate every unfamiliar patch of green. Our first shade of green fortune came from a little grassy islet, its rocks covered in pretty patterns of white bull's eye lichen. Tiptoeing barefoot through the thin patches of grass and squishy moss, I searched for wild edibles until I spotted something new.

"Hey, Micah. Check this out. We got onions!"

Reaching down I whispered, "Thank you, little beauty," carefully pulling out my first pink-flowering nodding onion. I peeled off the thin, papery sheath and took a bite. "Wow, is that ever good."

Micah's giant smile confirmed my taste buds.

Onions transformed even nasty meals into something palatable. We also found strawberry plants and wild roses, mustards and cresses, sedums and alumroots. Delicious raw, the budding yellow flowers of the winter cress tasted of sweet mustard. The bitter cress was spicy and became my favourite green to top off crab biscuits. We picked plump, crisp, reddish sedum leaves in small quantities to fry. Though juicy, this drought-resistant plant left our mouths puckered and dry; it was not the thirst quencher I had read about. The small-flowered alumroot grew on rock faces. Its soft, hairy leaves tasted like grass and became filler food, which I steamed or added to stir-fries. The islet became our local vegetable stand.

Following in the footsteps of the ancestors, we discovered many secret spots for harvesting fresh greens and medicines. In her book *Having Everything Right*, Kim Stafford wrote,

The Kwakiutl people of the Northwest Coast had a habit in their naming. For them a name was a story. We say "Vancouver," naming an island for a captain and we say "Victoria," naming a village for a queen. For them, a place's name would not be something that is, but something that happens… Their language shows connections where we have made separations.

A visit to Ralph Island prompted us to begin renaming islands, bays, and rocks, restoring our connection. The unknown legacy of Ralph, who sailed by 250 years ago, meant nothing to a starving survivalist. However, spying on a black-masked explorer, and nearly touching it, left a lasting memory. Ralph was renamed "The place of the Raccoon."

We named everything. Monkey Flower Island, Strawberry Hills, The Picnic Place, Wolf Track Bay, The Place of Willows, Bear Beach, and River Otter Rock. Tom Sewid had told us Native Anchorage was originally called Place of *Dzunukwa* (*joo-neh-qwa*). With long black hair covering her body and bright red lips, *Dzunukwa* whistles a tantalizing death call, luring children into the forest so she can stuff them into her giant basket. Apparently we were nestled in Bigfoot's backyard, and I had an inkling a wild woman had indeed recently moved into the woods. Me.

❧

In early spring the people of 'Mim'kwamlis would have prepared for the long voyage to their traditional river sites to harvest the eulachon, a small oily fish of the smelt family. They returned with hundreds of gallons of the precious eulachon grease or oil, and boxes of smoked eulachon. Eulachon grease smells like rancid, fish-scented, stinky socks. Most white people gag the first time they try it. Perhaps I have a few strands of Kwakwaka'wakw DNA spiralling in me, for I liked the taste of the foul-smelling grease, and so did Micah. The indigenous people dipped everything in it, from berries to the eelgrass grown on mudflats outside the village.

We also ate the tender, sweet roots of the eelgrass raw, harvesting them with Y-shaped hemlock sticks from the boat when we visited 'Mim'kwamlis that spring. We relished the treat, as we had nearly forgotten the taste of sugar.

The village was a wilderness supermarket. It had a produce section, prescription counter, cosmetic aisle, and entertainment centre. A large cedar-bark basket I had made acted as our grocery cart. We filled it with odd-smelling hedge nettle, pretty dove-foot geranium, small heart-shaped leaves of ground ivy, and sticky, pinwheel-shaped cleavers, which never successfully removed pitch from my hands as my guidebook claimed they would.

Of all the woodland plants, my favourite was the fringecup, not for its hairy, stick-in-the-back-of-your-throat taste, but for its divine scent. The slender wands of inconspicuous pink flowers emanated a perfume that demanded both deer and I stop, smell, and eat.

The village trail meandered through thickets of Himalayan blackberries, thimbleberries, and wild rose bushes. I nibbled on perfumed rose petals, which eventually yielded fat red hips I dried for a vitamin C-rich tea and spice. Ounce for ounce, rosehips are reported to contain a higher content of vitamin C than oranges, so they were vital for boosting our immune system and protecting us from scurvy.

We also found delicious dandelions and velvety plantains living in a field that wolves used as a playground. (They dragged pop cans, shoe soles, and rubber boots to the clearing to use as chew toys.) Although crushed plantain leaves steeped in boiling water produce a soothing treatment for inflamed lungs, the plantain family as a whole is like tough, dried-out, stringy celery and thus rarely made it into my shopping cart. Nor did I have success using the plant's veins as "emergency string," and the crushed "vitamin substitute" seeds did not taste like peanut butter, as many books stated. It vexed me that people would write about uses they had obviously never tried.

Under the cherry trees we located burdock, mint, and western dock plants, plus steaming piles of digested grass. The bears had woken up.

I encountered my first black bear in front of the bighouse frame. I nearly bumped into him as I sneaked through the tight trail. He nonchalantly turned

We designed a rack to dry our fish. We learned that it was important to preserve as much food as possible.

to look at me, and with the same indifference moved a couple of feet to the next clump of fresh new grass to continue munching. I wasn't interested in grass; I wanted the yellow dandelion blossoms found under the structure, so I began gathering my meal beside him.

We called the biggest bear on the island Wallace. He awoke with a patch of hair missing, no doubt stolen by a mouse looking for a comfy nest while he slept. Wallace regularly visited the village and our place at Native Anchorage. We had boundary disputes over dandelion blossoms. He loved them as much as I did. Sautéed, with their green bracts picked off, dandelion flowers tasted like candy. I would have fought the big guy over them had I a chance of winning.

I never tired of watching bears. I spent hours drifting inside *Gribley* or lying atop rocks, glimpsing their lives. I watched the resident mama bear teach her cub to roll rocks, uncovering small purple shore crabs, eel-like blennies, and other small critters living underneath. Ravens would often walk behind to eat any leftovers. I memorized the bears' every movement and studied the tracks when they ambled away. They became regular acquaintances at our tranquil wild supermarket.

Bears were a common sight at our camp on Village Island. We had to negotiate carefully over the sweet dandelion blossoms. We named the biggest bear Wallace.

The village provided a large array of salad fixings, too. With soft tread, I rambled in search of my favourite plants. I found the lemony burst of sheep sorrel, the bitter flavour of wall lettuce, the refreshing tang of chickweed, and the nutty taste of salmonberry shoots. Gold medal for the Best Organic Raw Leaf went to the small, teardrop-shaped Siberian miner's lettuce. Leaf by precious leaf dropped gently into my woven basket.

Many of the days I was gathering our wild salads, my soul sensed the ancestors' energy in the village. I felt blessed to follow the ancient trails, picking many of the same plants. The feeling deepened my understanding of how to be a guardian of the earth. We weren't just hungry survivalists looking for our next meal; we were reverent caretakers of the land, first and foremost. I tended nature the same way I would lovingly look after my own private garden.

Near a creepy building I suspected was haunted, I found a big patch of cow parsnip. Its Latin name, *Heraculeum lanatum*, is appropriate because it grows to a Herculean size. In the spring, its leaf stalks are tender and juicy. Cow parsnip is a member of the carrot family, distinguishable by white, umbrella-like flowers. Many plants of the carrot family are deadly poisonous, and cow parsnip has its own warning label. A chemical called furanocoumarin is present in its outer hairs, which can cause blisters and sensitivity to sunlight. We carefully cut and peeled the stringy, hairy skin off the stalks to munch on the crisp, sweet, peppery "Indian celery."

One afternoon, after snacking on cow parsnip, we decided to try our luck fishing. In a short time we lost our lures, tangled our lines, and caught the sea floor more often than I'd like to admit. While untangling the mound of knotted line, I recalled the ancient lore that said touching cow parsnip could prevent one from catching fish. I'm not saying the superstition proved true, but I never ate cow parsnip before fishing again.

As spring progressed, I had a hard time keeping up with the rush of new discoveries—unfamiliar plants were poking up for identification, and new bird songs to memorize floated through the forest canopy. The alder patches changed from reddish pink to bright lime green as hanging catkins gave way to leaves. Flocks of trumpeter swans bugled overhead, migrating to their northern breeding grounds, and a ruffed grouse began his ritual drumming somewhere behind our lean-to. Tufts of beach greens sprouted up through the white shells, giving us an abundance of vegetables. Crisp sea plantain, sparkling orache, and salty sea asparagus entered the soup pot or frying pan. And Gaia's candy, salmonberries, ripened for the robins and for us too. Micah created the best smile-maker recipe, crushing the berries into a dough of flour, baking powder, and creek water that he then flattened, rolled, and deep fried.

We also tried to preserve berries, though drying plump, juicy berries in what locals call "Monsoon June" or "Fogust" is as easy as walking on water.

Who wants to dry berries anyway, especially when it's been so long since I've tasted anything sweet? My basket's nearly empty by the time I get home. I just can't keep myself from eating them.

I found the best and lengthiest clue about First Nations berry preservation in my personal binder of notes on plants: "They dried the berries in square cakes in the sun." Not a lot to go on, but we figured if the ancestors had found a way, we would too. Whenever I felt discouraged, I reminded myself of what an elder medicine man said when a teacher of mine asked him the name of a bird. The elder replied, "What you are saying, is that you are too lazy to find out yourself." Micah and I were willing to learn the hard way.

After waking to another green and fuzzy berry-cake, Micah asked, "What if we cook them?"

"You're a genius, Micah. I bet that'll work. It should kill the bacteria and mould spores, and hopefully give the berries enough time to dry before more can settle."

We built a fire and boiled a new batch of berries, then spread the mash on the inner side of cedar-bark slabs, drying them successfully in the sun.

The term "berry-cake" leaves a heavenly impression on the mind of someone who hasn't had a chocolate bar in months. In actuality, however, the resulting cakes were hard to look at, dusty and smoke stained. Fortunately, the taste was divine to our palates, sweet, smoky, and tangy, even if it was slightly dusty—and even if we had to pick the occasional piece of bark from our teeth where the cedar slabs had become cemented onto the cakes.

We contracted "Morel Madness," a unique disease that compels fungus geeks to spend hours wandering through leaf litter as they hone their eyes to spot the highly prized, and highly camouflaged, black morel mushroom. We lived through many "demorelizing" days, returning home with empty baskets, but we finally trained our brains to stop filtering out the dark, honeycombed caps of the mushrooms. Small patches of morels started magically appearing where we had walked many times before. Mushroom crab burgers, with a garnish of wild onions, dandelion leaves and flowers, winter cress leaves and flowers, sheep sorrel, and miner's lettuce, were a favourite dish.

Most people are fungophobic, but once Micah and I became familiar with the amanita family, which comprises the most poisonous mushrooms in the world, we realized fungus hunting was not a dangerous pursuit. Many edible species are easily identifiable, and most symptoms of mushroom poisoning are mild, resulting in gastrointestinal upset that can be cured without a doctor.

Another myth proclaims mushrooms have little food value. In reality, they are high in protein as well as good sources of vitamins and trace minerals. And we sorely needed more protein.

TRAPPING BRUIN

I say bravo for coming this delicious distance with me in shedding your old dining prejudices against rodents.
—Calvin W. Schwabe, *Unmentionable Cuisine*

In our search for protein, I put our field guides to use, sure that the sea and shore would offer items to improve our unbalanced diet. The rocky shore did indeed house many edible creatures. None looked appetizing, but my protruding ribs told me to get over my pickiness. I had to learn to dine on whatever crawled my way. Wasting-away Micah had no trouble trying any of the new food. Every newly discovered creature, no matter its inedible appearance, was brought home for study and, if possible, the fry pan.

Chitons, finger-long black-and-white humps that cling to the rocks by a carrot-orange suction-cup foot, caught my attention first. These molluscs resemble living trilobites, with striking patterns and colours. Preparing to eat one, however, requires major hunger pains.

I cooked up the Black Katy chiton for the first time. It is the grossest thing I've ever seen. Gutting it with this slimy covering makes it stink. I think I may puke!

Using the shell as a baking dish, we cooked it, foot up, atop a bed of coals, simmering the chiton in its own juices. After brushing off the ash, I took my first bite of the chewy, rubbery meat. "Hmpff, it's not that bad," I said with surprise. I wrote, "Once most of the guts are scraped away, it's very good. It has a crazy crunchiness to it. It's so different to eat. You want to say you don't like it, but you do."

Rubbery California sea cucumbers literally grabbed our attention, as we started snagging them on fishing trips. Any weight on a fishing line is a blessing when you're hungry, even if it's a crimson, cucumber-shaped caterpillar of the sea, covered in bright orange rubbery spikes, that flops into the bottom of the boat.

When I picked up the cucumber, it felt like a jiggly, stress-relieving toy found at dollar stores. Cleaning one of the creatures, which are full of liquid viscera, with hundreds of tiny tube feet on the belly, was a sloppy job, but once I peeled off the five pinkish muscle strips lining its body and sautéed them with nodding onions, I forgot all about the goop and gore I had to wash off my hands. Sea cucumber tasted like crab.

Through all these experiments, we continued our efforts to catch a fish. Thanks to the book *How to Catch Bottomfish,* by Charlie White, we learned the technique of jigging. One of us would read aloud while the other practised. Charlie advised, "Drop your line until it hits bottom…Let your boat drift slowly with the wind, or tide…work your rod up and down to provide a darting, erratic action to the lure. Two quick jerks, followed by slack line to let the lure flutter down…"

It sounded easy enough. We'd row out to a kelp patch where fish supposedly lived and drop the "looks-good-to-me" hooks we had bought at a fishing shop before we left. We didn't have the rods Charlie talked about, but we did have one spool of thin fishing line and a roll of masonry string we had bought from the hardware store.

Micah caught our first fish on the first day of spring. We managed to bring two white-speckled greenlings and one brownish sculpin into the boat. To first-time fishers, they resembled a trout and a giant bullhead. It was a momentous occasion, like peeling back the wrapper of a Willy Wonka chocolate bar and finding the golden "You Win" ticket.

With our gift of fish, we rowed over to a nearby white-shell beach we named Hidden Midden, where I flipped through our fishing bible to learn how to gut and fillet the catch. We made a simple flour batter and celebrated the day with a spring picnic of fish, wild onion rings, and bladderwrack seaweed (which substituted for French fries), strawberry-leaf tea to drink, and deep-fried biscuits for dessert. Instead of bolting down our dinner while thinking of other things, we savoured the tastes and textures of our plain and simple food, eating with thankfulness and mindfulness, and didn't even miss the lemon juice, ketchup, or tartar sauce.

The taste of deep-fried seaweed surprised my picky tastebuds and became one of my favourite delicacies. It's called popweed for a reason: the gel-filled bladders explode in your face when fried. Fortunately, the gel has properties similar to aloe vera, and it worked wonders to relieve minor burns from oil explosions or sunburned lips.

That afternoon we let out a series of *oohs*, *ahhs*, and *mmms* we hadn't said in nearly two months. We dropped one piece of fish after another into the oil until our stomachs bulged. It was the first wilderness meal that left Micah feeling full. We kicked back on the warm beach, soaking up the rare afternoon sun. And we paid the price. Our shrunken stomachs complained well into the night. "We had quite the deep-fried stomach pain day," I wrote.

As our fishing skills improved, our favourite fish to eat became the quillback rockfish. The genus name for rockfish is *Sebastes*, meaning "magnificent." At first glance, though, "ugly" comes to mind. It has large, bulging eyes and dinosaur-like back spikes, more hideous than magnificent.

The true beauty of things is seen when I take the time to look at it really close. All of a sudden something rather strange becomes wonderful, something ordinary magical, and something beautiful becomes divine. Well, that's what happened when I took a closer look at these fish. It certainly doesn't make killing them easier.

All rockfish are slow-maturing and long-lived. A foot-long quillback reaches maturity at 12 and can live as long as 95 years. It gives birth to live young and protects small home ranges on shallow reefs, even returning to its original homesite . if released elsewhere. It deserves the name "magnificent."

I was a little nervous handling them the first few times because of the sharp, venomous spines along their fins. The first poke left me with a nasty sore on my finger for the rest of the afternoon.

We cooked rockfish many different ways. We tried roasting them whole on sticks, filleting, and pan-frying, but the most delicious method was clay-baking. I would stuff a gutted quillback with a handful of mint and mustard greens and six wild onions, then wrap it in thimbleberry leaves and a layer of green grass. I tied a frond of bull kelp around this bundle and covered the whole thing in a couple of inches of creek-bank clay that I'd pounded and moistened with water until malleable, being careful to seal all air holes. I'd bake this on a hot bed of coals, flipping it once, until the clay hardened (about 20 to 30 minutes), then crack the clay open for a feast.

We finally found Tom Sewid's hidden "teacup" hole, which I had marked on our chart, home to coon-striped shrimp and spotted prawns. Generally, prawns are found at a depth of 200 to 350 feet, but they don't live just anywhere on the bottom of the ocean. They are in small, localized "holes" or in larger areas stretching for a mile or more. All fishers have their own system for successfully filling a bucket with prawns, which usually depends on the temperature and colour of the water, the strength of the tide, the substrate and contours of the bottom, and, of course, the "best" bait to use.

Without an electronic fish finder, we had to resort to the old ways of measuring the depth of the water. We dropped a handline and counted how many feet to the bottom, over and over again. I'm not sure how many days we spent looking for that hole, but I'll never forget the moment we found it.

I finally counted out the magic number: 230 feet deep. Our arms ached by the time we shared the chore of hauling up the 400 feet of weighted rope hand over hand, but the sight of 12 prawns clicking and jumping around in the trap led to high-fives all around. Our menu expanded. We ate shrimp-fried rice, boiled shrimp, nori shrimp rolls, and head-shakingly delicious shrimp salads.

It was a gargantuan effort to row two miles to reach the prawn hole, and every time we went, we broke the cardinal law of food gathering: input must be greater than output. In our survival situation, it was not worthwhile to row four miles for our minuscule average catch. But we loved prawns. We took turns, one of us rowing there, the other back. Most days I would close my eyes to ignore the pain, plodding home one stroke at a time.

Scout often brought offerings for Micah and me. That's how I found myself plucking the feathers off a song sparrow one day. My modern conscience was comforted by the knowledge that, in the 19th century, thousands of songbirds ended up on dining tables. In his classic book *Birds of America,* John James Audubon wrote "that every gunner brings [American robins] home by bags full and the markets are supplied with them at a very cheap rate." He added, "48,000 golden plovers had been shot once in a single day for eventual consumption."

However, not much of a meal remained when I held the bald bird in my cupped hand, studying the pile of feathers in detail so I could recognize them again.

Scout supplied us with a small variety of sweet and juicy birds that we sautéed with herbs and onions, but I could barely stomach the idea of eating the deer mouse she gave us. The Swahili proverb *Kila nyama mayama tu* means "every meat is meat." In his book *Never Cry Wolf,* Farley Mowat describes how he lived off rodents. So we figured eating a mouse was worth a try.

...I gutted him, the stomach and intestines only, then skewered the fella and roasted him whole over the fire to singe off the hair.

Holding up a blackened stick that skewered a charcoaled mouse, I shook my head and passed the morsel over to Micah. "I can't do it. You go first."

Micah took out his knife and cut it in half. I got the butt.

In order not to miss any available nutrition, we had to eat the entire thing, bones and all. I barely wanted to pick it up off the table, let alone eat it. Micah just reached down and popped the head into his mouth without a hint of *yuck* on his face. Between chewing and crunching he said, "No, really, it's pretty good. Go ahead, try it."

I was leery of his positive review, since he ate the goop from prawn heads and the guts in crab backs, but curiosity took hold. I shoved the butt, tail and all, into my mouth without further examination. I wrote, "After I got over the initial thought of 'I'm eating a mouse, tail and all,' it just tasted like meat; a bit gamey, but not bad at all. I hardly noticed the bones."

For the Romans, mouse was a del-

Mouse on a stick was not a delicacy we sought out, but we were determined not to waste any food.

icacy. I wasn't looking forward to my next rodent meal with that kind of enthusiasm, but I knew this wouldn't be the last mouse I ate. Wastefulness was not a concept we condoned, and if Scout continued bringing us mice, we would eat them.

Shortly after the shish-kebab-mouse experience, we were rowing home after prawning by the light of a full moon when I was struck by the realization of how many lives we had ended. We killed something every day in order to live. Back home, when someone else did the killing, it was easy to forget this fact.

I looked into the bucket of prawns and watched the bright purple glow in their eyes slowly fade to black as they struggled without their watery environment. Then I tore off their heads. Grief welled inside me as I truly felt the sacredness of life and the sacrifice of taking a life.

I will always remember what a classmate said to me as we skinned a raccoon at a trapping course: "You need to get over the sadness you have for trapping animals. It's just a stupid raccoon." I refrained from slapping the guy and instead politely responded, "I don't have to enjoy killing something in order to call myself a trapper. I don't have to disrespect it either."

We lived with the philosophy of attempting quick, clean kills for all the animals and plants we harvested, honouring their lives as best we knew how. And yes, we extended this respect to plants. In 1973, Peter Tompkins and Christopher Bird wrote *The Secret Life of Plants*, a revolutionary book that described the work of Cleve Backster, America's foremost lie-detector examiner, who attached the electrodes of his machine to a houseplant and discovered that the plant not only reacted to various stimuli, such as tearing its leaves, but also differentiated between threats and real danger. His experiments suggested that plants were attuned to other plants, animals, and their human caretakers. Backster's work made scientists around the world begin their own experiments, duplicating and extending his findings. Science had proven what mystics and sages had known for thousands of years: plants are sentient beings who respond to various stimuli much as a human would. They just do it at a much slower pace.

Even with the added beach greens and tidal creatures in our diet, we still lacked the calories and fat needed to support our wild lifestyle. A lack of fat can kill survivors in the short term, while a deficiency of vitamins and minerals takes much longer.

We didn't often change our clothes down to bare skin, and when we did, we hurried, always giving each other as much privacy as possible. Around the 45th day on Village Island, I turned around too quickly and saw Micah pulling down his shirt. My mouth dropped open; I could see every rib.

"Whoa, you look like an anorexic, Micah," I exclaimed.

"Why didn't you tell me?" he scolded.

"I guess I didn't notice until it got so bad," I said apologetically. "I'm not staring at you while you're getting dressed."

"I know you're not. I'm sorry. I just need some real food. Clams aren't giving me enough energy. I need some meat."

Neither of us could keep wasting away another month, dragging our feet with every step in our chronic state of fatigue. We thought through our predicament.

To bowhunt a deer would take weeks of finding materials, creating weapons, and scouting deer trails. Alternatively, we could set a trap. But primitive traps are indiscriminate, and with fawns being born we dared not risk accidentally trapping a mama deer. We agreed to trap a bear.

Protective, wary female bears with spring cubs are often late in taking up residence near the lush, nutritious grass flats most bears seek after their winter sleep. They know the risk of both male and other female bears attacking and eating their cubs. This knowledge somewhat eased our apprehension of trapping in "baby time."

We turned to the few books we had packed to find some guidance on primitively trapping a bear. One paragraph in Stanley Hawbaker's 1974 book *Trapping North American Furbearers* shed some light:

> *Trapping Bruin [in a large cubby] is the most successful method. Make the cubby large and out of heavy timber. Nail them together, and against a tree to keep bear from tearing down the cubby and stealing bait from the rear. Cubbies should be 5 feet deep, 3 feet wide and 3 feet high.*

Building a trap with this amount of information was like asking a fashion model to assemble a diesel generator with only the parts list from the manual. Stanley failed to add necessary details of how the trap was assembled and how it worked. We would have to rely on our own minimal experience of setting deadfall traps.

We spent two days rowing and hiking, searching for the perfect place to build the cubby. A tiny, grassy meadow with a lot of bear sign in the vicinity caught our attention. A recently used bear bed lay hidden by the branches of a hemlock tree, with four piles of similarly aged grassy scat nearby, leaving a faint smell of tobacco on the air. A well-trod trail ran along the edge of the meadow and wound up the hill to a large salmonberry patch where tiny flies buzzed around fresher piles of scat. Evidence of bear-chewed grass and a tiny stream flowing through the meadow from a small pool of water convinced us we had found the trap site.

We spent another full day chopping down hemlock poles, hauling them to the site, cutting them to length, and sharpening the ends to a point so Micah could pound them three feet into the ground, four inches apart. I lashed them securely into place with several wooden crosspieces. After countless hours we stood back to examine the enormous cage we had built. Besides the substitution of cordage for nails, it perfectly replicated the cubby we had read about.

A deadfall trap system is designed to support enough weight balanced above to crush the prey when it is tricked inside the cubby. We needed to find and assemble the appropriate branches for the "trigger system." Specially carved sticks held up the weight of the crushing logs, using principles of balance and levers.

We designed a ramp made of sticks that the bear would step on. Micah excelled as our physics genius.

After assembling the trigger, we roamed the forest to chop the heaviest fallen trees we could carry. Every time we dropped a log in front of the cubby, I turned back toward the forest, wondering how I ever made it over the rough terrain. With a sigh, we dropped our heads and forced ourselves back into the trees to collect another. The more we needed, the deeper into the forest we had to hike. Together we carried five long logs.

We needed at least 500 pounds of logs to crush the bear. With twilight approaching and chores still to do around camp, we agreed to leave the last log for another day.

I'm beat. The last two nights rowing home, sitting in the boat freezing and exhausted, I could have fallen asleep. My arms kill. Cutting and chopping firewood for dinner just about did me in.

We awoke with aches and pains we had never experienced before. Our "Fibro" fatigue was at an all-time high. We made our way back to the trap site, with one mammoth log remaining. I could see the beast looming at the high-tide mark as the boat floated to shore.

I manoeuvred myself into position at the end of the log. With all my strength I heaved on my end of the log, but I could not lift it higher than my shins. I asked Micah for help, assuming that if I got it to my waist, I could manage the weight. Together we picked up the log.

Taking a deep breath like an Olympic weightlifter, I gasped, "Okay, let it go."

Crack! The log dropped from my hands as I yelled out in pain. It felt like my spine had snapped. I let out a series of pathetic laughs so I wouldn't cry. I don't know what had happened to my back, but it felt and sounded like a sledgehammer had mashed my lumbar vertebrae into my tailbone. I slowly straightened until I was standing upright.

The trap waited. Micah couldn't move that last log alone. When I could walk again, we hoisted one end of the log together, awkwardly swinging it around and walking the log to the trap site. During rests, I held my back and let out a string of relieving curses.

Carefully, we lashed all the logs to the main crushing beam so they wouldn't slip. We then covered the roof with sticks and branches, camouflaged the ramp with moss, piled brush around the back of the cubby to deter any bear from entering the wrong way, and hung a stinky fish in the rear of the cage.

Constructing this bear trap from local trees and fallen logs was an exhausting effort.

We set the trap to fall repeatedly so we could discover any unforeseen problems. There were many: the ramp wasn't steep enough to disengage the trigger, and the logs dropped too slowly, missed their mark, or ceased to fall at all. We didn't stop until we felt it was perfect. It had to kill the bear quickly and cleanly.

Kneeling down in front of the trap, we saw its true face: a monstrous death trap that could easily kill us if we were careless. It scared us, not only because of its sheer immensity, but because of what we aimed to do. However, our dream of primitive living would soon be out of reach if we couldn't obtain the meat we needed.

This was the moment we became true survivalists. We answered the question "Will you do what it takes to survive?" In the ensuing silence, we each said our own form of prayer.

In a dreamlike state, we rowed home. When we arrived at the lean-to, no firewood awaited us, dinner had not been collected, and the smell of a campfire meal did not waft down the beach to greet us. Too exhausted to do anything about it, we crawled into our sleeping bags. I thought about bears. I prayed for the perfect bear to come to our trap—not the biggest and healthiest bear, but just the size we needed. When I closed my eyes I heard a wordless song that was drowned out by the booming cadence of drums, pounding like a fast-paced heartbeat, from where I do not know.

I checked the bear trap from a safe distance every day, replacing the fish head each time the mink stole it. Days passed.

Our doubts, fears, insecurities, and unanswered questions tormented us. We shared our concerns long into the nights, wondering if the size of the cubby was correct, if the logs would fall properly, if we had wrangled enough logs to even kill a bear. Every night we prayed with all our hearts that the animal would not suffer.

A few weeks after finishing the trap, we sat beside our fire one night and listened to a pack of wolves howling and harmonizing from a nearby island. I felt as free as those wolves and wondered if the pack was celebrating a successful hunt.

The following morning I awoke to the first robin singing his morning song. Tiptoeing out of the lean-to, Scout and I headed to our secret place to take part in the enchanting moments of the dawn chorus.

When the symphony of birdsong petered out and life reverted to survival mode for all forest dwellers, I went back to camp to rouse Micah. I decided not to check the bear trap as I had done every morning. We planned to add another log to our crushing beam, so I figured we might as well go together.

The three of us hiked through the forest, looking for another gigantic log. At the moment Micah's axe swung back over his head to begin chopping our chosen log, I noticed the trap had been sprung.

My breath quickened. With featherlike steps we quietly stalked down the hill for a closer look. A black shape appeared in the cubby. I had pictured the scene in my mind a thousand times. I had prayed every day for the perfect bear. Now that it was there, I didn't know if I was ready for it.

The shape moved. We dropped to our knees. Our worst fear had come true; the bear was alive and suffering. If my heart could have healed that bear, I would have let him go that instant. We had to put him out of his misery fast, but how? We had two knives and an axe.

Then we remembered the gun Tom Sewid had left with us. Perhaps Providence had moved for the bear the day we accepted it. Like frightened deer we bolted back to camp.

The bear heard us return. He began bawling, a heart-wrenching cry. With gun in hand, Micah moved toward the trap.

Offended by his solo decision to shoot the bear, I tugged at his jacket and whispered, "Hey, I've shot a lot of guns too, you know. And I'm a pretty good shot. Why are you assuming you should shoot it?"

"Sorry, Nikki. You're right. What do you think we should do?"

With seconds to make a decision, we chose the fairest way we knew: Rock, Paper, Scissors. We counted aloud, "One. Two. Three." My scissors beat his paper.

Never before had my shoulders drooped from a win. I took the shotgun and switched off the safety, and we stalked to within 30 steps of the trap, hiding behind the closest large alder tree.

Where should I aim? I silently asked myself.

As if he heard my thoughts, the bear raised his head just a little to give me a shot. I took it. His head flopped down. I waited. A moan crushed my spirit. I pulled the trigger again. The gun jammed.

"What the hell?" I cried out. The slugs were apparently the wrong size and wouldn't automatically eject. Micah came to help. We frantically worked to remove the slug. Hours seemed to pass before I reloaded the gun.

I walked closer. *Boom!* The bear slumped. The gun, of course, jammed again, but this time I quickly removed the spent slug, aimed, and fired. The bear was silent.

Micah held the axe, raised above his shoulder, as we slowly walked over to the trap. I poked the bear with a long stick, just to make sure he was dead. He didn't flinch.

We immediately saw that Hawbaker's cubby dimension was wrong. The bear had had enough room to lunge forward when the logs began falling on top of him. Only his rear left leg had been caught in the trap.

I knelt down beside the beautiful animal. I felt I had failed. I dropped my head in my hands, ashamed. Our best wasn't good enough. Together we lifted off the logs, dragging the bear out from under them. With silent tears, we sat beside our gift of life on the grass, stroking his long, shiny black hair. I had never before touched a bear.

We spent the rest of the day skinning and butchering him. To our shock, the young bear didn't have even a tiny layer of fat for us to render. He must have been as desperate as we were for high-energy food. We cleaned up the trap area as night fell, rowing home in the dwindling light with hundreds of perch shooting off in all directions under the boat.

We immediately started a bow-drill fire. The firelight flickered against a giant ribcage that was propped up beside the flames to roast. A platform of sticks acted as our cooking surface to fry the tender heart. We shared a thanksgiving prayer in honour of the bear.

Back home I was a fickle vegetarian who ate a bit of chicken now and then, and never enjoyed the taste of meat. But when I gnawed into that first rib bone, my inner cavewoman burst forth. I became a meat-loving carnivore. Micah devoured nearly the whole rack of ribs himself. I think he gained five pounds overnight.

Stargazing that night, I spotted the Big Dipper, part of the constellation Ursa Major, or the Great Bear. I wondered if the young bear's spirit had journeyed there.

God blessed us today with perfect weather, a perfect young, skinny bear, and many lessons to think about. Not just on our trap design and how to butcher a bear, but much more, far greater than I can know tonight. Safe journey on your way to the light, brother bear. Forgive me. I pray to you.

The next morning we awoke to see four turkey vultures sitting on a small island in the bay. They gave me an eerie feeling, sitting side by side on the rocks, staring at camp, smelling death. They monitored our progress and the smell of fresh meat going rancid through the day. We cut the meat into jerky strips, an eighth of an inch thick and one inch wide, and hung them on the drying rack we had made of small poles lashed together with split cedar branches.

Trapping and killing the bear and then preparing the meat was an emotionally and physically difficult experience, but necessary for us to survive.

To preserve the bear meat we set up these drying racks to make jerky.

We had heard that hunters often soaked the carcass of a large animal in water to keep it fresher and to help remove the gamey taste. This didn't work for us. Instead, soaking the meat increased the speed of rotting.

We spent the entire day and night cutting up the meat. Flies gathered in huge buzzing numbers, and the small smoky fire near the drying rack did little to keep them away. However, once the jerky developed its glazed look, the flies would not lay their eggs on the meat, perhaps needing the moisture that was sealed inside. I could handle seeing fly feet on my meat, but the yellow eggs did not brush off easily, even when dried. They just smeared into the jerky.

The meat spoiled faster than we could process it, so we started grading it, from A to C, which came with a gag-a-maggot smell, suitable for desperate castaways. Starving souls can safely eat rotten uncooked meat. Only spoiled meat that has been previously cooked will kill.

We ate or preserved all the meat, no matter its stench or shade of green. Some scraps went into a stew pot we kept simmering over the fire. Scraps that weren't suitable for jerky went into mega stomach-bulging stir-fries, gristle, tendon, and all.

I didn't stop making jerky until I heard the first robin sing the next morning. Then I cleaned up the camp, cooked more food, and began the daily chores while Micah continued another sleepless day of cutting meat. Like zombies, we stayed awake continuously for three days, processing the meat as fast as possible. We could not dishonour the bear by wasting anything.

I washed and stretched the hide, with plans to turn it into a rug, and cleaned the claws for a necklace. Micah didn't share my enthusiasm for a necklace, but he cleaned out the intestines to stretch and twist into rope. The other organs had sat in the heat too long to be turned into water pouches. We wove the loose hair into a piece of cordage for a necklace, and scraped the bones to use as tools, sinking them into the ocean to let the sea lice finish the cleaning job. Days and nights blended together.

I slowly began to feel less ashamed of how the bear had died. Weeks later, when I was gathering plants for dinner by the creek bed, a mama and baby bear strolled out of the woods nearby to munch on greens, just like me. I sat down among the yarrow and bearberry to watch them feed. The bears taught me about forgiveness. I realized all I could do was my best; when I found it wasn't enough, I had to let go of judgment and forgive. The young bear had given us life and a chance to continue living our dreams.

EGO RETURNS

There is nothing that strengthens the ego more than being right… Every ego confuses opinions and viewpoints with facts.

—Eckhart Tolle, *A New Earth*

At long last our bodies' demands for protein had been met. We became health-ier, stronger, and more physically fit. The axe, which at first had felt heavy and cumbersome, became surprisingly light. We wielded it with greater accuracy. Our arms and hands became accustomed to the demands of rowing.

My compressed spinal discs slowly began to heal. Some days I couldn't even bend over to put on my socks, but I formulated several treatments to ease the fiery pain. I would wrap my back in a cut-up shirt soaked in a strong hot tea of anti-inflammatory chamomile flowers, soothing marshmallow roots, and a dash of stimulating mint leaves. Or Micah would rub in my homemade liniment (made with jojoba oil, St. John's wort oil, and three essential oils—rosemary, lemon, and spearmint) and place flat, heated rocks on my lower back to act as a hot water bottle. Covered with a blanket, I had the feeling a pair of healing hands rested on my injury.

The stored jerky decreased our food-gathering demands. We didn't know how long it would last, but having meat on hand eliminated the utter exhaustion we experienced every night when we were spending all our time gathering food. It also gave us the gift of free time. Our thoughts were no longer solely absorbed with survival. Having a couple of extra hours per day to explore, study, or sim-ply spend time alone gave our minds the opportunity to chatter and stirred our egos to life once again.

We weren't too tired to argue anymore. Our struggles with the little things began.

Broken Back Oil
1. 1 large, cleaned, heart cockle clam
2. 8 tsp jojoba oil
3. 3 tsp St. John's wort oil
4. 60 drops rosemary essential oil

It's funny how people will just bug you with what they do. Today I was out by the beach fluffing up cedar bark for extra tinder and listening to the sweet melody of the hermit thrush. Then Micah started sanding a shell. It might as well have been a freight train disrupting my peacefulness.

Micah and I spent nearly every moment together, either rowing in our little boat or crammed under our tiny lean-to, day after day after day. I wanted my own island, but we only had one boat. We were stuck with each other.

Some days his loud chewing bugged me. I was irritated with his obsession with licking every last morsel and taste off his plate.

"What the heck, dude?" I'd bark at him. "There's nothing left. The plate's as clean as it's gonna get."

Sometimes just looking at him exasperated me. We laughed at these annoyances, but deeper issues hid under the surface.

We were two extremely different people trying to live the dream we had both envisioned as children. We had to figure out all of our survival problems together, but we usually came up with different answers.

Three times in the first six months I declared I wanted to return home. I never meant it, but we argued about nearly everything, and our equally demanding stubbornness frustrated me into saying it. Sometimes we chose opposite sides of an issue or opposing solutions to a problem simply so we could argue. We were both defensive and always wanted to be right.

We argue I think because we are not comfortable with our failures, our lack of knowledge, and the truth revealed in the situation about ourselves. It is as if I am holding on to what I have learned in my life. We battle for what we think we know because our egos believe we have somehow worked hard for our knowledge and it refuses to let go or give in.

We even started questioning each other's character. Struggling to survive was stressful enough; fighting with the only human being we could talk to was insufferable.

Even still, we fought. Some days he brought out the worst in me, and I did the same for him. I tried to find faults in Micah, but I had to dig deep to find much of anything.

Most days we loved each other's company. We had to. A fight ruined our entire day. When we fought, an empty water bucket sat by the door, beach logs were not chopped, and dinner waited to be harvested. We couldn't run from our problems without real hardship awaiting our return. We lived in a 24-hour relationship seminar demanding honest communication.

To confuse and compound our problems, we also discussed where we felt our intimate relationship was headed. The story of an adventurous young couple living alone in the vast wilderness suggests a lovely, romantic sentiment. I'm a romantic myself, but living in Native Anchorage was like a Grimm fairytale turned inside out. The vision of two scantily clad lovers frolicking hand in hand, bodies entwined under sun-filled skies, with blossoms blowing on a summer breeze, was far from the reality.

We had soft, bright green beds of moss, like those of a fairytale, but in a rainforest these are usually damp and soggy. And lying naked together on a prickly forest floor, exchanging caresses with calloused hands, held no allure when we knew we'd be joined by mosquitoes sucking blood and black flies chomping skin. Desire was also stifled by our knowledge of how long each of us had gone without washing our stinky clothes and bathing our dirty bodies. I quickly stopped pondering methods of natural birth control and took to the idea of living like a nun under vows of poverty and chastity.

Kissing hasn't lasted long. It's like we have to get ready for the chapped lips, the dripping noses, the dirt smeared on faces, and the red-stained teeth from a recent alder twig toothbrush session. When your man pees off the side of a rowboat in front of you and then farts with the wind blowing in your direction, romance shrivels. Abstinence is the world I had created.

I knew I didn't emit the fragrance of lily-scented aromatherapy. We both reeked of wood smoke (not to be confused with the fondly remembered smell of a campfire). Fortunately, most of the time our noses were oblivious to our smoke-stained selves.

I finally brewed a fabric softener of boiled herbs to freshen our clothes. It cured my clothes, but somehow Micah's always smelled like the morning after a bunch of people who had been partying all night passed out in a tiny windowless room. Most of the time I felt like a seven-year-old whining, "Ewww, boys are gross."

Survival living is a good way to get over the commercialism and vanity of the city. You always have dirt under your nails, crap on your face, and gunk in your teeth. You have no mirror, so you never see yourself. Consequently you feel no reason to impress anyone with "good looks."

The reward for living through another tense day was squishing close beside one another near a smoky fire in the dark. We missed having a couch. We didn't even have enough space in front of the lean-to to lie down next to the fire. The one night I attempted such relaxation, I wriggled myself and a primitive couch I had constructed out of a slab of wood next to the fire, which promptly shot out a blazing ember that sizzled a hole in my pants and scorched my leg.

Most days, despite living with relentless discomfort and irritations, we were able to smile at one another. Deep down, we knew it was a blessing to share our adventures and lessons together. We had each found someone who challenged us, pushed us, and inspired us. We admired one another. We knew we had met for a special reason, even when our egos told us otherwise.

When I needed a little pick-me-up and relief from the hardships of life, I turned to the plants for a herbal spa. A little bit of pampering made all the difference. I called such moments my Mint Medley Day. The powerful, fresh fragrance of mint lifted my spirits. I described it in my journal as a "zippidy-do-dah feeling." First I steamed my face over a pot of swirling rose petals and mint leaves infused in boiling water. When my worries and impurities had dripped away, I smeared on a gooey softening and refreshing face mask made of simmered bladderwrack pods in mint tea, leaving it in place until my skin glowed and my spirit sparkled. For my greasy hair I made a stay-on conditioner by steeping mint leaves in boiling creek water for 20 minutes, then brushing the mixture through my hair.

11th day of unwashed hair
The upside to such greasy hair is that it nicely conditions itself, like its own hot-oil treatment.

When Micah invented an ingenious hand-drill with a flattened nail lashed into a cedar stick, I used it to drill holes into the bottom of a gourd, creating a showerhead. I wanted to remember what a shower felt like. I spent days preparing for the glorious moment.

Twisting long strands of fibrous, honey-coloured basswood bark, I wove a net to suspend the showerhead bowl from a tree branch, plaited a large reed bathmat to keep my feet clean, and pounded inner cedar bark to produce long, soft strands of fibre that I wove into a sweet-smelling face cloth. Then I waited for sun.

Finally, soft, warm rays tickled my eyes open one morning. I brewed a luxurious, perfumed tea using nettles, spruce and cedar tips, and wild roses. I hung my gourd showerhead on the high branch of a nearby alder tree, placed the bathmat below, and draped my cedar cloth on a limb. With bubbling excitement, I peeled off my layers of clothing. Sunlight streamed through the forest canopy onto my tingling bare skin. Positioning myself under the showerhead, I filled the yellow-skinned gourd. I expected squirrels to spiral down the tree to help pour the steaming infusion into the showerhead. Streams of hot spruce and rose water cascaded down my body. Song sparrows flitted about, and my toes giggled, squishing into the mat.

I had nearly forgotten the divine sensation. It was as if thousands of warm dew drops, scented by honeysuckle breath, caressed my body with a tender massage.

Sadly, I never enjoyed the feeling again. A curious bear came along the next day and ate the showerhead. I reverted to bathing with a pot, although I improved this bathing technique considerably much later in our sojourn when I was inspired to create the Paleolithic Back Scrubber.

Survivalists of the world, hear me. I have invented the greatest of all tools: the pounded cedar-bark back scratcher–washer. You can now bathe privately without the help of your fellow survivalist! It is soft, pliable, smells amazing, and exfoliates the skin nicely. I realized today that the things I don't have, the things I miss, like showers, are in a sense not as fulfilling as bathing the way I do now, with my gourd bowl, cedar-bark cloth, and sweet-smelling herbs simmering on the stove before me. Some modern conveniences, though nice, are often missing something intimate and personal.

No matter how brightly or dimly our spirits shone, two fat ripe berries picked and shared were often enough to cheer a droopy face and spark a moment of bliss.

VOICES, VOICES EVERYWHERE

Captain Hill afterwards told me that he never saw anything in the form of man look so wild as I did when I first came on board.

—John R. Jewitt,
The Adventures and Sufferings of John R. Jewitt, Captive of Maquinna

The summer months brought sun-tanned faces, westerly winds, red thimble-berries, blades of seaweed...and boating tourists. A strange transformation happened. Our peaceful, solitary island of bears and berries became a holiday village, with at least four groups of tourists coming through each day, some yelling out, "Hello bears, coming through, bears," with pepper spray in their holsters. (To us, bear spray seemed the most ridiculous form of protection to use on an ornery critter. Every time I imagined using it, I saw the wind blowing it right back in my face. I saw myself running in a blind panic, trying to wipe the burning cayenne pepper from my eyes as I bumped right back into the bear. Using bear spray would have been a last resort for us.)

Tom Sewid and his crew moved into a little floathouse he built on the village docks and began offering historical tours. Our bay became a popular spot for yachts and sailboats to drop anchor; the travellers would then launch their small tenders and head to the village to hear Tom's stories, snap photos, or look for artifacts along the beach.

Instead of waking to the cry of an eagle, we awoke to rumbling engines. Quiet walks through the village, harvesting salad greens and tracking wolves, ceased. The wolves' rubber-boot chew toy was even thrown away, mistaken for trash. We tried to continue focusing on our preparations for the primitive year ahead, drying plants, weaving baskets, and carving bone tools, but with increasing interruptions this became difficult. The intrusions overwhelmed all of us wild critters.

I must have been a savage sight for the tourists when I popped out of the brush with matted pigtails under a cedar-bark hat, wearing a grubby, smoke-stained wool sweater and toting a basketful of weeds. Once I spooked two guys hunting seals who thought I was an ancestral ghost.

Tourists were astonished at our chosen way of life. And their lives were nearly foreign to us by now. After six months in the bush, trying to recall modern living was like looking at heat waves rising from a far-off desert oasis. An invitation to dine aboard a 50-foot yacht, which we accepted without much thought, highlighted the differences.

The idea of eating city food, with someone else doing the cooking, was an opportunity we didn't contemplate turning down, not even with thoughts that we were "cheating." As Micah and I walked with our hosts down the dock, we casually excused ourselves to wash up for dinner. Kneeling, we dipped our hands into the salt water, rubbed them together, and stood up, wiping them dry on our dirty pants. Then we followed the couple to their million-dollar yacht, oblivious to our faux pas.

However, as we stood in front of their home on water, I had a revelation. As if I had been zapped out of my body, I saw the entire scene in one quick flash: smelly, starving survivors meet tidy, technological tourists. Micah and I fit nicely in our woodland surroundings, but the moment I stepped onto the white deck of that spotless yacht, I knew we were in for a ridiculously uncomfortable situation.

I hesitantly removed my gumboots, cringing at the state of my socks. I couldn't remember the last time I had changed them. We were at an all-time low with our hygiene.

Micah took off his boots, stepped into the immaculate galley, and walked toward the table, twigs, sand, leaves, and all sorts of debris trailing behind him. Our host immediately picked up a small broom and dustpan to sweep up after him. But he could do nothing about Micah's feet, which reeked. And this wasn't the average smell of stinky feet but the stench of nasty, weeks-old socks living in damp, rank rubber boots.

An awkward moment ensued in which none of us knew what to say or do. I can only speculate that our hosts were regretting their invitation, but they graciously began setting out their lovely ceramic dishes and sparkling clean glasses without saying a word.

Admiring the exquisite west coast artwork and rich teak interior, I glanced down at myself with renewed self-consciousness. Afraid of how I might look, and smell, under my brown alpaca wool jacket, I never unbuttoned it, even when I felt the stickiness of sweat on my back and when my cheeks burned with a deep red glow.

I tried to come up with the fastest, most polite way out of our situation, but the moment my nose sniffed the wafting, mouth-watering aromas of the kitchen, my senses overwhelmed any rational thought processes. We couldn't leave then.

Our hosts served a delicious meal of salmon soup with seasoned crackers, creamy butter, and Caesar salad. I held my face down over the plate, sniffing the unfamiliar scents like a dog before shovelling and slurping the food. "Ohh, this butter is soo delicious," I repeatedly commented, lost in my senses' delight. I regained my memory of proper manners when I noticed the cloth napkin folded neatly by my plate, just after I had finished wiping my mouth with the back of my hand and my nose on my jacket cuff. Nudging Micah below the table to ease his feeding frenzy, I unfolded my napkin and placed it neatly on my lap.

When the dessert cupboard opened in front of us, I could barely control myself. I wanted to rush over, filling my arms with all those cookies, crackers, and chocolates, and dash off the boat. In slow motion I saw the bag of chocolate cream-filled cookies pulled off the shelf. It was torture. Our hosts had no idea of the agony we felt nibbling politely on two measly cookies when we could have devoured that whole bag in minutes.

Wishing to give our hosts something in return, I offered them all I had, holding out a scrunched-up ball of wilted mint leaves mixed with lint. To my astonishment, they courteously declined. I obviously had slipped back to my wild ways, as no one but a desperate forest dweller would dare to drink any tea housed in my woollen pocket.

Equally graciously we said our goodbyes, slipped on our rubber boots, and headed back to our ten-foot yacht, *Gribley*.

To my surprise, as we left the yacht, I realized that instead of leaving me longing for a modern life, our mingling of worlds had only strengthened my love for our wild ways. Despite my sweet tooth and the delicious dinner, I knew that 200 bags of cookies could not have enticed me to walk away from the feral life waiting for me. Something had changed inside me. My body yearned for the healthy, pure food I found in my meandering on animal trails. When I saw the Chateau in the distance, I couldn't wait to start a fire and sip on a warm cup of mint-lint tea.

❦

Of course, we spent an enormous amount of time and energy harvesting mint and other plants for winter food, and with continued interruptions from question-filled tourists, time was running out. We were no longer graced with 18 hours

I spent days harvesting cedar bark for the preparation of our primitive adventure. I carried the strips home with a backpack made of cedar-branch straps.

of light each day; nourishing plants were wilting away, sending their energy back to their roots for winter storage; and behind our lean-to, a busy squirrel was depositing spruce cone after spruce cone for his winter larder. We too maniacally harvested seaweed and berries, essential for a mineral-rich diet and for taste buds longing for something sweet.

With constant care and a bit of luck with the weather, we successfully preserved many other plants by drying them in the sun on logs. We dried stinging nettle leaves for food and shampoo and their stalks for rope, mint leaves as a digestive tea, yarrow flowers for cleansing washes and blood-clotting bandages, dandelion and dock leaves for winter greens, and dandelion roots for a liver tonic tea. We followed one rule to monitor drying time: everything had to break crisply before storage. If it didn't, it would spoil in the damp, rainy climate.

In June and July, the sap runs through the western red cedar trees. Known as the "Tree of Life" or "Long Life Maker" by the Kwakwaka'wakw people, it touched our spirit more than any other plant. In the book *Cedar*, Hilary Stewart recounts the origin of the cedar tree:

> *There was a real good man who was always helping others. Whenever they needed, he gave; when they wanted, he gave them food and clothing. When the Great Spirit saw this, he said, "That man has done his work; when he dies and where he is buried, a cedar tree will grow and be useful to the people."*

The First Nations used the rot-resistant, straight-grained, easy-splitting wood for their bighouses, canoes, bentwood boxes, tools, weapons, masks, rattles, and culinary dishes. They peeled the soft, pliable inner bark for baskets, boxes, hats, bags, blankets, mats, ropes, clothing, and ceremonial regalia. The strong, flexible roots and smaller branches or withes were split for lashing, basket-making, and sewing. The fragrant, sacred boughs created sweet, insect-free bedding, purifying smudges, and powerful medicines.

A primitive survivalist's dream is to find an old cabin hidden in a wooded glen where an elderly medicine man or wise woman apprentices her in the old ways. I never had an elder walk through the forest with me, pointing out the perfect peeling characteristics of a cedar tree. My teacher lived in my back pocket, speaking through a couple of photocopied paragraphs. The greatest teacher of all, however, is nature. I learned from the cedar tree herself.

Not every tree will give its bark to the basket-maker. To understand the language of trees I had to listen with all my senses. I scrutinized every nuance of my chosen tree, from its shape, colour, and size to the thickness and pattern of its bark. Before I cut into the bark, I always took a few steps back from the tree to ask myself if the tree would produce perfect long strips of bark. Then I asked the tree.

I noticed how my body reacted, paying attention to any thoughts popping into my head. If I felt unsure about anything I scanned the tree from top to bottom again. Injuring a cedar without receiving its gifts was nearly as heartbreaking as finding a live bear in a trap. I wrote: "I argued with a cedar tree today trying to convince her she'd be good for basket material, and of course, in the end, I lost."

I roamed the mountainsides to find perfect peelers, trees approximately one and a half feet wide with slightly thin, straight-grained, smooth, greyish brown bark, free of branches or thick knots on one side. Many times Micah and I hung onto the bottom of a 40-foot-long strip, swinging like Tarzan and Jane, trying to yank the tapered end off the trunk. A tree can provide only two strips of bark before it dies.

Once the long strips tumbled to the forest floor I separated the inner cambium layers from the woody outer bark with a peeling technique that, as a side effect, built lumpy wrist muscles. The fibrous outer bark turned into survival newspaper to start friction fires. Folding the strips into bundles and stringing them on cedar branches, I backpacked them home the old way.

🌿

A relationship with a tree is clear-cut and down-to-earth; a relationship with another stranded survivor is something entirely different. Micah and I had no desire to continue living next to the Chateau in Touristville any longer. Tension had built between us. We snapped at each other like a bitter married couple and stressed over our meagre amounts of dried food goods.

A person is deemed "bushed" when he or she has gone crazy due to isolation. If someone serves guests mouldy cookies, is seen twirling naked with arms outstretched in his yard, carries around teddy bears, or hangs a full deer carcass in his house until it rots (and still eats it), he's bushed.

I considered myself bushed at the end of summer, not from isolation, but from visitors. I escaped for a week-long getaway, living in a cave with only my knife and bow-drill kit. I lost another five pounds. I needed a new home.

❧

Providence moved once again, and this time it brought us a new friend. We had heard of a man named Billy Proctor who lived in a place called Echo Bay. He had spent his life among the islands, hand-logging, trapping, and fishing. He went from rowboat trolling as a "boy-kid" to high-lining aboard his own wooden trollers. He had started a salmon hatchery with other community members, turning his attention to saving the last of his pristine country. He had spent 70 years wandering the beaches, looking for artifacts. His collection rivalled those of the best anthropology museums, and we could hardly wait to visit his famous museum. Rumour had it that Billy Proctor knew everything about the Broughton Archipelago, or, as he called it, the Mainland, and everything one needed to know about how to live in it. Though we were skeptical, when we finally made it to Echo Bay to meet him, we discovered it was all true. Billy Proctor was the real thing.

He didn't know much about me when we first met. Enthusiastically I told him, "I'm bringing back the rowboat fisherman, just like you used to be. My friend and I are looking for a new area to survive off the land and sea. We want to live a primitive lifestyle."

He shook his head, looked down at the ground, and chuckled. "I've heard that story before. Another crazy hippy with a dream."

I wasn't the first to share with Billy Proctor the "I'm going to live off the land" dream, although ours was a little more extreme. The Mainland has a long history of draft dodgers, hippie kayakers, fugitives, and back-to-the-landers who simply wanted to escape to the wilderness, arriving with little more than dreamy enthusiasm. Billy had met many of these wide-eyed dreamers and waved goodbye to most of them within a few weeks.

In spite of his skepticism, he did not hesitate but began naming numerous possible locations where we could move. I quickly snagged a scrap of paper lying beside

I never dreamed I would find lifelong friends in the wilderness, but Billy and Yvonne Proctor were like the grandparents we always dreamed of having.

his hatchery donation box and scribbled notes as fast as I could, astounded at his detailed memory of people, places, and dates.

One name stood out from all the rest: Booker Lagoon. This had been our second choice during the long days I pored over maps, searching for our forest home. I turned to Micah with a grin as Billy began sharing stories about the place.

Over the years a few people had lived in Booker Lagoon. Bob Boise, a retired sea captain, settled a homestead near the entrance. A man who made clay bricks, known as the Clay Trapper, lived on the western shores. Elmo Wortman, a father of rescued orphans and shipwreck survivors, built a house at the northern tip of the lagoon. In 1972 he moved off the land and onto a floating dock bound for Alaska. And ten years later the 'Namgis First Nation started an oyster farm in the same general area that never amounted to more than sunken floats and mesh bags full of dead oysters.

The possibility of pottery clay, a grassy homestead clearing, and oysters sounded promising. Micah showed more excitement about the oysters than I did. The long winter of choking down shellfish was still too fresh in my mind. And oysters brought back childhood memories of Christmas parties featuring platefuls of awful-looking meat speared on fancy toothpicks. I was leery of slurping oysters but excited about pearls.

With a stick, Billy scratched a map in the dirt, showing us good fishing spots for halibut and lingcod. He also described salmon resting spots with detailed landmarks and told stories of cockle clams, starry flounders, wind patterns, currents, and the wildlife he had seen or hunted there. We had found a treasure chest in Billy Proctor.

When the time came to leave, he told us, "Always treat everything with laughter. If you can find the funny things in something most people complain about, you'll always be happy." We took his advice to heart as we set out to explore the locations he recommended.

We weighed the pros and cons of every place we visited. There were a lot of cons. Then we made a trip to Booker Lagoon, located far north and to the west of Native Anchorage on Broughton Island. It sat facing two major bodies of water, Queen Charlotte Strait and Fife Sound. Both were far more dangerous than any stretch of water we had yet rowed.

When we entered a sheltered area called Cullen Harbour, southeast of the lagoon, we saw a glossy black bear in a little grassy bay that we immediately named Bear Bay. Rhinoceros auklets and mew gulls bobbed around several large kelp patches, where we expected small rockfish or kelp greenlings to live. A few small islets grew our favourite wild edibles.

As we approached a narrow channel that led into the lagoon, we saw a small human figure made out of boulders on a rocky point. We had no idea how long it had been standing there, but judging by its tattered, grey, mouldy lifejacket, this fellow was a veteran. It reminded me of a pirate skeleton.

The Inuit call such a rock statue an inuksuk (ee-nook-sook), meaning "a thing that can act in the place of a human being." Depending on how and where an inuksuk is built, it can help people in many different ways, communicating essential knowledge for survival. It can indicate where food caches are stored or the location of successful hunting areas, good camping spots, or places where people are remembered. Specific inuksuit (the plural form of the word) warn of danger or point the way home. I wondered what the Booker Man had to tell me as we rounded the corner into the narrow passage. Luckily, we had arrived at slack tide, avoiding the torrent of whitewater, tide rips, and whirl-pools that formed with the turning of the tides.

The lagoon itself is a large body of water approximately one mile long and two miles wide, with five "arms" extending in all directions. Booker Lagoon was a harsher environment than Native Anchorage, but its isolation was ideal. We continued to weigh the pros and cons of moving here until we came upon a hidden bay with a white-shell beach, protected from the winds by two small islets.

Two belted kingfishers rattled their territorial calls back and forth as we entered the tiny lagoon. We could see the remnants of a small clearing on the embankment, overgrown with thimble and salmonberries. Carefully manoeuvring through the rocks of the shallow beach, we pulled ashore and climbed up the short steep midden, stopping to stare unbelievingly at a tiny, rundown, three-walled shack. What a treasure.

Trash and metal littered the ground, and a battered tarp hung as a makeshift wall. Inside, the planked floor was stained with a dark greasy residue that reeked as if I were standing in the oil pit of a garage. Thick moss covered the roof, but the shack, which was definitely vacant, looked surprisingly sound and somehow inviting. We considered it a step up from our leaky lean-to next to the trash-trailer. Booker Lagoon would be our new home. When we passed the rock man on our way out, I knew it would always point the way home.

With excitement, we packed up our things at Native Anchorage. We had only one problem: we couldn't afford a water-taxi to transport us to Booker Lagoon. The universe blessed us with another new friend.

Roger Laton owned a private fishing resort next door to Billy Proctor's childhood home site. With incredible generosity, Roger helped us transport our things to Booker Lagoon, including hundreds of pounds of cedar planks we had stashed in various places around Village Island. He even surprised us with an unusual housewarming gift: an old wooden dock and two small windows.

Though at opposite ends of the spectrum—Billy, a highline fisherman on the coast, and Roger, a retired CEO of a high tech company—both men freely gave their hard-earned knowledge to anyone willing and interested in learning, with patience, excitement, and passion. I had never dreamed I'd find lifelong friends such as these while trying to survive in the middle of nowhere.

PART THREE
BOOKER LAGOON

BLESSINGS AND HAUNTINGS

We change the world not by what we say or do, but as a consequence of what we have become.

—David R. Hawkins, psychiatrist and spiritual teacher

Day 163
So here I am, sitting on a white-shell beach in front of my new home in Booker Lagoon. It is so beautiful here; it's a dream come true.

The solitude was perfect. Our new, oil-stinkin' three-walled shack was far from ideal. But a metamorphosis had taken place inside me; I never cringed at the thought of moving into another dumpy shelter. My heart beamed with thankfulness.

Renovations commenced. We set to work turning the wall-less generator shed into a habitable shanty. I built cedar plank shelves, drying racks, and an all-purpose bed/desk/table. Micah straightened rusty nails we found on the beach and used the old dock boards to build a fourth wall. Roger's two windows turned the dark, dank cave into a slightly brighter one.

Nearly every night we burned a single taper candle for about an hour. I had harvested a red-belted bracket fungus clinging to the side of a dead tree, and we used it as a primitive candle holder, nailed to the wall. The soft glow created the type of reading light many believe will cause blindness, but by then we functioned perfectly in shadow light, as if our owl eyes had formed more rods for night vision.

The candle cast a mellow light on coiled roots, baskets, bows, quivers, and primitive projects hanging on the walls. Shadowy bundles of cedar bark, nettle stalks, arrow shafts, and rolled deer hides flickered in the rafters. In classic woodsman fashion, animal-skin rugs lined the floor, and fragrant herbs hung from the ceiling. The shack had become the ultimate clubhouse we dreamt of as kids, even though it smelled like a musty dog bed. To freshen the air, I boiled evergreen boughs, smudged our home with burning cedar bundles, or lit the essential oil burner I created from a hollowed sea urchin shell. It lit the place with brilliant geometric patterns.

We hiked the forest and beaches searching for large, plankable cedar logs. The knot-free, old-growth wood split beautifully down its even grain. We lugged the boards, three feet wide, six feet long, and two inches thick, through the forest, often rowing them home from another island, until we had amassed a sizeable pile. Micah built a stylish porch with the sweet-smelling new planks, giving us a place to work on projects in the rain. We lived in raingear from head to foot throughout September and October, wondering if the drizzle would ever stop. I was no longer turning into a raisin from a dry, smoky fire; I was wrinkling like a prune from all the rain.

Scout demanded a morning hug each day. She was always ready to play or attack us, even while building our cedar-plank porch.

I lashed together some of the cedar planks to create a wobbly picnic table and set up a primitive cooking area with a rock-encircled firepit, lined with several inches of sand and shell to prevent underground fires. We dug a three-foot-square pit to use as an oven, covering it with a large cedar plank and heating it with round cooking stones. I lashed driftwood poles together in a tripod so we could hang pots over the fire, allowing us to simmer soup and fry fish at the same time. A planked board by the firepit served as a crude, tailbone-crushing couch, keeping us off the wet ground without comforting our weary bodies. At least we had room to stretch out beside a fire.

Our survival camp would not be complete without a first-rate smokehouse. We lashed five-foot poles together for the frame and used cedar planks for the walls and roof, creating a sturdy structure resembling an outhouse.

A stylish outdoor toilet with a covered roof and driftwood toilet seat, perfectly shaped to fit bare bums, completed the camp.

We longed for a comfortable chair, but our luxury came with a cedar-plank backrest and the space to stretch out next to the fire.

Micah combined a rusty 55-gallon drum we found in the bushes with a discarded electric stove to make a hobo-style cook stove for use inside the shelter. There was only one problem: we couldn't stand upright. Even though we built a stone chimney cemented with creek clay, the chalky white smoke that billowed into the shack from the homemade stove forced us to live as hunched-over dwarves.

We knocked heads together, literally, trying to figure out how to create a proper draft system. Nothing worked. After several weeks of smoky torture, I gave up. One night in bed I rolled over to face Micah, wiped the tears streaming from my smoke-stung eyes, and blurted, "The stove's moving out or I'm moving out. I'm coughing all day long and hacking up gobs of nasty yellow phlegm. I think my eyeballs are burnt. I'm done."

Micah pulled back the blanket covering his face and turned to me with a runny nose and smoky, tear-filled eyes, laughing. "I can't wait to chuck the thing either."

After seven months saturated in swirling smoke, we modified our dreams of relying solely on an open fire and opted to use the emergency woodstove my godfather had built for me by welding together two small propane tanks and giving it legs and a vented door.

I remembered Jack loading it into the back of his truck. "I built you this little woodstove," he said, "just in case you ever need one." I distinctly remembered my reluctance to take it, rambling on about how we wanted to live 100 percent primitively. Thankfully, he ignored me. The stove worked perfectly. I thought of him almost daily, wishing to hug him again for the gift.

The stove did cause one of our worst health crises. I would stoke the fire until the metal tank emanated a bright red glow. Sweat poured from my forehead as I lunged in and out of the heat waves to quickly stir meals. One night I dashed forward to add another piece of wood, then jumped back, yelling, as my skin sizzled on the hot metal.

The soreness left as quickly as it came, but in the wee hours of the morning my seeping burn cried out in excruciating pain. I couldn't fall back asleep. The centre of the burn, about the size of a quarter on the corner of my elbow, had turned into a yellowish pus-filled wound. The surrounding area was covered in lesser first- and second-degree burns. The whole thing became dangerously infected.

For days I experimented with herbal concoctions. Nothing worked. The infection worsened. A thin scab formed over the custard pus of dead cells, sealing the infection. I had to scrape and peel off the crust daily to clean it out. My entire elbow throbbed. I jumped and cried out at the slightest touch to the area. A bandage only made it hurt more. At night I softly sobbed myself to sleep.

After seven months of living in a horribly smoky environment, we finally opted to use our "emergency" homemade wood-stove to heat our shelter and cook on when escaping nasty weather.

One morning I woke knowing I didn't have long before the infection went systemic. I was paranoid that I would see the telltale sign of red streaks up my arm. I needed to either administer the emergency antibiotics my doctor had given me before I left, or row eight hours to Echo Bay for an emergency floatplane evacuation. I searched for signs that the poison had hit my bloodstream. When I found none, I gave myself one more day to find the plants that would heal me. If that failed, I would need to swallow the pharmaceutical drug. I talked to roots. Listening to my feelings after my one-way verbal conversation, I concocted a remedy.

I made a paste from mustard-yellow powdered dock root, fine clay, and Oregon grape root tincture. Gently I smeared the cooling balm over the burn. By evening it had started to draw out the infection. To stop the scab from re-forming, I prepared a healing salve with soothing anti-inflammatory oils that kept the wound soft and moist.

The burn took a couple of weeks to heal, but it left me with nothing but a nickel-sized scar on my elbow.

Since we no longer had to press our faces up to the cracks in the walls for gulps of fresh air, we spent a couple of days chinking the drafty gaps with pounded clay harvested from a nearby creek. We neglected to add moss as a binder, so the clay eventually dried, cracked, and fell out here and there, but compared to the leaky, breezy, lean-to, the shack vaulted to four-star status.

Like a mischievous sprite, the howling wind would blow through the shack and puff out the candle. When that happened, I'd fumble around in the dark, put my journal away, and hit the sack, knowing neither of us wanted to go through the agonizing process of lighting it again. Some nights when the baskets swayed on the walls and the shack shook in gale-force winds, I imagined being one of the three little pigs, hoping the big bad wolf couldn't huff and puff it down.

Once the main structures were built, I finally began unpacking and organizing all the things I had tucked away in storage at Native Anchorage. The happiness I felt at insignificant happenings continued to surprise me.

One night, sitting on the bearskin rug next to the warm, smokeless stove, I wrote, "This place is like a palace compared to Native Anchorage, especially when I can take off my shoes and change into cleaner 'house clothes.' The shack is a real step up in the world of survival shelters."

It was a small palace, like a 10-foot by 15-foot closet, but it was dry and warm, two conditions we had lived without for a long time. Smaller yet was the three-foot-wide bed we somehow managed to squeeze onto. Micah could fall asleep midway through a conversation. I couldn't.

I have the worst sleeps, a real step down from my hemlock mattress in Native Anchorage. I never imagined it could get worse. Sleeping on the ground is almost soft and giving, in a way. This wooden bed is about as soft as a rock. Really therapeutic for my aching back! I wake up every hour and roll over to keep my shoulders and hips from cracking.

My first comfortable night came 30 days later. It's a mystery how it happened. I wrote, "I didn't want to get up. I just wanted to savour the moment. Who knows, it might not come around for another month."

As a kid, I had always pictured myself sleeping in a buffalo hide, but when I couldn't obtain a hide before I left, I adjusted the dream. I traded tanning lessons with my neighbour for six woolly sheep hides, which I eventually sewed into a deluxe sleeping bag. I stuffed cattail down I had collected from a faraway pond into a pillow—a once-familiar luxury my head had not enjoyed for over eight months. When I snuggled up in warm, comfy hides like a primitive princess for the first time, I couldn't stop giggling.

However, even in thin, synthetic sleeping bags, Micah and I barely fit on the teeny wooden bed side by side. The heavy monstrosity that was my new sleeping bag engulfed the bed. Nearly every morning we woke feeling as if we had been squashed up on a car seat all night. Like the best friend he was, Micah chose the bear-skin-covered floor and gave me the multi-use table. Though both spots were drafty and hip-crackingly hard, we instantly experienced the restful sleeps we had taken for granted back home. It was almost like having my own bedroom again.

We modified *Gribley* too. We cut out the back seat to make more room for our gear and installed the second set of oars that we had bought during our move from Native Anchorage. Micah sat in the bow, I in the middle, and Scout roamed back and forth, dodging the oars to avoid a *thwap* on the head.

It took a lot of practice to become synchronized rowers. Micah's oars walloped my kidneys and spine over and over again. Bruises of all sizes appeared in record numbers when our timing faltered. I wore my lifejacket as body armour until we became coordinated. The day we aced it, I turned to Micah with a smile. "I think we're ready for the Olympic rowing team. Can we ever haul ass." It was like we had a two-horse Yamaha on the back.

In modern terms our lean-to in Native Anchorage would be considered a condo in the city, while our shack in Booker Lagoon was a house way out in the country. We discovered we had to travel farther than we had gone before to find the food and supplies we needed.

We located the local vegetable stand right away, on a nearby island we dubbed the "Produce Section." It lacked the abundance of the old village but offered three new veggie selections: the sweet-tasting roots of silverweed, the ambrosia-like scurvy grass, and delicious elfin saddle mushrooms. We also identified many other places worthy of names: Punk Rock, Oyster Arm, Giraffe Passage, Seagull Islet, Dock Rock, and Spa Bay.

We enjoyed our new sense of freedom, but the transition to Booker Lagoon also caused a lot of stress, gloom, and disagreements. Approaching the second winter, our situation appeared bleaker than it had during the first. This time we were facing the whole winter, rather than arriving in February with the knowledge that spring would come soon. By mid-September we had nearly depleted our food bin, which housed nothing more than a couple of Ziploc bags filled with

Patch and Crease, our dolphin neighbours, would play with us every time we left home, whether we were in our boat or swimming with them in the water.

horrible smoked clams, tiny amounts of rancid bear and fish jerky, and several bags of dried plants and berries.

When Roger Laton ferried us to Booker Lagoon, he gazed around the place and commented, "You know, there's only one good thing about the 'good ol' days.' They're gone." He also suggested we stockpile ten cords of wood for winter, but at this point we didn't even remember what a cord of wood looked like. Our routine of chopping two giant armloads of wood every day had so far kept our shack toasty warm, but the task of stacking huge amounts of wood for the long term moved to the bottom of our seemingly never-ending and overwhelming list of preparations we needed to complete before November. (Later we learned that folks in Echo Bay had been laying bets that we wouldn't last the winter.)

The negativity sucked our spirits into a downward spiral, and both of us started questioning our rationales. On Day 170, Micah finally said, "I sometimes can't remember why I'm out here. Do we ever have good times?"

I shrugged my shoulders, whistled for Scout, and sat under an overhanging bank on the beach, out of the rain. I hugged my knees and cried. But somehow, just posing the question put me back on track. I vowed that I would not continue letting dark thoughts dampen my heart's inner knowing. I would relearn what modern society had encouraged me to forget, and discover all that nature had to teach me. We couldn't give up.

Scout rubbed up against my leg. I stroked her damp back, smiling at the glistening, crystalline drops of rain hanging on the tips of berry branches above my head, gently pulled by gravity's fingers, plinking and plopping by my feet.

Living in Native Anchorage had taught me to treasure the small joys, often overlooked, that occurred every minute of the day. Now, in Booker Lagoon, it didn't take long for Micah and me to laugh again, living in the moment and flowing with the changing situations.

For one thing, negativity could never spoil a day when dolphins splashed in our front yard. Patch and Crease, two Pacific white-sided dolphins, had moved into Booker Lagoon and never ventured out. They greeted us whenever we went for a row, their grey dorsal fins slicing through the water toward us, swimming like torpedoes under the boat, rocking us back and forth. *Gribley* didn't kick up a large enough wake for big action, but they were clearly as desperate as we were for entertainment. We cheered them on as they surfed the baby waves, bow-riding beside the boat, leaping, flipping, spitting, and splashing.

Patch and I swam together on my birthday, the first day of fall. I jumped off the boat into the chilly water and patted my hands on the water's surface to call the dolphins closer. I dunked my head under to see Patch swimming toward me. When he was a few feet away he stopped, cocked his head, and then came closer. Our eyes locked. The moment I gazed into that dolphin's eye and he searched mine intently, I truly came to believe the old proverb that says the eye is the window to the soul. With a flick of his tail he jetted away, leaping out of the water in front of me, splashing me in the face with his spray. I felt like a mermaid being kissed on the forehead by heaven.

Micah jumped in too. We lay on our backs, soaking up the magical moment as the dolphins jumped in tandem around us. Graced by *kulutas* (*khew-loo-tahs*).

We didn't think life in Booker Lagoon could get any better until we caught our first coho salmon. We celebrated with a traditional barbecue, roasting the filleted fish on a cedar rack system called the *tlupsa'yu* (*gloop-sigh-you*). When the shiny silver skin bubbled and the drips of fatty oil turned into caramel, we removed the fish from the fire and relished the tender, mouthwatering flakes of salmon.

We boiled the head, bones, and fins in creek water for a delicious soup stock, then stirred in chopped dandelion and silverweed roots, sliced angelica, nodding onions, and dried crumbled bull kelp and stinging nettle. It looked disgusting, but once we strained it to remove floating eyeballs, Fish Head Soup started my saliva running. We ate it with a side dish of nori crackers.

We caught a total of six salmon in two weeks outside the lagoon. We discovered if we left the fillets overnight to "firm up," we could trim off a higher quality of jerky. Thin, one-eighth-inch reddish strips hung on small carved cedar sticks in the smokehouse. We tended the alder-wood fire for two days. Once the fish darkened to a desirable smoky colour, we hung the jerky on racks above the woodstove until the meat cracked when bent.

Our hooks caught three spiny dogfish too. Most commercial and sport fishermen consider these relatively small sharks, averaging three feet long, the scourge of the sea, as they often steal bait from more desirable quarry. Sport fishermen who admit to eating them are looked down on.

Russ Mohney, in *The Dogfish Cookbook*, wrote, "Our research on the edibility of the common dogfish was carried out under a dark cloak of secrecy. On one occasion we made the mistake of cleaning and dressing a dogfish in full view of a praamful of dedicated salmon fishermen…Unfortunately, we soon find that the path of the intrepid explorer is often paved with the hoots and catcalls of a doubting public."

Many people believe dogfish urinate from their skin, making their flesh unfit for the dinner plate. This is false. They have a normal excretory system, but unlike most other fish, these ancient sharks have solved the osmotic problem of living in sea water. Since fish continually drink salt water, they are constantly battling dehydration and must expend energy to excrete salt from their gills. Dogfish retain nearly all the urea and organic compounds in their blood, preventing their bodies from absorbing excess salt from the ocean. The retained urea means ammonia is released into the flesh as it is cooked. I never noticed a disagreeable taste, but I had also lowered my standards to that of a survivalist. Those with a flare for rarity can marinate the fillets overnight in a weak vinegar and lemon juice solution to render the steaks fit for the finest tables.

Smoking and drying the oily shark flesh turned it into a chewy, greasy wad in our mouths. We concluded dogfish taste better fresh. The rough shark skin became our sandpaper, and we rendered their oily livers into a nourishing wood oil.

Though we knew more meat had to fill our bins, we were still able to enjoy the comings and goings around us. I often watched mice sneak through Scout's cat door as if they were part of the family. Scout enjoyed playing with them inside the shack, and they naturally escaped to hide under the boxes and baskets stashed along the walls. Rejoicing at their good fortune, they often invited their whole families into our shack. Luckily the mice didn't take over, probably because we lived with a feral cat, who would leave their bodies lying around the shack for us to deal with. She preferred seafood. Often Micah blinked open his eyes in the morning to see a fuzzy brown dead mouse four inches from his nose. One of Scout's presents.

Then came the night we first felt a drip on our heads. The shack had a leak-proof roof.

I just pray it's not a mouse peeing on us. Micah's come up with all kinds of better scenarios, but I'm always telling him, "Whatever makes you feel better." Deep down, we know we're being attacked. Maybe it's because Micah ate his friend for breakfast. "Piss on you guys!" That's what the mouse is saying, laughing all the way to his numerous food stashes. I found a stash in my rubber boot this morning.

Eventually, after feeding our little guests tiny portions of scraps outside, we began experiencing happier living arrangements.

An otter family of six lived on the opposite shore, bringing me a spirit of joy and playfulness when I needed it most. *Ma̱tsa* (*mah-chah*), the mink, lived on a tiny, forested island beside us, while the great blue heron, *k̲wak̲'wani* (*kwa-gwa-nee*), hunted at low tide in Little Lagoon. Two eagles joined us nearly every evening to watch the setting sun, and the continuous bellowing roar of distant sea lions drifted to us on the south wind's breath. We even heard rumours that we should watch out for the neighbourhood Bigfoot.

"You seen the Big Fella yet?" local Natives asked whenever we met out on the water. My journals were packed with eerie stories of the supernatural beast. Perhaps it was all the legends, the unnerved look on people's faces as they recounted their stories, or the spookiness I felt in the old villages now and again. Possibly it was the forest itself, for on shadowy, gloomy days the dark-barked trees draped in long witch's hair lichen murmured of an untamed wildness within. Whatever the reason, I began to feel like a kid sitting around a campfire listening to ghost stories. The controversial creature became real to me.

❦

One night I drifted off to sleep and found myself visiting a village filled with standing totem poles, at the end of a mighty river estuary. I was staying in a small, one-room cabin planked in cedar. I thought the two doors on opposite ends of the cabin rather peculiar. I always kept the back door closed and the front open so I could watch the activities of the village. I was living inside an Emily Carr painting.

I was sitting in the middle of the floor watching the children play outside when the hairs on the back of my neck stood up. I swivelled. Like a ghostly being, *Dzunukwa* passed through the closed door. In two giant strides the black, hairy figure loomed over me. She bent down, her long hair swishing forward over her face to cover a haunting pair of blood-red lips. Grabbing hold of my right leg, the enormous creature swung me around on my back, dragging and bumping me along the cedar-planked floor toward the open door. Once into the sunlight she picked up the pace, her long strides extending into a slow jog. The villagers noticed her at once.

"*Dzunukwa* is here!" Their screams echoed through the village.

In slow motion, *Dzunukwa* turned her head to look at me; her deep, fearsome eyes pierced my soul, as if a black widow had just injected her deadly poison into me. Her full, crimson lips curled up in a horrific snarl.

I began to sing. Kwak'wala words poured from my heart. Words I did not know, from a song I had never heard. *Dzunukwa* paused. A look of horror and astonishment enveloped her as she dropped my leg and fled. I watched her effortlessly and gracefully disappear into the forest.

An elder from the village ran to me and knelt down. With a quizzical look, she asked, "How do you know that song?"

"I don't know," I replied. "It just came out."

"What you sang is a sacred, ancient song very few of my people know," she said softly with a smile. "It is a song of protection against *Dzunukwa*."

✿

At these words I woke to the yellow-stained windows of the shack in Booker Lagoon. Lingering between the worlds, a part of me was shocked I wasn't in the village, but another part grasped at the wisps of notes and words of the song. As the seconds ticked by, my memory of it faded.

Even with the dream song, I constantly battled my illogical fear of these supernatural beings who are so tightly woven throughout the history of the Kwakwaka'wakw nation. I continually had powerful dreams of *Dzunukwa* and *Bakwas*. I wanted to believe the protection song still lay hidden deep inside me, like a locked music box that would open when I needed it.

WOODEN SPEARS

If the air is jam-full of sounds which we tune in with, why should it not also be full of feels and smells and things seen through the spirit, drawing particles from us to them and them to us like magnets.

—Emily Carr, artist

The wheel of seasons turned. Autumn painted the Broughton Archipelago in every imaginable shade of green. The monochrome landscape made me miss the brightly coloured streets back home, littered in shades of red and yellow from fall leaves dancing to their deaths. The only splash of red in Booker Lagoon came from the tiny, inconspicuous leaves of huckleberry bushes dotting the shoreline.

When I first arrived on the coast, the trumpeting calls of swans heading to their northern breeding grounds brought an intense feeling of adventure. Their returning bugling in the fall, accompanied by grey young, bestowed a new form of excitement. I felt the peacefulness of home. Living close to the earth made the natural markers of seasonal change more apparent to me than ever before.

My new life and home filled me spiritually but not physically. The chilly fingers of mid-autumn urgently prodded us to continue stockpiling food for the winter, but we hit another wall in our ability to obtain the protein-rich food our bodies craved and needed to survive. Our fishing skills failed to produce the larger fish that would sustain us through the windy winter, and our tiny rowboat would not withstand the stormy waters and allow us to continue fishing. With anxious hearts we agreed to harvest another bear.

The painful memory of our first primitive bear trap dwelled in our minds. Nervous about repeating our mistakes, we unpacked the wire snare given to us by an afternoon visitor at Village Island. He claimed that every bear he had trapped lay dead upon his arrival. Trusting his stories, we decided to set it up. But where? We had seen a minuscule amount of bear sign in Booker Lagoon. Were these bears more wary and wild than those on Village Island? Had they travelled to distant salmon-spawning creeks? Were the salal berries keeping them in the forest, or had they already headed to higher ground in search of a cozy den? Finally, we set the snare in the only place we had seen a bear thus far, Bear Bay, the tiny grassy bay outside Booker Lagoon at the mouth of Cullen Harbour.

I hated checking that snare. I crept up the beach, clenching our homemade fishing gaff in one hand and a small hatchet in the other—both weapons that I knew would be useless if I needed to defend myself against an angry bear that was caught but not strangled to death by the snare. Taking one last breath of courage, I bent down and peered into the tangle of thick cedar branches, hoping a big black paw wasn't about to bat me on the side of the head. It seemed ridiculously dangerous.

Micah and I took turns embarking on this daily suicide mission, and every time I cautiously peeked through the branches with my little axe, my intuition screamed for me to make a wooden spear. I didn't know why, except for the logical reason that a longer weapon might better protect me. Oddly, I ignored this sound advice for a couple of weeks, until one day I told Micah, "We're never going to catch a bear unless we make a spear. I can't explain it, but I really believe this."

"Hmm. Okay, I guess we should make some spears."

After two weeks of wasted effort, with other activities taking priority over making spears, we took the snare down. Sticking to what we knew, we spent three full days of hard labour building another primitive deadfall trap, based on the one we erected at Village Island. We improved this trap by shortening the length of the cubby, lowering the main crushing beam, increasing its falling speed, lowering the trigger ramp, and waterproofing the roof in hopes that this would prevent rain from drowning out the foul scent of rotting fish.

Precise, calculated teamwork was necessary to manoeuvre 600 pounds of logs into position to remain perfectly balanced on a six-inch trigger stick. We set the trap, tripped it, and watched it fall over and over, scrutinizing any possible flaws. When we knew our bodies could not exert themselves one more time to lift the logs, we quit.

I walked away feeling a mixture of trepidation, worry, sadness, and hope. Once again, I prayed for a clean, quick kill.

Our worries about the fast-approaching winter encouraged us to reset the wire snare a mile up the mountain on a small, tunnel-like trail. It was a steep hike, filled with treacherous hidden holes, slippery logs, and thick brush, but the game trail looked promising.

It took at least two hours every day to check the traps, breaking all the survival laws regarding conservation of energy. Days passed, then weeks. No bear. We talked about giving up as the nights grew longer.

On our 196th day I saw a big, healthy bear rolling rocks on the beach a hundred yards from the trap. I rowed closer until *Gribley* eased up to the shoreline. I sat quietly admiring her beauty in the downpour, listening to her munch the tiny crabs she had uncovered.

The bear's black fur shone with a dark indigo hue, as if reflecting a light that glowed from within. Raindrops glistened on her shiny coat. I fell in love with her magnificence. After I observed her for a blissful half hour, the bear slowly made her way to the edge of the forest, toward the trap.

"Is this our bear?" I asked the universe. I thought it would be impossible for her not to sniff out the rotting fish, and I reasoned her instincts would compel her to enter the trap for the rare treat of putrefied salmon. "How could she not?" I mused.

As if hearing me, the bear turned her head. She stared straight at me. "Do you think you're the only one who is taken care of?" a voice echoed in my head. The question surprised me.

The bear immediately sauntered into the forest. I rowed closer to the trap's location, sure I would hear the crash of falling logs. The moment felt surreal.

I strained to hear the sound of the trap over the loud plunking and plopping of raindrops. Instead I heard music. Lovely music. Like an orchestra playing a heavenly symphony that only I could hear. The gloomy green landscape shone with an unearthly electric radiance. I felt my chest vibrating with a surge of energy, as if butterflies were fluttering at light speed in my chest. Captivated by the music, I spoke softly aloud, "If angels had come down from heaven, this is the music they would play."

My logical self could not accept ethereal music playing in the forest. My deeper, heartfelt self was thankful. Half of me wanted to pull ashore to investigate, while the other wanted to stay put so as not to startle the bear. My rational mind picked up the oars and rowed home. As the music began to fade, I prayed for the blue sparkling bear, torn between a wish for her safety and my need for winter food.

I didn't know what to say to Micah. When I stepped into the shack to tell him about my experience, I felt bombarded by hard-fact reality, as if the shack were sucking away the enchanted feeling that quivered through me. Micah had gotten used to my "dropping of the veil" stories. When I told him of the blue bear, his eyes widened and he beamed me a non-judgmental smile. He motioned me outside and lifted up his newly carved hemlock spear.

The next morning I heard footsteps running up to the shack. The door flew open. "Come quick," Micah panted. "The bear triggered the trap."

Shocked, I blurted out, "What? Is it dead?"

"No, it's gone. Let's go."

As I pulled my raincoat off its nail, I glimpsed the large, Rambo-type survival knife hanging near the door. We had never used it or even carried it before, but for some reason I grabbed it, strapped it to my belt, and tied it around my leg.

I rushed to the boat to catch up with Micah. With a heave I pushed *Gribley* off the beach and jumped in, hoping the bear tracks wouldn't tell the story of a wounded bear. Micah's heavy, six-foot-long spear lay across the boat seats. I let out a sigh of relief. At least one of us had finally carved one.

Approaching the trap area, we tracked the large depressions the blue bear had left in the soft debris the day before. They paused in front of the trap. Long claw marks tore into the main crushing beam, which now lay on the ground. She had pushed over the immense log, climbed over it, walked to the back of the pen, ate the fish head, sauntered away to the creek for a drink, and then ambled up into the forest, unharmed. To our disbelief, the bear had figured out how to dismantle the trap without getting hurt, a difficult task even for us.

As a hunter, it's easy to be caught up in the illusion that humans are the ones taken care of by the spirit that moves through all things and that this divine energy is on "our side." The magical bear taught me otherwise. The world needed her to live more than I needed her as food. The revelation humbled me.

We reset the trap and then trudged up the mountain to check the snare. After a half hour of slogging and bushwhacking through the dense foliage, we came to a flat area crowded with straight cedar saplings.

"Hey, Micah, would you mind going on ahead to check the snare? I'll be able to make a perfect spear with one of these saplings. I'll try to hurry."

"No problem," he replied. "I'll whistle if I need you." We imitated a few birdcalls to relay messages when human verbal communications could disrupt the forest.

As the tenth wood chip fell from my spear, I heard a strange lamenting sound filtering through the forest. I cupped my hands behind my ears to amplify the noise.

"*Fee-bee-bee, fee-bee-bee.*" Micah's chickadee call interrupted my straining concentration. I quietly followed his whistling. When I spied Micah crouching behind a gigantic log, the mysterious sound abruptly changed. It no longer held the same melody. I dropped my head and closed my eyes, listening to the now familiar sound of a bawling bear. I crept behind Micah, placing my hand on his arm. He didn't have to say a word. The look on his face said enough.

As we sharpened our spears, we whispered a quick plan for assessing the horrifying situation that lay ahead, then crawled over the log. Gripping the spears, and in a thigh-burning crouch, we silently stalked toward the snared bear.

I felt like Ayla, the main character in one of my favourite books, Jean M. Auel's *Clan of the Cave Bear*. Ayla ran away from her adopted Neanderthal clan to venture alone into the vast unknown. In her journeys she became proficient with the sling, discovered how to make fire, tamed a sabre-toothed tiger, and trained a prehistoric horse. She was a Paleolithic superhero.

Unfortunately, I didn't feel a drop of heroism in me as I prepared to risk my life to spear a bear. I trembled. My heart pounded with an ancient fear that throbbed in my wrists and hands. Every rustling leaf caught my attention, every faint crack of stick sounded like cymbals crashing beside my ears. A primal fight-or-flight sensation rippled through my body as feral instincts passed down from distant ancestors surfaced. I was about to fight a cornered bear with a wood-tipped spear. Red ochre rock paintings of stickmen spearing woolly mammoths came to life in my imagination.

The bear's continuing cries stabbed my heart and sent shivers throughout my body. As we drew closer, the distress calls rippled farther through the forest in concentric rings of sound. The forest predators would be coming.

We quietly climbed up a 15-foot bank for a better vantage point. Micah led in the point position, choosing our route and focusing his vision forward. I took the rear guard position; my awareness encompassed all that came from behind and beside us. I followed Micah without hesitation, a perfect scout team.

Reaching the top of the bank, we belly-crawled to a rotten log for cover. We peered over the mossy log through a tangle of tree branches. On a forgotten, over-grown logging road, tied by the neck to a small hemlock tree, lay a young black bear.

Horrified, I scrunched my eyes so I didn't have to face our situation. I didn't want to accept the fact I was causing such misery again. Pain swept through me as my heart beat with heavy sorrow. But I knew no magical song would wake me from this nightmare; I had to open my eyes and end the agony we all felt. I inhaled a deep, powerful breath. With regained courage, I surveyed the scene in detail.

The bear held her front paw up by her neck in an awkward, unnatural position. From our vantage point it was unclear if she was caught by her neck, her foot, or both. We saw no indication of injury. Torn plants, bent saplings, and other signs of disturbance told us the young bear had struggled to free herself but had reluctantly given up. She had not yet detected our presence. As her frightened cries ceased, I looked down at my roughly carved spear.

Lying on the forest floor we whispered our concerns. We couldn't decide how to kill the bear. The longer we talked, the more confused we became. Ignoring my intuition to use our spears, we decided the safest decision would be to run all the way home for our bows and arrows. We bolted down the mountain.

We reached the cabin quicker than I thought possible. In seconds we gathered our hunting equipment, then launched *Gribley* as we could return to Bear Bay and the trap more quickly by water. On the way back, we began to question our rash decision. I had only recently finished my hickory longbow, a 40-pound test bow, legal for hunting deer, but Micah had yet to make one. He held my 35-pound practice bow. We each had just a stone-tipped arrow and one pointed practice arrow.

Powered by adrenaline, we sprinted back up the mountain, stopping to stalk the last distance so the bear would not detect us, and arrived at the mossy log in record time. We leaned our backs against the log, taking a few moments to slow our laboured breath and racing minds. Groans and gruff cries from below made us turn to each other. We did not speak. Our haunted eyes conveyed everything we felt as we turned to look down the bank.

The bear paced back and forth, lunging forward again and again with all her might as she tried to break the cable, clearly demonstrating that the snare's loop was firmly cinched around her neck. The cable had a locking mechanism that prevented the noose from loosening, but for some reason the snare had not tightened around her neck. We had to finish the job our modern equipment had failed to do.

We picked up our primitive bows and arrows. Nothing less than a perfect shot to the heart would do. Through the thick foliage we each took aim, though we knew the odds were against us. I had to find the place inside myself where miracles did happen. Nodding our heads to count down, we jumped up, simultaneously drew back our bowstrings, and shot.

As if standing outside time, I saw my arrow in slow motion pierce the bear's skin right behind her shoulder, a perfect shot to the heart. As quickly as it hit, the arrow fell to the ground. She barely flinched. Micah and I stared at each other in disbelief.

Now that the bear had seen us, she began struggling harder and bawling louder. We restrung our bows and shot again. Micah's arrow hit her spine and mine her vitals, but once again they bounced off as though we were using toy arrows with suction cups instead of pointed tips. Our bows were woefully inadequate to give our arrows the force needed to penetrate the thick bearskin.

"Look," I finally exclaimed, "I knew I had to make this spear for a reason, and I'm going to use it."

Without a second thought I charged down the hill toward the bear, unafraid and wholly focused on what I aimed to do. Micah skidded down the hill after me, then charged ahead. This was his bear.

Holding our spears in front of us, we faced the bear. I could feel the aggression building in myself and the animal. A bear with ready claws can overwhelm its prey with a surprising burst of speed. I knew she could charge us at any second.

Micah advanced upon her. She backed up as far as the noose allowed. Each time Micah tried to manoeuvre into position to spear her heart, she countered his moves, lowering her head, batting at the spear with her powerful paws.

"This isn't working, Micah," I said. "She has six feet of movement in all directions. She could easily get you. Why don't I push her back as far as she can go on the noose, and then you come at her from the side."

With knuckles white from the tight grip I had on my spear, I slowly walked toward the bear, jabbing at her from the front and carefully avoiding her swiping paws, while Micah eased up to her side. The plan worked. The bear was focused on me and less on Micah. But when he lunged at her with all his might, his wooden spear bounced off without leaving a scratch.

We backpedalled as fast as we could, shocked, horrified, and sagging with despair. The sorrow we felt was all for the frightened bear.

Tears welled in my eyes. I tilted my head back, asking for guidance, and felt something heavy knock the side of my leg. The knife. I had forgotten about the monstrous survival knife that hung from my belt.

"Micah, use the knife," I yelled.

I quickly handed over the nine-inch blade, and Micah unscrewed the base of the knife, emptying hidden survival items I didn't know existed. He pushed the spear point into the hollow handle and lashed it securely to the staff with the string from my hood.

We advanced on the bear again. I prodded her with my spear as Micah moved in from the side.

I whispered, "I'm so sorry, bear. We never meant to torment you."

Micah thrust the knife-tipped spear. It pierced her heart. The bear fell dead as her life's breath blew out of her.

We rushed to the limp body, skidding to our knees. Cradling her, we pulled the noose from around her thick neck, gently laying her heavy head on my lap. As our fingers gently stroked her brownish black face, the dark sheet of rain clouds blanketing the sky parted for the first and only time that day. A radiant sunbeam streamed through the trees, casting long, ethereal rays directly upon her body. The bear gleamed against the mournful gloom of the surrounding forest. Tears of relief and sorrow dripped down my face. Her spirit was finally free.

The clouds slammed shut and the shafts of light vanished as quickly as they had appeared. Minutes passed in sacred silence.

My intuition finally spurred us into action. "We should leave, Micah. The cries of the bear have travelled throughout the forest. I don't want to have to defend our bear from a cougar or pack of wolves trying to steal it. I have a feeling something is on its way."

We cleaned up the area and, using the drawstring from my raincoat, tied the heavy bear to Micah's spear. Heaving the spear up onto our shoulders, we began the long hike down the mountain.

Whether I held the head or the butt, I couldn't see where I was going. Micah's height forced the weight to tip to my end of the spear. A monster bruise spread on my shoulder with each agonizing step. My legs dropped into hidden holes countless times, and I continually slipped on mossy logs. Often I ended up flat on my back, with arms and legs splayed out in all directions under the heavy bear. As I spat her hair from my mouth and tried to breathe under the weight, Micah rushed over to prevent the bear from squishing me.

At a trickling stream surrounded by thickly mossed logs and rocks, we took a break, folding salal leaves into small cone-shaped cups so we could sip the refreshing water. I stared at the bear hanging from the spear. Many friends back home had teased me before I left, saying I would become a modern-day Ayla, with Micah taking the role of Jondalar, Ayla's Cro-Magnon man. I had laughed at the notion, but gazing at my dirty, blood-stained hands as I sat next to a speared bear and a man I loved, I realized the novel had come to life.

Without serious injury we made it to the seashore, where we honoured the bear with more prayers and a small reverent ceremony before gutting her and rowing home. In the fading light, Scout greeted us on the beach with tiny meows.

We cleaned up to the sound of an owl, "the bird who snatches away souls," whose hoot foreshadows a death.

The sky was too dark, and we were too exhausted, to butcher the bear for dinner, so we covered her with a cedar branch and left her floating in the boat for safekeeping until morning. Instead, we ate some dried fish jerky and collapsed into our sleeping bags.

Over the next week we used bone and obsidian tools to skin, de-fat, and butcher the bear. We found the bone skinning tool far superior to any modern knife. The sharp obsidian blades, however, took twice as long as our modern knives to produce ragged, thick jerky. We used the antler-chipped stone knives for a full day and then switched back to metal knives to speed up the process. Neither of us could bear to see any of the meat spoil simply because our dream of primitive living pushed us to use stone tools.

> *Have been working on the bear all day, literally. It's so late now and we are nearly ready to go to sleep. We had our only meal of bear heart and snapper soup, and some unripe apples Billy Proctor left with us on his first visit. They are giving me diarrhea but I'll continue eating them anyway. They are such a nice treat! All the work out here requires constant squatting, bending or kneeling. If I'm not crippled by the time I leave here I will be very surprised. Forget the smoke and lung condition. My back and muscles are going to be so wrecked I'll have to be wheelchaired around for a month when I return. I have a huge bruise on my shoulder from carrying the bear and shooting pains in my thumb, forefinger, and the muscles along the side of my hands from making all this jerky. My lower back is about to give in and I'm just praying I don't get nasty infections in all my cuts or worse, trichinosis from eating the bear meat. All and all, I sure do love it out here. I wouldn't trade it for a thing right now.*

We dined on scraps every day, cooking the meat for a long time on high heat to avoid contracting trichinosis—a parasitic disease caused by ingesting round-worm larvae (*Trichinella* spp.) from undercooked meat, especially pork or bear.

The bear was the perfect size for our needs, and unlike the skinny spring bear, our chubby fall bear had put on a thick, insulating layer of fat for the winter. Her fat reserves would now supply us with the energy we needed. Two pots brimmed to the edges with chunks of greasy fat. One contained the clean, creamy white pre-mium fat, while the other held the bloody, hairy, not-so-premium fat. It looked disgusting, even to a seasoned mouse-eater. I was leery of the bubbling concoc-tions, but the idea of spreading bear butter on the next biscuit was appealing.

We cooked the oil on relatively low heat all day until deep-fried golden rinds formed on top. These yummy rinds became our dessert. Their oily centres gushed and melted in our mouths. I couldn't eat many at once but the caveman in Micah devoured them.

The oil resembled light-coloured honey and smelled a bit like old doughnut grease. All we needed was a container, and the empty five-litre sour cream tub we found on a nearby beach was perfect. We longed to live with only primitive tools and crafts, but, in reality, plastic containers were a lot better than the cedar-bark baskets we had made.

Scout was thrilled when the last morsels of meat hung on cedar sticks in the shack's rafters and the bones were sunk into the ocean for a sea lice cleaning. The constant sight and scent of bear had put her on edge, so she was startled by even common noises around camp. I felt some relief too.

The deaths of both bears draped a thin, dark layer of sadness over my heart. Hunting hurt. We needed both bears for survival, and their lives were traded for ours, but I couldn't help wondering…if fear were replaced in every cell by true, perfect love, perhaps evolution would create a world where there were no carnivorous animals in existence. I knew I still walked with fears and would hunt animals again. No matter how much I honoured my prey, I always felt I had to seek forgiveness. And if the spirit of our young bear did forgive me, I felt it while caressing her face in the brief sunbeam that shone through the forest.

With each new struggle, however, I came closer to understanding life's truths. I found answers not only from life-threatening challenges and blue bears, but also in small, unremarkable moments, like skinny-dipping in a hidden pool with countless shimmering blue dragonflies zigging and zagging overhead, or frying a piece of dogfish on a hot rock. Booker Lagoon graced us with a freedom I wish everyone could experience.

SEA MONSTERS

Faith sees the invisible, believes in the incredible, and receives the impossible.
—Unknown

The smell of rain tickled my nose. The marshmallow clouds I observed a day and a half earlier had forecast the dismal, dark grey sky now hovering over Booker Lagoon. My ears had turned into barometers, alerting me to changing air pressure with degrees of popping and clogging, reminiscent of airplane descents.

I plugged my nose with my fingers, blew hard to ease the pressure, and whistled for Scout. Her head popped through the cat door. We went to our new secret spot. It wasn't exactly a secret place, only 50 steps down the beach. But it gave me adventures of all sizes.

We climbed onto the tallest lichen-covered rock we could find and sat side by side, staring across the water. I attempted to still my talkative mind. Scout grew bored with such an easy task, wandering off to investigate a hollow log the mink used as a dining room.

The resident *tsik'wi* (*chee-quee*), herring gull, soared just overhead. Low tide signalled breakfast time. The seagull's handsome white head was streaked with brown winter plumage; seeing his change of dress reminded me of our skimpy stash of winter food and triggered images of Micah and me grovelling in the mud for sandy clam dinners as vicious gales howled around us.

The bird distracted me with a peculiar two-flap bobbing dive. Seagulls are too buoyant to submerge themselves far underwater, and this one's awkward dive reminded me of a kid jumping onto a beach ball floating in a pool. The technique was effective, however, and he flew to a nearby rock with a tough ochre sea star sticking out of his beak. The rigid purple star was the size of my outstretched hand, too big to fit the seagull's mouth, or so I thought. For several minutes the seagull rearranged his hold on the creature until all five legs were neatly folded together into the perfect swallowing position. He then began a series of convulsive, painful-looking, swallowing movements. It was like watching a bizarre act at a freak show. I held my breath as he tilted his head back in one last jerking gulp. Down it went.

For another ten minutes he stood with an uncomfortable expression as pokey sea star legs bulged out from the sides of his neck. He ate five whole stars in an hour and a half and taught me a lot about seagulls, things I had never read in my field guides. I didn't want to leave, even when the first raindrops began to fall. Patience always rewarded me with intimate encounters with wildlife that captured my heart and touched my soul. Sitting at my secret spot sometimes seemed more important than gathering food, but slack tide approached. Today Micah and I needed to check the fishing line.

Fishing took priority in the month of October, since our feast-and-famine routine would not get us through the winter. For *Gribley*, the large open bodies of water surrounding us meant long, potentially dangerous rowing conditions, but it had become imperative to start catching bigger fish—lingcod or halibut—before they disappeared to deeper waters in November. We needed to preserve large quantities of fish, and the small troutlike greenlings and tiny sole fillets we were catching were not enough.

Living off the land and witnessing the miraculous work of nature, we naturally came to possess a strong faith in a Creator, a universal energy, that assisted us when we asked. We believed all our needs would be provided as long as we listened to our intuitions, worked for these needs, and seized the opportunities that arose.

But at the end of another fruitless day of fishing and record-setting rain, when we found ourselves rowing six miles home with nothing once again, our faith was shaken. Our hands and toes didn't warm up until we returned to the shack and I fumbled around in the pitch black, with frozen white fingers, trying to bust out a bow-drill fire. On nights like this I wished I had Micah's morning fire duties.

We spent the next morning at our individual secret spots, pondering our unproductive fishing trips.

When I returned, I found Micah already back from his walk, awaiting me in the shack.

"Hey, I thought of something this morning, something about worrying," he said.

"Me too, you go first."

He paused. "Well, perhaps the actual act of worrying only negates the faith we think we have."

"You've got to be kidding me. I just thought the same thing. I decided worrying about something is only telling the universe my faith is a lie. And look how quick we lose this faith when our needs aren't instantly met."

We decided to stop worrying. I had to practise constantly. When I caught myself fretting, I let the thoughts go, reminding my ego I would receive all I needed. Not agonizing about the same things over and over was enlightening.

We spread the charts out on our multi-use table and brainstormed, drawing on all the knowledge we had gained about tides, depths, and fish over the past eight months.

A new enthusiasm glowed in us as we set off the next morning for another long day of fishing. The abnormally sunny day also brightened the faith we had in ourselves.

Like a private aquarium, the entrance to Booker Lagoon was carpeted with white-frilled anemones, pumpkin-orange corals, and pink coralline algae. Rainbow-coloured sea life clung to every inch of the rocky walls and ocean floor. We hung our heads over the side of the boat, mesmerized by the diversity.

I was reminded of distant days when I was learning to identify roadside plants. I could name a weed at the side of the freeway, even when I was passing at 70 miles per hour, and would slam on the brakes for any unidentifiable plant. We carried on the same tradition in *Gribley*.

"Whoa, hold up!" one of us would yell. "We have something new over here. It may be a Nudie. Let's turn around." ("Nudies" were nudibranchs, beautiful sluglike creatures.)

After examining the find, we picked up the oars and plodded on. Arriving at our chosen fishing spot, Micah bent over the side to grab our buoy. We didn't have a bright orange buoy to mark our rope. Instead, we used a short log with a hole in it. This primitive method had one drawback; sometimes driftwood littered the ocean like rocks in an asteroid belt. Some days it was nearly twilight before we found the marker and line.

Once we'd found the marker, we took turns pulling up the longline. Twelve hooks were spaced at least 20 feet apart on the sea floor, approximately 150 feet down, anchored with two large rocks at either end of the rope.

Humungous fish live at the bottom of the sea. Halibut can grow to 450 pounds and can sink a boat or break a fisherman's leg with one flap of the tail. We never talked about what we would do if we ever caught the "big one," but we secretly thought about it. My anticipation of the white belly of an enormous fish surfacing next to *Gribley* was mixed with anxiety at the thought of landing such a monster in a tippy boat. *Gribley* was sturdy, but some days I saw her as nothing more than a tiny wind-up toy plunked down by a giant in the middle of the sound.

On this day, Micah leaned over the side, pulling the rope hand over hand, unclipping the empty hooks, and handing them to me to re-bait. I cut up small pieces of yellow-tail rockfish, known as "brown bombers," and speared the chunks onto curved halibut hooks.

"We got something!" Micah yelled.

"What is it?"

"I don't know yet, but it looks big."

He kept pulling up the line. I could almost smell the growing tension.

"It's a skate," he finally called back. "A big skate."

I handed him our homemade gaff hook, hoping it wouldn't snap when he lifted in a fish the size of a kite. Luckily, skate are relatively docile, perfect for gaff hook beginners, as we were.

With a ferocious swing, Micah gaffed the flatfish in the jaw, grunting as he heaved it aboard. I quickly ended its life with the back of our axe, which doubled as a fish-bonker.

A few seconds later, Micah yelled, "We've got another one, another skate."

He pulled the second aboard with little fight. Just when the second fish stopped flapping, Micah called out, "I can't believe it. Here comes another one, and it's huge."

I glanced down at the two fish already filling the bottom of our boat. I wasn't sure I wanted to see a bigger one. Precariously tipping the boat to one side, I leaned over to admire the strange yet impressive-looking fish gliding to the surface, its giant wings gently flapping beside the boat. It was as wide as *Gribley*.

When all three fish were sandwiched into the boat and the last anchor rock was banged aboard, we flopped back onto our seats. In silence, we stared at the boatful of *bagwani* (*bah-gwa-nee*). They looked prehistoric, triangular flying fish with large bat wings, long spiny tails, and catlike eyes. Shades of grey and purple dappled their shiny skins. Carefully I tipped back each skate's hard, pointed nose, removing the hooks from their frightening flat shark mouths. We reset the line in search of *po'yi* (*poi*), the halibut.

A lot of work lay ahead: cleaning, processing, smoking, and drying all the fish. We increased our speed, tugging deeper on the oars and belting out

Johnny Nash's hit "I Can See Clearly Now." (Our tiny repertoire of songs would torment most people. Worse, we could easily recall countless commercial jingles promoting coffee and cleaning products.)

The skate won the prize for the strangest fish jerky. Their slimy, gritty, sharp skin hangs loosely from their body, like an elephant's. Handling it turned my fingers into sandpaper. Their flesh is layered in long, round strips that peel apart like string cheese. Trying to slice the rubbery chords into thin strips was nearly impossible and produced poor-quality jerky. When we cut the wings into chunks to stir-fry, it turned into a tough, slimy mass that I had to force myself to swallow. Boiling the fish helped to minimize the goo. Much to the disgust of my taste buds, I ate a lot of skate.

The *bagwani* sparked a new beginning for us as faithful fishermen. We continued to check the longline every day, and on Day 204 I was cutting up bait fish when I heard Micah shout, "We got something. I can feel it tugging the line."

My stomach knotted with trepidation as Micah continued to pull the rope over the stern, piling it in the bottom of the boat. He glanced back. "It looks like a halibut. And Nik, it's huge."

I clambered over the tangle of rope, peered over the edge, and felt my stomach move into my throat. My jaw dropped.

A monster halibut, at least half as long as our boat and just as wide, swam forebodingly back and forth under us. I felt like the cartoon fisherman in *How to Catch Bottomfish.* He sits in a tiny boat next to a humungous pair of eyes lurking on the surface of the water. The caption reads: "There is a sign on the dock at the Alaskan capital city of Juneau which warns boaters not to bring large halibut aboard small boats…Several boats have had hull planking smashed open, and the boats have gone down with loss of life."

Any confidence I had in our wee boat or our fishing skills plummeted. The plan we quickly hashed out must have been motivated by past hunger pains and our perfect record of heaving every fish onboard because it was stupid, driven by emotionally charged memories, instead of slowly processed logic.

I stood up on the middle seat, balancing myself in the rocking boat and holding our improvised fishbonker above my head. Just enough time elapsed for my brain to start firing neurons in the logic department. I began to wonder where Micah would fit once the halibut came aboard.

Before I could say a word, my partner, deep in survival mode, started counting aloud. "One!"

I can't believe I'm standing on the seat; the fish still isn't going to fit in here.

"Two!"

Isn't this fish-bonking axe a little dangerous?

"Three!"

Holy shit!

His arm swung down. I held my breath.

"Oh no, the gaff tore out!" he shouted.

"What? Is she gone?"

"Nope, she's still hooked, but diving for the bottom."

The rope reeled over the side of the boat. Micah scrambled so as not to get tangled in it and whipped overboard. The line slackened. Again, our emotions blocked our reason and even our intuition. Not once did it occur to us to cut the line. Instead we started slowly pulling her up again.

I concentrated on two thoughts. First, I prepared myself for the big plunge overboard I reckoned likely to happen when the fish hit the top of the gunwale. Second, if we didn't tip, I knew I needed to end the life of this fish quickly before it bashed us to pieces.

The halibut appeared below the boat. Up came the gaff hook, bent and empty. She dove again.

This fish was going to shore.

I picked up the oars and started rowing to the nearest island, pulling the halibut along beside us. Within a minute I realized the current was moving faster than I could row against it. The intended beach quickly whizzed by as we sped down the sound. Calculating our line of travel, I aimed for another island, one with a tiny bay not engulfed in a tangle of bull kelp.

My questionable calculations sped us right past the target, toward a giant, twisted mat of kelp. The halibut thrashed wildly when we reached the shallower waters. Micah had to let out more rope so she wouldn't rip out the hook. She dove and swam to deeper water, towing *Gribley* with her.

I grunted and groaned with each stroke, edging us closer to shore, barely winning a tug-of-war with a fish as big as I was. When the boat rammed ashore with a loud crunch as metal scraped barnacle-covered rocks, I hopped out and quickly tied it to the nearest boulder.

Micah climbed out and carefully began pulling the fish closer. Kelp wrapped around the line, the fish, and the hook. Time ticked closer to darkness. We decided to yank her ashore. We risked ripping out the hook, but if we continued slowly manoeuvring her through the jumble of kelp, we wouldn't be able to see to gut her.

Micah wedged himself in the rocks and braced his feet against a big boulder, pulling with all his might. I stood ready with the axe. The hook held. As my eyes adjusted to the dwindling light, the outline of an enormous halibut came into view.

Apprehensively I waded into the water to cut the tightly wound kelp that held the fish. I knew one powerful thump of her tail could break my leg. I felt my heart pounding in my temples as I inched beside her. Micah heaved again, I swung the axe, and before we could blink, the fish lay flapping wildly on the rocks. I hit her again, cut the base of the tail to bleed her, and stood back to appreciate the incredible fish in the dim light. She lay still.

I knelt down to touch her. The diamond-shaped halibut is considered a flat fish, but she was remarkably thick and dense.

It was nearly impossible to see the landscape around us by the time we gutted her, loaded the boat, and headed home. After five minutes of silent rowing I stopped and turned to look back at Micah. Smiles slowly crept upon our faces. In jubilation, we high-fived. We rowed back, singing, "We caught a hali, hali, hali, hali-but!"

When we entered the lagoon, Patch and Crease were glowing. The phosphorescence turned the dolphins into streaks of bright green lightning, torpedoing back and forth under the boat, leaving behind a fantastic trail of flashes. When they leapt out of the water, green sparkling lights coated their skin, like magic fairy dust.

As we reached shallow waters, the dolphins turned around. A comfortable silence ensued until I noticed Micah's oars had stopped slapping the water.

In hushed tones he asked, "I wonder why we rejoice at the death of a fish, but not of a bear?"

Our egos had been caught up in the glamour of catching the big one. Now a blanket of shame covered me.

I bent over and stroked the fish. My tears dripped on her slick, dappled skin. I wished all humans could hear the cry of a fish as they do that of a bawling bear.

Scientists have proven through extensive experiments that fish can feel pain. Like humans, they have specialized pain receptors throughout their body, including nearly two dozen around their face and mouth. Injured fish demonstrate reflex responses and changes in physiological states, such as loss of appetite and increased breathing rates. Victoria Braithwaite, researcher and author of *Do Fish Feel Pain*, wrote, "If we already accept that mammals and birds are sentient creatures that have the capacity to experience positive and negative emotions—pleasure or suffering, we should conclude that there is now sufficient evidence to put fish alongside birds and mammals…[and] extend to fish the same welfare considerations."

There is something alluring to the ego about the "big catch" in the world of sport fishing. It's about obtaining bragging rights. Studies consistently show that half of all throat- or gill-hooked fish die when caught and released, with many more who are caught and escape dying from the physiological stress and exhaustion caused by the struggle many fishermen are looking for. With hundreds of fishing lodges and marinas along the coast of British Columbia, an enormous number of fish are wasted. I've seen dead salmon thrown overboard when a bigger one was caught; hundreds of spawning salmon caught and released in a small pool during a single afternoon; and female halibut too big for boat freezers thrown off docks after the picture is taken, when the fishermen think no one is looking.

My ego had always told me I was better. My rejoicing at the 120-pound halibut lying on its back in front of me told me something different. I knew that if a time came when I didn't need the food for survival, I would never keep another big one again if it could be released safely. I felt a responsibility to choose wisely.

The halibut taught me to examine my actions and goals, to make sure I wasn't doing things for the wrong reasons. I realized how many thoughts, words, and actions were ruled by my gloating ego's triumphing spirit.

❦

A cold, blustery rain fell the last day we went out to check the longline. Before entering Fife Sound we tied the boat onto a group of bull kelp to assess the situation. Large, choppy, white-capped waves from the sound rolled into the usually calm waters of Cullen Harbour and warned us to turn around.

We usually followed the safest course on the water, rarely taking chances, but when the need for food was so great, turning back hardly felt like an option. It spurred us to take risks.

"It doesn't look too bad," I commented. "I don't think we'll die. Let's try."

We put on our lifejackets, nosed the boat into the angry, spraying waves, and spent the next half hour searching for our log buoy. When we found it, I cautiously leaned over the bouncing stern to grab the log. A wind-whipped wave crashed into the back of the boat, nearly toppling me overboard. I felt the water drip down my neck and wiped the salt water from my eyes. "Things aren't looking too good after all, are they?" I said to Micah.

We could barely lift this halibut off the ground. It was powerful enough to tow us and *Gribley* down Fife Sound. The jerky we made from her fed us all through winter.

One of our favourite meals was fish head soup. It definitely tasted better than it looked.

I grabbed the heavy line and started pulling it in. The wind steadily increased, challenging Micah as he worked to keep the boat facing into the waves. I unclipped the hooks, tossing them into the bucket as quickly as I could, until the line stretched taut and wouldn't budge.

I handed Micah a section of rope. Together we heaved as hard as we could. Nothing. I braced my feet against the stern of the boat, leaned back, and tugged from every angle. Nothing. Finally, through more grunting pulls, it gave. Backwards I flew, landing hard against the metal seat.

At the seventh hook I saw the white belly of a fish. "Get ready, we have something!" I yelled. A medium-sized skate calmly flapped to the surface. I unclipped him from the line and hung him off the side of the boat, hoping he would stay calm until we rowed to safer waters.

The wind and current increased, and waves came level with the stern. We needed to get out of Fife Sound quickly. I pulled the line as fast as my bulging forearms could go, but stopped when the familiar shape of a halibut appeared hooked to the line.

Worried that two fish tied to the boat might be able to tip us over if they thrashed around, I gave the 45-pound halibut a few feet of slack line and continued to pull the rest of the rope into the boat.

Another empty hook came aboard before I felt heavy jerking on the line. I turned around. "Micah, there's something big down there. Something's fighting pretty hard." I heaved on the line. All my muscles burned. Trying not to lose my balance in the bouncing boat, I leaned over the stern.

The biggest lingcod I had ever seen was fighting the line, spinning like an alligator. Its enormous head thrashed back and forth as it tried to free itself. Its gaping mouth, filled with inch-long teeth, could have swallowed my head whole.

Micah continued rowing us to the safety of a sheltered bay while I managed the line. I couldn't tell if it was sweat or rain dripping down my back as I strained to pull up the taut line. When the monster ling reached the side of the boat, I saw another farther below. It was even bigger.

Reaching the shore, I waded into the water until it was just below the top of my gumboots, gaffed each fish, and heaved them on the rocks for Micah to club.

We sat down in relief, oblivious to the tumultuous wind and heavy raindrops dripping from our hats. The speckled brown ling were nearly five feet long. We beamed with an immense sense of appreciation, knowing we had all the food we would need for winter.

🌱

Everyone in the neighbourhood enjoyed the bounty of the fish. The mink ravaged the carcasses, and I befriended a Steller's jay who ate from my hand. Young Jay woke us nearly every morning, tapping on the window for his morning treat. He followed me everywhere, much to the annoyance of Scout.

Fish 'n' Seaweed Chips became our specialty. We skinned, stretched, and dried the halibut hides for future projects, such as waterproof clothing, basket lids, or knife sheaths. Bones and teeth were saved for experimental needles. I knew I had become wild when I decided to save every fish eyeball for a necklace. The clear marble found in a fish eye reminds me of a beautiful crystal ball. To my disappointment, however, the beads crystallized and crumbled by the time I had collected enough.

When puffs of smoke no longer billowed daily from the smokehouse, strips of golden brown smoked fish hung in the rafters on cedar sticks to continue drying, and our bellies were bloated from all the deep-fried fish binges. There were some drawbacks.

I think the tendonitis has gone up my arm now, if that's even what I have. I'm not sure what ailment to fix first or which is more chronic! With all the repetitive motion of our marathon of fish jerking, my right hand has developed a serious injury.

Shooting pains ran from the outside of my thumb past my elbow to my triceps and rendered my writing hand useless for three days. With hot water I moistened yarrow flowers and mullein leaves, and mashed comfrey roots to form a mushy poultice that relieved the inflammation, soothed the pain, and sped the healing.

Then we survived a bout of rotten halibut-head soup poisoning. After that, we leaned back against our cedar plank bench and stretched out by the crackling fire. Our struggles for food had come to an end. I shivered in delight, wondering how our wild life would evolve when we didn't need to hunt for food full-time.

LATIN FOR DUMMIES

Jesus realized that that for which he was seeking was right within himself. He knew that in order to be the Christ he must declare that he was. Then with pure motive of life, thought, word, and deed, he must live the life he sought, in order to incorporate it within his physical body.
—Baird T. Spalding, *Life and Teachings of the Masters of the Far East*

The struggle for survival had finally metamorphosed into the primitive living experience we had dreamed of. Thankfully, the days of smelling like smoked lingcod and eating mice had come to an end. I preferred sautéed squirrels.

We ate a squirrel for breakfast with biscuits. Now how's that for wilderness pop-tarts?

We filled our days with whatever we wanted to do, completing primitive projects, exploring wherever we chose, and eating whenever we felt hungry.

Gradually, we transformed our little shack, exchanging modern items for those we created from materials around us. Large, folded cedar-bark baskets and boxes, sewn with split cedar roots, replaced the Rubbermaid bins that had stored our clothes, basketry materials, and fire-starting supplies. We also made cedar canoe bailers. However, the plastic bleach container we had scavenged seemed far more reliable for that task, so our handmade scoops held our journal supplies, project pieces, and other miscellaneous items in the shack.

After hours of practice, I eventually mastered the art of basket weaving and could produce a single checkerboard-style cedar basket in something between 5 and 20 hours, depending on its size and design. I designed each basket with colourful patterns using natural grasslike materials that I dyed with roots, lichens, and leaves. I used shiny, red cherry bark as a decorative overlay to contrast with the golden bark, and chose different rims—wrapped, folded, braided, or tucked—for particular uses and styles.

We spent countless hours creating a huge array of cedar-bark projects. Nearly every tool or craft we needed to make for survival depended on the cedar tree. I gained a deep understanding of why it is sometimes called the tree of life.

Harvest baskets had to withstand abuse. I wove double-walled baskets for heavy loads, weaving in handles of thick twined raffia, cedar bark, or basswood cordage, which Micah had brought from the eastern United States. I created large, rectangular gathering baskets with thin strips of bark and minimal twining for maximum airflow to keep plants fresh. These hung over our shoulders. A smaller on-the-go basket, with a lid and bone clasp, looped into my belt. Others I carried like backpacks, with specially crafted shoulder straps. Berry-harvesting baskets were seven-by-seven-inch squares for easy handling. Once the small baskets were filled, they could be dumped into the larger one carried on my back.

Day after long day, with pitted, golden-stained hands and tender finger pads, I decorated our spartan shack with beautifully crafted baskets, each as unique as a snowflake. Various sizes and shapes lined the shelves like the ancient baskets in museum display cases that I used to sketch. But mine were not empty relics. Eagle, heron, owl, and raven feathers, collected for arrow-fletching, mingled in one. Lengths of coiled cordage material was stuffed in another. I filled the flat, rectangular basket with my sewing kit.

I was excited about that kit. I had spent hours carving and sanding bone needles, sharpening bone awls for punching holes, and pounding dried deer tendons for thin thread. To complete the kit I added thorn needles from the hawthorn bush, string from the yucca plant, and a spool of nettle cordage. I cheated by keeping a pair of scissors for precise work, rainbow seed beads from home, modern necklace clasps, and thin, metal beading needles.

It took 15 hours to twine a beautiful little basket with orca whale designs for my jewellery box. I had become desperate for anything pretty. Necklaces and bracelets filled the void, with claws and teeth replacing my diamonds and rubies. Small elderberry stems, hollow bird bones, and empty white tubeworm casings turned into beads. Using sharkskin sandpaper, I sanded shimmering abalone shells I had found near a river otter den to create beautiful pendants.

It was out with the new, in with the old, as primitive gear replaced the modern. Folded cedar baskets, some four feet tall, replaced our Rubbermaid storage bins.

I taught myself to bead the bottom portions of eagle feathers. One rainy afternoon I was humming to myself before stopping to take a drink of water. When I picked up the feather again, I moved to turn on the radio before realizing the radio was me. I missed music that much. *Uh oh. I'm bushed.*

On Day 230 we took our first day off. We did absolutely nothing, simply sat and mildewed the whole day. We loved it so much that when we awoke the next morning we did exactly the same thing: Nothing.

I clung to the notion that to feel worthwhile I must be productive, and to consider myself productive I must always be doing something. I needed this act of nothingness. It allowed my imagination to play and my dreams to surface, and created stillness for inner reflection. Wild places gave me permission to linger in this state.

However, reflection brought me back to my search for "goodness." I told myself that I was a good person, as good as can be expected anyway, making a million excuses for my negative behaviour and thoughts. I aspired to become perfectly good in all manner of things, during both tough times and happy moments. Effortlessly good, without having to work at it or remind myself. But as I continued to slip and act in ways I didn't think were good, I began to question what the true meaning of "good" was. I could see bits and pieces of a definition, but I still lacked a full understanding. My heart told me I had to look beyond the highest virtues to find this divine wholeness.

One day, walking to my secret place, I slumped down in despair.

What is this goodness, I asked myself, *and how shall I begin to change into it?*

In my mind's eye I saw myself running my fingers over beautifully scribed Latin words on a scroll of papyrus. It reminded me of two goals I had not yet accomplished while living in the wilderness. 1) I wanted to teach myself Latin and 2) I planned to read the Bible.

I had no idea how learning to speak a dead language could help me discover divine goodness, but I decided to start there. I wandered back to the shack and dug out the *Latin Made Simple* workbook I had packed. After practising my first pronunciation lesson—"Pater noster qui es in caelis" or "Our father who is in heaven"—I picked up the Bible Micah's father had given me.

I zipped through the opening pages with little mental pain, but, as had happened every other time I tried reading it, I couldn't get past Genesis 4:18: "Irad was born to Enoch. And Irad became the father of Mejujael. Mehujael became the father of..."

I put down the book, wondering why I felt compelled to read it. I didn't consider myself religious, nor was I searching for a religion, but still I felt embarrassed and ignorant that I was 30 years old and hadn't read the most famous piece of literature in the world. I tried again. This time I started at the back, opening the New Testament.

"A record of the genealogy of Jesus Christ...."

I stopped again. *My God, how am I going to get through this?*

I told myself to start again with an open mind, not to bring along my judgments or prejudices. I had a lot of both when it came to religion, the church, the Bible, and Jesus. I wasn't concerned with the accuracy of those who wrote or translated the Bible. I didn't care if Jesus was a real man, if his miracles truly happened, if he had died for my sins, or if he was the road to heaven. I just wanted to know what the book said. Micah had taught me to question the words of others. He had to test everything for himself, not because he thought he was better than anyone else, but to find out if what was said made sense to him. I picked up the small brown leather book once more.

And this time I couldn't put it down. I read the whole day, until my eyes couldn't stay open another second. I was astounded at what I read in the Gospels. The message was straightforward, simple, and loving. I was shocked that religion had tormented millions of souls as a result of the inspiring words singing from the pages.

The example of perfect goodness set by Jesus was going to prove harder to live up to than I had imagined. I realized how powerful my thoughts were, not only for measuring my goodness but for creating the life I dreamed of. Living with the belief that my secret thoughts had little impact on the universe was over.

I put the book down, flopped onto my back, and whispered aloud, "Great, I'm screwed."

I realized I couldn't turn back to the illusory world I had been taught to believe in. It scared me for a moment. I could feel my ego clinging to its comfortable understanding of the world like a little kid clutching a shabby security blanket. But I knew my thoughts often emitted dark vibrations and undertones of lack and limitation that could only halt my progress to the perfection I sought and the miraculous life available to me. Jesus may have been the son of God, but I was God's daughter as well. I saw no reason why I couldn't achieve such mastery of life.

I treated it as I would breaking any annoying habit, becoming vigilant about observing my thoughts. When I noticed a dark thought, no matter how insignificant it seemed, I forced myself to stop mid-sentence without judgment, let it go with a sincere apology, and, if necessary, change it to one of abundance and possibility. I practised thinking miraculously.

I recognized that if I truly wanted to discover my goodness, I not only had to bravely face my fears, but I had to start looking honestly at a part of myself that was easily ignored. I also realized that when we live alone, it is easy to create a comfortable illusion of personal perfection; living with someone else reflects our darkness within. I had planned to get to know my lower human ego, and I couldn't have done it without Micah. I forced myself to reveal my darkness to him.

I believe we have been brought together not because of our skills, but to reveal our shadow sides, which lurk deep inside us.

One night I admitted, "You know, Micah, this goodness stuff is a lot harder than I expected."

"Yeah, I know. I'm starting to question whether my actions to do good come from my true heart or if it's just because of the way my parents raised me."

We agreed to help one another become aware of what we were saying and doing, vowing not to give up on ourselves or each other.

I had run to the woods with the illusion that by living simply and purely in nature, I wouldn't have to deal with the temptations or distractions that bombarded me in the city. I thought becoming a truly good person would be a lot easier in the forest. I quickly discovered that anything can become a distraction. I had plenty of them, even in the middle of nowhere. I am who I am no matter where I dump myself off. For example, I would cram information into my head, searching for my life's answers. Sometimes after stuffing this knowledge into me, I could trick myself into believing I had gained true understanding. But as I continued to read, I realized there's a point when the student must close the book and open her heart to the universe's teachings without a mediator.

After spending many rainy days and nights curled up on sheep hides, reading and writing, I ventured outside. I opened the creaky, heavy door to the shack and stepped out onto a new life path, a road that led me toward the person I wanted to become. I didn't find religion in the Bible. I found a truth that resonated with my soul. I discovered a way to goodness.

TENDON FOR TWINE

We journey into the world of stone-age skills, and we return with the knowledge, wisdom, and strength to enrich our lives in contemporary society.
—Thomas J. Elpel, *Participating in Nature*

My slow, even breaths puffed with misty vapour as I meandered down an ancient deer trail on a chilly winter morning. My feet were thankful for the damp leaves littering the forest floor, which allowed me to stalk quietly. I fox-walked tenderly along the deeply grooved path until my brain finally registered what my senses had already noticed about my surroundings: the forest was strangely still.

I paused to listen beside a grey alder tree covered in an intricate patchwork of crusty lichens. I cupped my hands behind my ears to imitate the tall, amplifying ears of a deer. I heard nothing. A hush came over the forest. It stopped breathing; no branch swayed, and no sparrow rustled in the leaves.

I caught a slight movement out of the corner of my eye. Imperceptibly slowly, I turned my head. A pure white deer stepped out from behind an evergreen tree. An ethereal shaft of light streamed through the boughs, illuminating the doe's glistening white coat. I stood spellbound, enchanted by her loveliness.

She gazed at me with deep, chestnut brown eyes, as if the entire world's gentle, loving power pulsated within her. The white hind then drifted down the trail. I followed, mimicking her moves. Her snow-white body shimmered against the dark emerald green forest. At the edge of a leathery-leafed thicket, she paused. Her head turned back toward me, beckoning me to follow. I hesitated. Then awoke.

Through the yellow-stained window of the shack, a bright crimson sunrise dazzled my sleepy eyes. Without stirring I watched the colours spread out to paint the sky before fading to pale rose. My chest fluttered, thinking of the otherworldly white hind who had visited me.

Deer have been revered by many cultures, not only for the abundant gifts they bestow upon hunters, but for their qualities: the doe's grace and gentleness, the stag's fertility and power. Deer have captivated man's imagination for millennia. I remembered stories of ancient Celts led on incredible adventures by white hinds. The sight of a white deer was considered by many to signify a mystical encounter, foreshadowing a sudden change in one's life.

I loved deer more than any other animal. But now I planned to hunt one. I snuggled farther under my sheepskin, closing my eyes in a state of confusion and excitement.

For weeks Micah and I had prepared for what I considered my first deer hunt. Micah had gone bowhunting the previous fall but never took a shot. I had killed a deer before, but I couldn't call what happened hunting.

Four months before I left for Native Anchorage, I was standing in a heap of big-leaf maple leaves, scraping fat off a deer hide that leaned against the tree, when I heard a terrible commotion coming from my secret spot on the hill above my rented cabin. I dropped the scraper and ran across the meadow.

At the edge of the forest I caught a glimpse of my neighbour's husky-wolf cross running into the brush. A crippled doe lay in the middle of my secret spot, blood dripping from her neck. She had a dull, mangy coat, and I could see mucky brown stains oozing down her back legs. Piles of runny scat dotted the area. The old doe was sick, and dying from more than the dog's bites.

I slowly approached her, talking in hushed tones to ease her fright. The skinny, sickly deer stumbled back into a dense blackberry thicket. She could barely walk. I got down on my hands and knees, took a deep breath to calm my racing heart, and then proceeded to squeeze through the tight, thorny rabbit trail with no thought of what I would do once I reached her.

The scared doe lay 15 feet ahead, her crippled back legs splayed behind her.

"Whoa, little girl. You've got to get out of this thicket. I can't help you here." A strong force compelled me to end her suffering. I couldn't walk away to let the coyotes ravage her, but I also couldn't do anything while she hid in the tangle of sticker bushes. I picked up a dead bramble branch, leaned forward, and poked her in the back.

The doe turned with lightning speed, bolting straight for me. She pinned back her ears as she awkwardly leapt forward, scrambling, crawling, and dragging her legs behind her. Sharp black hooves floundered in all directions as she rushed toward me. I somehow remained untrampled, crammed inside the rabbit trail, then belly-crawled out, unscathed except for a few minor scratches and missing strands of hair. *What was I thinking?*

The doe had flopped down ten steps away, scared and exhausted by the trauma.

I slowly stood up and inched toward her. As I neared, she lunged forward with enormous effort, trying to distance herself from me, falling back each time onto her side. I could see the dog had torn a back leg muscle.

I realized I knew this deer. She visited my secret spot often.

In a calm voice I whispered, "Whoa girl, whoa girl. Be still."

She collapsed for a rest, her neck arched back at a horrible angle as if she were having a seizure. I felt for my three-inch carving knife. It was the only weapon I owned. I questioned whether I had it in me to kill her. Tears welled in my eyes.

Only a few feet separated us now. The doe took another pitiful leap. That was all I needed to summon up my courage and rush forward, tackling her to the ground. In her panic she tangled herself in a single blackberry vine. I saw the fear in her eyes, and I knew she saw it in mine. In a flurry of kicking hooves and thrashing arms, with the help of the vine, I somehow managed to pin her to the ground with my body. I raised myself up, with my right knee on her side and my left hand on her neck, and stabbed into her heart.

Stroking her cheek and neck, I blubbered, "Please, die faster."

I felt her body convulsing under my hands until her eye blinked without fear and she let out her last shallow breath. The doe's warm body relaxed. Her chocolate brown eye glazed over. Lying next to her, I threw my arms around her neck and buried my face in her soft hair, sobbing over the loss of my friend.

At the time I had only read about such events in books written by outdoorsmen who were braver, stronger, and certainly more experienced than I. This incident convinced me that the attributes we bestow upon our heroes are inside us all.

I made a vow to myself that day. I decided I would never shoot a deer from farther than eight steps away. I felt this was an honourable thing to do. I wanted to become a hunter in the truest sense, not simply a killer. I felt if I couldn't get that close, I didn't deserve to take the life of a deer.

🌿

Micah and I practised daily to get to the point where we felt we were ready to bowhunt. I remembered having a hard time pulling back my bowstring to a full draw at home, but living in Booker Lagoon changed that. Geronimo, my bow, shot like a dream.

I named my longbow Geronimo, secretly hoping to instill the energy and skill of the legendary warrior into myself and my weapon.

Scout and I snuck through the woods daily, pretending to be Geronimo, the legendary Apache warrior, choosing target after target to shoot. "Bull's eye!" I'd cry out after the perfect shot.

It had taken patience and many long, gruelling hours to transform a stick of wood into a primitive longbow. To maintain our beloved handmade bows, Micah and I oiled them with dogfish liver oil we had rendered in September. We attached squirrel hides to the ends of our bow strings as silencers, and though I doubt it helped, they sure looked cool—like decorating my first bike's handlebars with flashy streamers. I used dried walnut hulls, boiled for ten minutes, mashed to a soft pulp, and then simmered for 15 minutes or more, to stain the wood in camouflage patterns.

Combining our knowledge and ideas, we discovered the art of making beautifully straight, feather-fletched arrows with knapped obsidian points. After working with different types of branches, from Nootka rose to ocean spray, we found straight-grained cedar driftwood made the finest arrow shafts. Unlike arrows made from branches, those carved perfectly round from chunks of cedar never needed straightening again, a huge benefit in the soggy conditions of the coast.

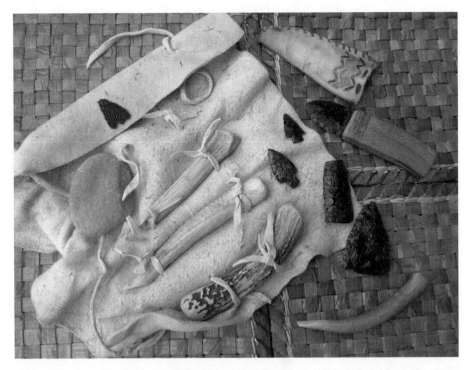

I tanned a deer hide to use as a soft leather carrying case to hold my flint-knapping tools, which I used to make stone knives and arrowheads.

Though cedar is not the densest wood, arrows made with cedar flew straight and fast enough, at my eight-step shooting range, to hit their mark.

Our fletching came from feathers we found on our travels. One day at Native Anchorage I watched a mother eagle atop a bulky nest preening her feathers. She gently pulled each feather through her beak, straightening and joining the tiny microscopic barbs along the edge of her feathers, as if zipping up a zipper. With a gentle pluck, a white tail feather dropped out of the nest and floated toward me. I caught it in mid-air and wrote, "I hope this feather that once guided such a majestic bird will guide my arrow someday." Mama's feather now adorned my primary hunting arrow.

Feathers are flawlessly constructed to become the fletching of an arrow. A long groove down the mid-vein or middle of the feather guided my knife to split it evenly in half, as if it had been designed to become a human's tool. I gained a deep under-standing of, and intimate connection with, the natural materials I used and the items I made from them, something I didn't receive when I bought them in a store.

We had to perfect many skills to make our primitive hunting gear effective.

After the feathers were trimmed and cut to length, we chipped obsidian arrowheads, as primitive humans had done 100,000 years ago. In general, flint-knapping, the nearly forgotten science and art of making stone tools, forced us to learn patience and nonattachment. An excruciating amount of effort, time, and blood is needed to create a thin, even, functional, and artistically crafted knife or arrowhead, which can break in half with just a tiny miscalculation when it is nearly complete. Creating stone arrowheads was a bit like playing chess. It took strategy and precision to strike or pry flakes of stone off a large rock to form an arrowhead, and each flake that was removed set me up for the next move, until the vision was manifested.

To put everything together, I gently pounded hard, golden deer tendon with a stone until I had a bundle of long, white, fibrous strands of softened sinew— nature's perfect duct tape. Sinew loves saliva. Spit seems to bring out the sticky gluelike properties of sinew better than water. I dangled the putrefied Achilles tendon of the doe I had stabbed in front of my face, stuffed it into my mouth, and began tenderly chewing the tough fibre. When the tendon became as soft and floppy as a wet noodle, I used it to lash the arrow and feathers into place. No knots were required. The taste is usually bearable, but not always.

> *I can see myself skinning the rotten deer legs and pulling apart the thick tendons back home. I'm thinking, "What the hell happened to me. How'd I go from show-jumping my beautiful horse to flicking off maggots?" I can't believe how awful these tendons smell and taste. I'm certainly not swallowing my spit. It's sometimes bad enough for a bit of a gag. The things we primitive dreamers do!*

To finish the arrow, I needed pitch to coat the sinew for waterproofing. I collected perfect sap "pearls" from the ring of small holes drilled in trees by sapsuckers, then melted and hardened these pearls over a fire and spread the resulting pitch over the sinew. Though the drilled holes cause damage to the tree, they benefit not

I longed for a bathtub to soak in, but our sweat lodge was a beautiful replacement. We wove cedar branches into a sturdy frame until only golf-ball-sized holes remained, and then covered it in clay.

only the outdoorsman, but also many other animals. I have often watched the first returning hummingbirds feeding from these wells. Sometimes they follow directly behind the red-breasted sapsucker doing the drilling.

Eyeballing the finished arrow down the shaft to ensure perfect straightness, I marvelled at the first *Homo sapiens* who was divinely inspired to chew tendon for twine to create such tools.

With sinew and bone tools I sewed a coonskin hunting cap, feeling like Daisy Crockett. Micah wove a cedar cap. Quivers of folded cedar bark held our sharp, obsidian-tipped hunting arrows and antler-tipped practice ones.

Even if you don't hunt, making your own bow and arrows, and then stalking around in the woods shooting stumps is so much fun. It brings back all those fond childhood memories of playing "Cowboys and Indians."

In honour and memory of the old ways, we built a sweat lodge, a sacred ceremonial sauna, to cleanse our bodies and purify our minds, hearts, and spirits. As usual, the project turned into a gargantuan effort.

First we dug a firepit in the centre of a marked circle. We then collected curved branches from a recently fallen cedar tree and lashed them together, forming a small, rounded dome and weaving smaller branches and boughs throughout the frame until barely a hole remained. We pounded bucket after bucket of clay from a nearby stream into a workable consistency. Smearing the clay over the dome, we hoped to seal in the steam and heat from the hot rocks that we would bring inside and douse with water.

"Only 15 or so buckets to go, but I've been saying that for days," I wrote in my journal. By the time we had collected, hauled, and pounded over 50 buckets of clay, only three-quarters of the lodge was covered. Then a heavy night of rain left the lodge "melting." Micah turned to me with weary eyes and said, "Let's use the tarp."

I laughed. "Yeah, I'd like to finish it this year too."

There had to be a better way than using clay in a rainforest. Months later Micah found the answer in a book we had. I flopped on my back laughing after he told me.

"We should have dug a hole and covered it with cedar planks."

We spent a full day preparing the sweat lodge the day before our hunt. We stoked a huge fire outside the lodge, gathered large Grandfather Stones, and heated them in the fire until they sparkled with a red glow.

I knelt down with bare knees on the spongy, cool ground and bowed my head in front of the lodge. "To all my relations," I whispered, and crawled into the sacred space. Micah pushed stone after stone into the lodge with a stiff branch, and I rolled them into the pit with a special deer antler, saying, "Welcome, Grandfathers." The dwindling fire flickered darting shadows on the inside walls as the strong, sacred scent of cedar filled my nostrils. Micah crawled in, sealing the doorway. The only light penetrating the darkness was the glowing stones. My naked body, flushed from the heat, was moist with sweat.

I dipped the bundle of cedar boughs into the bucket of fragrant water and tenderly splashed the rocks. *Shwooosh.* Scorching-hot steam erupted into the lodge, saturating every pore. Misty sweat poured down my back and dripped off my nose. My nostrils and eyes stung from the searing heat. It was impossible to take a deep breath. Both of us humbly bowed to the ground in prayer, returning to a time far removed from our civilized roots, to whisper unspoken words to angels and the ancestors of the land.

The lodge was like the womb of the earth. We crawled out to the cool, refreshing air, newly born to the world. The next morning we were bound for Gilford Island to find deer.

SHAPE-SHIFTING HUNTERS

Grandfather of all Scouts.
Teach me to be the eyes of my people.
Teach me to move like the shadow.
Allow me to become the winds, the rocks, the soils,
and the life force in all its forms.
                    —Excerpt from an Apache prayer by Shadow Walker

Our island had little deer sign. Gilford Island, on the other hand, was a patch-work of clear-cuts of various ages, providing perfect deer-feeding areas.

Our 261st day in the wilderness gifted us with a gorgeous, bluebird sky. Like a strange feral family, Micah, Scout, and I shoved off in *Gribley* for our December deer hunt. Scout yowled her annoying high-pitched meow for ten minutes before she gave up and quietly settled in for the long ride.

Our excitement dwindled the longer we pulled on the oars, lost in the mono-tone greens and blues we passed along the shoreline and in the bitter cold that numbed our hands and feet. The squeaky thud of the oarlocks distracted me tem-porarily, but my thoughts always returned to the ache in my back and rawness of my butt, a malady I termed the "Rower's Rub." At the halfway mark we hit the Tidal Vortex. Even with the tide in our favour, the surface water continued to run against us and we had to buck the flow the rest of the way. Moving at a sloth's pace, we pulled up on a dark, muddy beach after nine hours of non-stop rowing.

I'm sitting under Gribley, *which is propped up by a stick, next to a little fire, roasting a female mallard duck that a mink killed before Micah luckily scared it off. I never thought we would find an ocean "roadkill" out here. We could hardly believe the good fortune.*

We had found no suitable quick shelter near our hunting area—no hollow stump, no decent log, no overhanging bluff, and no piles of leafy debris—so we dragged *Gribley* farther into the forest, flipped her over, propped up the bow, and set up our hunting camp. I felt like an old cowboy, sitting in my long underwear next to the smoky fire, gnawing on greasy bones. Only one thing kept the moment from being perfect: my sleeping bag had fallen into the ocean upon arrival. I couldn't decide what was worse, sleeping in my wet bag or in one of Micah's.

Micah always slept in two sleeping bags, both of which looked like they had been found under a freeway overpass. One didn't zip up while the other had a gigantic hole in the bottom. By using both, he managed to sleep warmly. Now he stood up holding one tattered, dirty bag in each hand.

"Which one do you want?"

My eyes darted back and forth. "Neither." I knew where they had been, how they smelled, and how they were taken care of. However, I also knew about long, shivery nights in a wet sleeping bag, so I hesitantly reached for the zipperless bag.

I was as eager for morning as a kid on Christmas Eve. We wanted to arrive at the hunting spot by the time the indigo hues of twilight welcomed morning, so I didn't want to miss the first second of predawn, the moment when eyes adjust to the subtlest stirrings of morning's twilight sky. The result was that my internal clock kept waking me through the night.

"Hey, you up?" Micah said.

"I am now."

"Do you think it's time to go?"

"I'm not sure. I've woken up so many times tonight, wondering if it's getting light, and it's still dark. Let's just get up."

Careful not to smack our heads on *Gribley's* seats above us, we crawled out of our bags and lit a small fire beside the boat to warm our numb toes and chilly noses. Scout was not impressed at the nighttime rise and curled herself back into my sleeping bag. Micah and I painted on our camouflage before we crept off for the hunt.

I needed no mirror or light to paint my camouflage. From years of practice I knew the lines, the shadows, and the shapes that allowed me to blend into the landscape. I filled seashells with ground charcoal, gooey mud, and clay the colour of yellow ochre and burnt sienna, resembling the shades of dying deer ferns and dropped cedar tips. For realistic stencils, I had an assortment of leaves, ferns, and branches gathered on our reconnaissance mission the day before.

Camouflage is a form of art. We use it to dull shiny areas, blend sharp lines, and break up our human forms. I dipped my finger into the moistened charcoal and began the transformation, smearing charcoal, dabbing clay, and splattering mud with a hemlock branch on my skin and clothes. Half an hour later, as I put the finishing splashes of colour on my wool pants, rubbed forest floor duff into my hair, fuzzed up my jacket, and charcoaled the back of my ears, I asked Micah to critique my work. He dabbed some mud under the tip of my nose and I touched up the bare spot under his chin.

I admired Micah's masterful makeover and let my mind drift to remember the coyote who trotted over my hand, the squirrel who sat on my leg, the turkey vulture whose wing touched my head, and the hiker who screamed when I suddenly moved to avoid becoming her seat. Then I reminded myself that the most important invisibility tactic wasn't the camouflage; it was quieting the relentlessly chattering mind. When I still my mind into a place of sacred silence, I need no mud or charcoal to vanish from the view of others. If I wanted to get within eight steps of a deer, I needed to breathe in this space of invisibility. Camouflage merely kept my logical mind focused, helping it believe the impossible.

At the same time Micah and I both noticed the small change in our eyes' ability to detect shapes in the landscape. Dawn approached.

Owl-light had turned to daylight by the time we crept up to the edge of the clear-cut. We had chosen a poor vantage spot for surveying the area. When our heads poked around the trunk of a tree, a doe and buck were already staring at us. Busted. The pair trotted up the hill with the white undersides of their tails flashing, signalling to everyone that humans were in the area.

There are three ways to hunt deer: 1) drive a truck along logging roads, hoping to spot a deer within scope range; 2) hide along a trail, waiting for one to walk by; or 3) quietly stalk by foot, searching for one. We chose option two and played Rock, Paper, Scissors to determine who got the bottom portion of the clear-cut, then set off, a little unsure of what to do next.

At the first deer trail I came to, I bent down and carefully studied the tracks and sign. There were plenty of fresh, heart-shaped deer hoofmarks and browsed vegetation, as well as the resident buck's antler rubbings on a thin alder sapling. I decided to follow this promising trail and sat down in the first place I found with decent cover.

I broke a few hemlock branches to set in front of me and sprinkled handfuls of leaves around my feet and on my pants. Settling into my shooting position, I slowed my heart rate, stilled my mind, and ignored the discomforts.

To keep from shivering I took deep, slow breaths of the crisp, stinging air, and to ensure my fingers weren't frozen when the time came, I repeatedly pulled my bowstring back, slowly, almost imperceptibly.

A small flock of golden-crowned kinglets came by to search for insects. One landed on my ready-aimed arrow to take a rest. I marvelled at the detail of the tiny bird's feathers as she blinked, cocking her head to the right and left to keep an eye on her friends. The kinglet's sun-yellow forehead, outlined by a black stripe, beamed against her olive grey body. My hand moved undetectably to touch her. My finger rested just below her belly before my visitor flew off to start feeding again. Hours later, a glossy black raven flew in to pick at what looked like a portion of squirrel remains beside me. Not a single deer came into view.

When my right leg had fallen asleep, I couldn't feel my toes anymore, and I could barely move my fingers, I decided to stalk around to memorize the landscape. I smelled the buck rubs and scent posts along the trail. They left a slight peppery, gamey odour. I felt like a buck with an acute sense of smell, detecting the slightest scent on the smallest twig. For better or worse my nose had become as sensitive as a dog's.

As twilight approached I finally spotted two does meandering up an overgrown logging road. Micah and I had agreed not to shoot during evening twilight, in order to avoid losing an injured deer in the darkening light. I let the deer fade into the alders.

I arrived back at camp to find Scout trotting up the hill to meet me. "Hello, kidder cat," I called out, reaching down to stroke her soft back. "Let's get some firewood." I brewed up a pot of winter tea, with licorice fern root, mint leaves, and rosehips, to welcome my hunting partner.

December's cold breath kept me close to the fire as the last hint of light faded from the sky. I was anxious to see Micah. I imagined the tawny body of a deer slumped over his shoulder as his tall form appeared in the flicker of firelight.

More than an hour later, twigs snapped, leaves crunched, and Micah came into view. He slumped down beside me with a broken bow in his lap, but no deer. His strung bow had taken a bad set from the dampness, and when he tried to bend it back into shape it snapped in half. As I moved to the fire to cheer him up with a gourd of hot tea, I stepped on my arrow and cracked it in two.

We shared the day's stories over a small stir-fry of dried food until we were both too tired to talk. Without cleaning off our camouflage, we wrapped ourselves in our sleeping bags. Scout found it necessary to kill a white-furred ermine before crawling under my covers, reeking with the pungent scent of weasel musk.

The next morning I headed up the darkened logging road alone while Micah stayed back to make a new quick bow, called a "Father and Son." Instead of a traditional single branch bow, this one has a smaller curved stick tied to its back.

Like a shadow I moved into a new hiding spot in the open clear-cut, just as a torrential downpour began. I had a few hours before my thick wool clothing was completely saturated.

After sitting perfectly still for hours, watching raindrops drip from my bow and body, I finally heard my spirit whisper, "You're not thinking like a deer." I envisioned a little doe dry and warm, hunkered down under the upward-sloping branches of a cedar tree, while a young buck browsed nearby in the protection of the deep forest. Stiffly, I groaned into a standing position and headed into the forest. By the time I noticed a drop in the light, I hadn't glimpsed a deer. I headed back to camp.

Back at camp Micah greeted me with a dejected look on his face. His new bow had also broken. I lent him mine for the rest of the day, but he returned later with nothing but a bunch of wet clothes. Neither of us dragged a deer back on day three either.

On the fourth morning, the old road sparkled with a thick layer of crystallized frost. Our feet scrunched on the icy path. Along the way we picked a few spruce needles to chew for a lemony pine-tasting breath freshener.

Learning from our previous mistakes, we belly-crawled the last few feet to the clear-cut. I caught my breath as I peeked over a log. The opening glistened, a frosty, winter wonderland. I imagined nibbling the frozen plants, like a fern Popsicle.

"I think the deer will wait until the frost melts before moving in," I whispered.

"Me too," Micah replied. "Let's try somewhere else."

We decided to try hunting option three: stalking. I was to enter the clear-cut from the top of the slash, while Micah would enter from the bottom. However, no matter which route I took, I hit a jungle of salal bushes. After hours of trying to get through the thick brush I had lost all chance of a stealthy approach. I wiped the sweat from my brow and smiled as I remembered a story Billy Proctor had told me about a man who was found cutting up salal leaves with a pair of scissors. "Salal can do that to a man," Billy explained. I could finally relate.

The first ray of sun peeped through the brush; somehow I had to get to the sun-drenched clear-cut.

I continued bushwhacking through the salal, hacking at the noisy foliage with my arms and lunging onto the dense branches as if swimming through the brush, until I sprang onto the road as if I had been popped from a can of exploding streamers. I took a minute to compose myself and then headed back to the clear-cut. As I entered the open forest, I melted back into the landscape.

I love stalking. It is not just about stealthy movement through the forest, avoiding crunchy leaves and snapping sticks. It is dancing. It is about flowing over and around those things without focusing on your body. Moving with the landscape in a poetic dance of silence. When you shift into this space of invisibility, animals and people no longer see you, even when they stare right at you. Perfected stalking is like walking with the feet of an angel.

I moved low and evenly from tree to tree, stump to stump. Then I saw her.

The stillness came if only for a moment's time, but indeed it was enough. For shimmering in that golden light, with eyes so soft yet deep and knowing, there stood my friend and perhaps my greatest teacher.

Her tail flicked as she dropped her head to continue feeding. I stood in the shadows, watching the solitary doe. Scanning the terrain, I wondered if I could reach her before dark as I envisioned the painstakingly long, slow stalk. Silently I asked the universe, Is that the deer for me?

A voice responded, "You came here to hunt, didn't you?"

As I stepped out from behind the cover of a hemlock sapling, my left eye caught a tiny movement. I froze. It was Micah.

I slowly motioned to meet behind a large cedar log. In hushed tones I told him my plan. He whispered, "I'll stick around down here. If you spook her, maybe she'll run toward me. I might be able to take a shot, too." It seemed like a plan, albeit not a detailed one. Without further discussion we headed our separate ways.

After crawling over and under the piles of discarded logging debris bordering the clear-cut, I found a well-used deer trail winding through the open clearing. A small trickle of a stream bordered the edge, with a steep cliff in the centre of the slash. I kept myself concealed behind small shrubs and stumps up the cliff line.

Inching my way up the slope, I stopped behind a stump to visualize my next move. Like a worm, I crossed the open ground to a hemlock sapling in minute increments. The tiny push-ups left my arms burning and my stomach muscles painfully tense. No doe.

Where is she? I knew a deer could freeze and blend perfectly into its surroundings in a fraction of a second. I had played this waiting game countless times before.

My heart pounded in my ears as I lay motionless under the tree, awaiting the twitch of an ear. It never came. Misgivings rolled in. *She left. I took too long.*

She heard me. She saw me. I recognized this pattern of doubt and ignored it, keeping perfectly still for at least half an hour.

Two bald eagles and a couple of noisy ravens caught my attention on the hill above the slash. I reckoned the ravens had called in the eagles to open the body of a hunter's lost deer. I couldn't resist the mystery. Up I stood. Out stepped the doe. Simultaneously, my head and the doe's turned in disbelief.

Without thinking I reached down to pick the nearest plant, popped it in my mouth, and started chewing. I glanced her way. She bent down and snatched some grass with her teeth. Before I swallowed I closely examined the plant I was chewing. It was the seed from the common rush. Edible. I picked more and continued to move slowly, searching for other edibles.

The doe also continued feeding. When she stopped to look and listen, I too stopped and listened. When I stopped to listen, she did the same. She nibbled deer fern and I chewed hemlock needles. We moved together under the warmth of the sun's gentle winter rays.

She disappeared behind a small hemlock sapling. Through the foliage I saw her beautiful brown eye staring back at me. My heart melted. When she again emerged into full view, nipping twigs off a huckleberry bush, my mind screamed. *How many shots have I already passed up?*

I knew what I had to do, but my inner dialogue continued. *How can I deceive her like that? She trusts me.*

I glanced down at the bow I had forgotten I was carrying, reminding myself of my earlier intentions. I anticipated her next moves and positioned myself in plain view for a shot. Three more steps and she would be in my eight-step range.

One… Two… A little closer… Three. Her body was in the perfect position for a heart shot. *Take the shot. Take the shot.* Instinctively, I raised the bow and drew the arrow back in one motion, then released the shot. I saw the arrow whiz through the air and miss her heart by an inch. Stunned, I watched her bound away with the arrow deep in her side.

I sank to my knees. I had missed the mark, but it was a kill nonetheless. I felt confident I had hit her liver. A hunting teacher's voice echoed in my mind: "One of the most important things to remember is to sit and wait for at least half an hour before tracking a shot deer. You don't want to spook it further. A deer will run until it reaches cover and then bed down to rest. If you wait long enough, it will die where it lies."

I waited about two minutes. Then I jumped up, ran to the cliff line, and scanned the gully below. She was gone. I followed her tracks.

A huge logjam, a jumble of slippery logs and debris, blocked the way down the gully. It looked ridiculously impassable. I turned away, systematically tracking every inch of the bank leading up to the forest. I found nothing. I re-tracked the area.

I began questioning my instincts and skills. In this moment of uncertainty it became easy to discount a minute detail the size of a sunflower seed as nothing but guesswork.

I sat down to clear my mind and give my strained eyes a break. My teacher's advice continued: "You are taking the time to wait, not only for the deer's sake, but for your own. The half-hour wait is to calm down, get focused, and step back into that place of awareness." I wished I had listened.

The light faded. I was torn between tracking farther down the gully and returning to camp. I didn't want to spook the deer from its bed. I mournfully hiked back to camp.

Micah had not returned. Only Scout greeted me. Sitting down under *Gribley*, I picked up my kitty to receive her twice-daily hug. I needed one. Her paws stretched around my neck while she rubbed her face along my chin. Scout always comforted me when she sensed my sadness. We foraged semi-dry wood and I mustered up the rest of my energy to start a bow-drill fire to guide Micah home.

At dark, Micah plopped down next to the fire. When the fire lit up his face it looked as gloomy as I felt. We exchanged stories of the day's events over the last crumbs of dried food we had brought.

"I waited down at the bottom of the hill the whole time until I saw the doe bounding towards me," Micah explained. "I figured you spooked it. She appeared in good health. I saw her enter the woods and bed down under a small hemlock tree."

"What side did she lie down on?" I asked.

"Her right side."

"That's the side I shot her in. Did you see the arrow?"

"No."

"Why would she lie down on her wounded side?"

"I don't know, but after several minutes she stood up, peed, and then lay back down. That's when I started stalking her," Micah continued. "I got within range, but she noticed my bow rising to shoot. She stood up without effort and walked nonchalantly back into the clear-cut. I repositioned myself and took the shot. The arrow deflected off a teeny branch that I hadn't seen in the fading light. I let her walk off. I didn't want to risk losing her in the darkness. If I knew you had already wounded her, I would have tried again. Believe me, she appeared totally normal."

Silence ensued.

The night was colder than a frog in a frozen pond. I lay awake most of the night, shivering beside Scout, imagining the doe leaping over the 8-foot-high, 15-foot-long logjam—a move I had discounted as impossible—and landing sure-footed on the slippery, mossy logs with an arrow in her side. Deer move like the wind. I should have known better.

The next morning we hiked straight to the deer bed. I expected to find a lot of blood and an easy trail to follow.

"Well, this doesn't make sense. I don't see a drop of blood anywhere. Are you sure this is where the doe bedded down, Micah?"

"I'm positive."

We dropped down on our bellies and scanned every hemlock needle, cedar leaf, and dirt pile in her bed, but found no trace of blood.

We backtracked and discovered the arrow lying on a clump of rush where she had pulled it from her side. A light maroon fluid remained on the shaft, but nothing else.

Dumbfounded, Micah asked, "Where's all the blood? A shot to the liver produces a lot of it. Did you miss?"

"No, I saw it go in. I can't erase the image from my mind."

It was easy to pick up her heart-shaped hoofmarks in the mushy, wet ground at the bottom of the clear-cut. I measured her stride and foot length on a stick to ensure I didn't start following another deer. She had meandered through the clear-cut, nibbling here and there, before entering the forest. Her tracks revealed a normal walking pattern, without strain or effort and definitely no sign of limping, dragging, or stumbling. She had effortlessly jumped onto a gigantic log that I had to crawl up and over, an action we thought she would have avoided with a hole in her side.

We followed her tracks all day, through all types of soil and debris. Our eyes burned from the strain of searching; no amount of rubbing could fix the blurriness.

By the time we felt the temperature drop and noticed the first dimming of the sky, my head pounded from the focused concentration. I was weak from hunger too. We hadn't packed enough food for this length of hunt, so we took advantage of the last bit of light to gather some. We could pick up the trail tomorrow.

The forest gave us a meal of yellow-foot chanterelle mushrooms and bladder-wrack seaweed. Scout could catch a mouse.

We rose early to find the last known hoofprint. I knelt down, traced my finger along the sharp edges of the depression, and recited the Tracker's Prayer, which had been passed down from teacher to student through the ages.

Grandfather, Great Spirit,
Master of all things, you who are called by so many names,
and worshipped in so many ways;
Allow me to become the Earth,
teach me to surrender to the tracks,
so that I may become that which I follow,
and if I am worthy,
allow those tracks to lead me closer to You.

As the sign aged, it became harder and harder to spot the tiny indicators she had left behind. I pressed the side of my face into the dirt for a better vantage. When I couldn't find a tiny broken stick, a bent fir needle, scuffed dirt, or the faint mark of the tip of her pointed hoof pressed into an alder leaf, I placed my tracking stick over the last known sign, sweeping it over the debris to guess where her next footfall should be.

I knew she would seek another bed. Finally, near the end of the day I found it under an old log, protected from the wind and rain. She wasn't there, nor was there any sign of struggle or injury. Next to a fresh pile of droppings, I picked up two hairs. They bent into a v-shape: deer. Exhausted, I plunked down in her bed and called out in a soft voice, "Where are you, little deer?"

I cocked my head, startled by the name I had used. I had always called myself Little Deer when I was a small girl. I whispered, "I'm so sorry, sweet doe. Please forgive me."

The story she had left in her tracks told me she was fine, but it was hard to believe. My arrow must have slid between her diaphragm and liver without damaging an organ or piercing a vein. A miracle shot. I had to let her go.

Micah and I had followed separate trails in the afternoon. I knew he would be making his way home soon with the last of the season's mushrooms. When my pockets were filled with licorice fern, chanterelles, and spruce tips for tea, I climbed up on a large, moss-covered boulder next to a beautiful hoof track of *giwas* (*ghee-wahs*), the deer. I cried.

The primitive hunt is a masterpiece of skills. All my years of training had come together in this one, and I revelled in the feeling. Though I didn't come home with a deer, I returned with something greater than food: knowledge. I had become the shadows, the stumps, the soils, and that which I followed. I had viewed nature from the inside out. Sitting on that rock, I understood where my life came from, not because I was trying to take a life from the world, but because

I was living with it. A sudden change occurred inside me, as the white deer in my dream had foretold.

I gave thanks for my life to the earth, the water, the plants, the animals, the sky, the sun, the moon, the ancestors, the future generations, and my creator.

Hiking home I came across the skulls of a young buck and doe, side by side under a cedar tree. The last track of a deer. It wasn't the doe I had been following, but somehow I felt closure.

We packed up the next day and pushed off for our long row home in the pouring rain. Greeting us at the entrance to Booker Lagoon was the age-old rock man. We stopped rowing. I wiped my runny nose and brushed the rain from my eyes. Home was near.

I twirled out a friction fire, warmed up by the stove, cooked a song sparrow that Scout had given us for dinner, and flopped into bed.

THE 70-MILE ROW

Living rough in the wilderness is a salve for the soul. Ancient instincts awaken; forgotten skills are relearned, consciousness is sharpened and life thrums at a richer tempo.

—Lawrence Anthony, *The Elephant Whisperer*

We took stock of our winter food supply. It was impressive. We felt secure, as if our bank statement showed a seven-figure balance with no bills to pay. As the deer's rut season was nearly over, and we had enough food to last the winter, we decided not to hunt again. We had gained enough. We even stopped working on our seal-hunting arrows. We didn't want to take a life just for the experience. It was time to experiment with primitive cooking.

In order to get all the nutrients they need, survivalists expect most meals to consist of grey, murky stews with bobbing carcasses and bits of blackened charcoal floating on top. Our stash of dried meat, fish, and plants encouraged me to take cooking to a whole new level. My mission was to invent gourmet primitive meals.

Dear Mom,
I'm not too sure if the little herring fish faces and eyes looking back at me from the fry pan would go over too well with anyone but Micah and me. I think the low-light situation in the shack gives the presentation of our food a some-what enticing feeling. In the daylight, even I am taking a second look, dishing out a rather strange jumble of "who knows what" and "no, that can't be."

In the modern world I was encouraged to eat a low-fat diet. In contrast, the Kwakwaka'wakw who had lived in the lagoon long ago had a diet high in eulachon grease, and both Micah and I found ourselves craving fat—our bodies needed it. We drenched our stir-fries in the bear fat and the vegetable oil we had brought from home. We used the eulachon grease as a special topping. (We had obtained a supply by trading a basket and arrowhead at the Native village where *Gribley*

I named all our newly created recipes. Giant horse clams became our plates, mussel shells our spoons, and hollowed gourds our bowls and cups.

was rescued after she had floated away.) The nutritious wild foods and various oils made us fit, strong, warm, and healthy.

I had researched enough about other food items the Kwakwaka'wakw considered delicacies to know that I didn't want to replicate many of their meals. Rotten salmon eggs kneaded into a deer's stomach until the mixture achieved a cheeselike consistency was not my idea of a tasty snack.

Because we didn't have an extensive variety of dried foods, our taste buds detected the slightest new flavour. Simply by replacing one ingredient, we created a rave-worthy new dish.

We made good use of seaweed, which is abundant on the Pacific coast (more than 600 species) and one of the most nutritious plants on the planet. It is divided into three groups, red, green, and brown, with red and green providing easily digestible carbohydrates for energy, and brown giving us our fibre content—we called it our Raisin Bran. All seaweeds are edible, each with a distinctive taste and texture. Our favourites were the purple laver or nori and the bull kelp. We spread the thin, brownish red sheets of nori on the rocks to dry, and it became our potato chip and soup cracker.

From its rootlike holdfast, bull kelp grows an average of five and a half inches per day, sometimes attaining a length of 118 feet to reach the ocean's surface.

The rainy fall season transformed the forest into a mushroom buffet. We dried huge quantities of fungi.

Known as "Indian radar," the large underwater forests of kelp fronds warn of shallow water and rocks. They also support an incredible diversity of life: their thick tangle of gently swaying fronds creates a nursery for young sea creatures and a safe haven for fish and sea mammals. Nutritionally, kelp contains all the essential fatty acids necessary for human health. Kelp became our healthy, salty seasoning. I cut the long, hollow portion of the stem or stipe to use in soups and stir-fries, and we hung the golden brown blades, cut from the bulb end of the hollow stem, to dry in the wind and sun.

We also gathered a variety of mushrooms on our fungal forays. Day after day, from September to November, we brought home basketfuls of delicious orange chanterelles, stringy-stemmed honey mushrooms, sweet-tasting angel wings, dark-capped elfin saddles, and funnel-shaped yellowfoots. We snacked on gooey witches' butter and rubbery, toothed jelly fungus. We transformed the shack into a gigantic dehydrator, with a colourful array of spongy woodland mushrooms drying on woven cedar-branch trays above the stove, while clumps of onions dangled from the rafters.

One day we traded our fresh fish for leftover powdered milk from a group of kayakers. Ecstatic, I made a delicious dessert with jelly fungi.

Leathery turkey-tail polypore became our gum. Though chewing on a tough mushroom is not remotely close to blowing Juicy Fruit bubbles, it entertained us when we were hiking.

Our first oyster mushroom burger was one meal we never forgot. The large, murky-grey oyster mushrooms growing on trunks of alder trees looked sketchy to first-time fungo-geeks, but after discovering the colour of their spores, we decided to try them, hoping we had properly identified them. I wrote a death note in my journal before I cooked them: "If I am found dead you'll know I died from the mushrooms I found on the fallen alder by our clay quarry." Then Micah baked two fresh biscuits, while I sautéed the large questionable mushroom with kelp, topping it with fresh greens. The oyster mushroom burgers were delicious, not deadly.

Our Favourite Dishes

Appetizers

Woodland Salad
Freshly picked miner's lettuce tossed with tender dandelion, dock, and dove-foot geranium leaves, drizzled with an infused nettle vinegar dressing, and topped with grilled elfin saddle mushrooms.

Bear Buttered Biscuits
Two toasted whole-wheat rosemary biscuits sprinkled with cattail pollen.

Main Courses

Fall Harvest Rice Bowl
Sautéed spot prawns, nodding onions, chanterelles, rosehips, dried bull kelp, and chopped apple wedges served over rice and garnished with hazelnuts and dried thimbleberries.

Dandy Root Stir-fry
Freshly dug dandelion and silverweed roots stir-fried with wild onions, mustard greens, and bladderwrack seaweed fronds, and served with freshly caught clay-baked lingcod.

Plain Jane Delight
Boiled spot prawns served with nodding onions, nettle seeds, and crushed bull kelp fronds on a bed of steamed rice, dribbled with rosehip syrup.

Coho Salmon Loaf
Large biscuit stuffed with smoked coho jerky, coon-striped shrimp, angel wing mushrooms, wild onions, and baked in a Dutch oven.

Bitter Surprise
Boiled limpets and frilled dogwinkles mixed with sautéed oyster mushrooms, dandelion leaves, bittercress, and plump sedum florets. Served over rice.

Clam Cakes
Six cockle clam patties pan-fried with wild onions, honey mushrooms, and kelp seasoning.

Dessert

Bear Pie
Flaky-crusted pie filled with prime bear meat, rosehips, dried thimble berries, alumroot, and nodding onions.

I mastered fish-and-crab tacos, sushi rolls filled with the gonads of spiny red sea urchins, fish and onion perogies, breaded oysters, "survival pizza" (without cheese or sauce, it was aptly named), bear meatloaf, stuffed pita pockets (using sea water as yeast), and every kind of stir-fry imaginable.

But I cooked up some "gagger" meals too.

The nettle loaf was undercooked and really awful. It was a hungry-man series recipe, and though it was filling, only a real hungry man would want to eat it.

Nonetheless, we forced down our worst meals. Even though we had an entire winter stash of food, we wouldn't waste a morsel.

We ate nettles almost every day, since they are one of the best known sources of vitamins and minerals in the plant kingdom, rich in vitamins A, B, C, D, and K, as well as calcium, magnesium, iron, chlorophyll, zinc, chromium, and numerous trace minerals. The plant is armed with hollow, stinging, hypodermic-needle-like hairs that arise from a small gland containing formic acid, histamine, and two neurotransmitters that increase nerve sensitivity to pain. This cocktail of chemicals resembles insect venom. Any part of the plant can leave a small, bumpy rash on your skin, along with a painful, prickly sensation that can last for hours.

Cooking the plant pops the stingers and dilutes the poison, providing tender, tasty leaves that are safe to eat. I used nettle in my pot-bathing water and as a nourishing hair rinse, steeped it for a nutritious tea, sprinkled the seeds in biscuits, stripped the skin from its stalks for rope, and boiled the whole plant for a green dye.

Nettle Hair Rinse

1 large handful of fresh nettle leaves
about 1½ cups of water
Place just enough water to cover leaves in a pot. Cover pot. Simmer for 15 minutes. Cool and strain.

When I did get stung I either rubbed brown spores from the sword fern (found under its fronds) on the affected area; smeared it with crushed, juicy dock leaves; or carefully folded a nettle leaf in a tight wad, bit it with my front teeth until mashed, then rubbed it on the rash.

During the winter I attended what I dubbed the Booker Lagoon Raincoast Naturalist University. My desire to live off the land had fostered an addiction in me to learn about every aspect of the natural world. The lagoon provided me with the perfect place to study.

It was no ordinary bay. Our front yard was an ancient clam garden, built thousands of years ago. A small rock wall barricaded the mouth of the lagoon. A few stones had been removed in the middle of the wall to allow passage for a single canoe. Removing rocks in the bay to build the wall had produced a sandier beach, giving the clams more room to grow and an easier digging substrate while also preventing erosion of the beach. The old wall created a wondrous tidal pool to explore.

I identified at least 50 different critters living along the garden wall. Scout and I spent hours watching colourful life under the sea, sometimes for most of the day. It reminded me of an alpine meadow in bloom. My silent, patient observation taught me more than what my field guides offered.

Day 365
We've been out here a whole year now and it doesn't seem that long when I sit here watching this fire, hoping these hot rocks for the pit cook [our underground oven] don't explode and impale us with rock chips.

We celebrated the momentous day with a sweat lodge and feast of fresh fish and silverweed roots under the full moon.

We shared the task of making a spiked rake from yew and a cedar-rope dip net, which proved far outdated when we journeyed to the herring spawning grounds.

By mid-February, herring were on their way to spawn. These tiny, silvery, schooling fish not only provide people with food and bait for other fisheries, but also make up the bulk of ingredients for fertilizers. They are a keystone species of the ocean, and many fish, birds, and mammals rely on them for food. We wanted to follow the old ways, replicating the seasonal migration patterns of both the fish and the people who followed them. We spent days constructing primitive fishing gear—a cedar-bark dipnet and a spiked herring rake.

I think we've twined somewhere between a couple hundred and what seems like a couple thousand feet of cedar-bark rope for our dipnet. And still we need more. My fingers are so sore. Working with cedar is hard on your hands. It leaves them dry and pitted looking. I can twine cordage incredibly fast now. My fingers look like spider legs spinning a web.

Micah and I had to travel a lot farther to the spawning grounds than the people of the plentiful past. In 1973 the homebound herring that once spawned throughout the Broughton Archipelago were wiped out due to overfishing. Fishermen continued to fish with floodlights until their once-overflowing nets yielded only a bucketful of egg-filled herring. The herring never returned.

Today the fish only spawn along the shores of the major sounds and inlets of the area. Wakeman Sound was the closest to Booker Lagoon. Including detours, exploration missions, and zigzag rowing, we estimated a trip to Wakeman was 70 miles.

We expected to find massive schools of herring and plentiful eggs to harvest and dry for our soups and stir-fries. A single female can lay up to 20,000 eggs. When the males fertilize these sticky newborns, the surrounding water becomes milky white, and the mixture can be seen for miles.

We imagined ourselves piercing plentiful schools of herring on our rake, plunging our dipnet into flashing silver balls of fish, and harvesting egg-encrusted seaweed along the shores. The only problem is that the spawn can coincide with either the new or the full moon in either February or March, which gives fishermen a guessing game: when to go? We chose to arrive by the new moon.

Day 376

We woke to a morning one would expect to see on the coast. The sun was glowing behind a blanket of fog. When the fog began to lift and burn off, it wrapped itself around the mountains. Wisps of it trailed around the islands. The flat, calm water shimmered like liquid mercury. It was a beautiful sight, the perfect way to begin our voyage.

On our way out of the lagoon, two snorting sea lions convinced us to take a new route past their usual haul-out spot. The *tlix̲'an* (*glhee-ghan*) always bask, bark, play, and scratch on the distant rocks of Eden Island. We drifted back and forth past the 1,500-pound bellowing bulls' nose-plugging rookery until we suspected we had worn out our welcome.

Not a breath of wind rippled the water. The fog closed in around us as though we were moving through a dense cotton ball. We used our compass to stay on course.

After three hours of rowing, the fog finally lifted, revealing a gorgeous, Smurf-blue sky. Oarlocks squeaked and arms burned as we rowed on and on and on.

We fell into a natural, recurring pattern. The first few hours we laughed and joked, enjoying the scenery and animals we encountered. The following hours combined laughter and pain as we shifted into new positions to ease our aching joints and muscles. I developed the sideways row, the forward row, the squat position, the kneeling position, and the head-back "I'm about to die" position. The next couple of hours were silent ones. After these, the wall showed up. I didn't want to talk, nor did I want to hear a single peep from Micah. The wall eventually disintegrated as laughter began again, our bodies disbelieving that they were still rowing. This pattern repeated over and over until we reached our destination.

A rower's view of the coast is on a closer, slower scale than that of most boaters. We no longer rushed. We loved knowing we could travel anywhere we wanted for free, propelled by our own bodies.

When we were only a couple of miles from the mouth of Wakeman, we spotted two large schools of herring beside the boat. My heart leapt, knowing we had successfully followed their ancient route.

"We'll see you at Wakeman Sound, little fellas," I called out, as I hung myself over *Gribley*'s side.

We had packed little food for the trip, just enough to energize us during the arduous row. Like ancient paddlers we snacked on lingcod pemmican during the row.

I have to say our pemmican made the most delicious lunch. It is amazing how much energy we got from it.

I leaned back, licking my greasy lips, stretched out on my seat in the warm sun. My whole body smiled at the unknown ahead. I wondered if the early explorers felt the same way when they sailed along these shores for the first time.

"I hope this isn't the best thing I ever do in my life," I told Micah, "because it's going to be pretty hard to beat." I didn't want to end up like the mountain climber who continuously craves higher altitudes until there are no more peaks to stand on. Where would their life go from there?

Micah replied, "We can't let that happen to us, Nik." Silence followed.

At the mouth of the sound we let our oars drag to a stop. Wakeman was the wildest, vastest landscape we had ever seen. Tall, white-capped mountains swallowed up the sky. Thundering waterfalls cascaded down the canvas of steep crags, as tiny rainbows danced in the spray.

I dipped my finger into the brownish green water and licked it.

"It's hardly salty," I said. Before Micah could reply, we spotted a huge group of dolphins jumping our way, a sight that banished all thoughts of the discomforts of long-distance rowing.

Scout's eyes nearly popped out of her head when the first dolphin leapt beside the boat, within arm's reach. Seconds later, hundreds of shiny grey dolphins, glittering in the sunlight, were whizzing every which way under the boat, rocking us side to side. Dozens leapt in unison in a spectacular feeding frenzy. They were also here for herring.

When the dolphins had left us to continue their hunting loop of the sound, we rowed on to Corson Creek.

What a great way to end the day, sitting on my new, diagonally woven cedar mat by the warmth of a fire, listening to waterfalls and mystery animals cracking odd sticks around camp. I am blessed in the heart of such wonders.

On the second day of the herring trip, I wrote in sloppy printing:

Whoa, what a day. I am totally exhausted. I am so tired that it is an effort for me to write. We had another huge day of rowing. Wakeman Sound is a humungous place and somehow we never factored that in. We imagined a lush river estuary full of the first new greens of spring and herring spawn as far as we could see, but it turns out our visions are imaginary.

We saw no herring, no eggs, four eagles, and a few seal heads popping up for air. The grass flats several miles away offered nothing green to eat. We found nothing but winter-worn bladderwrack seaweed, not a single algae-eating limpet, giant barnacle, dogwinkle, clam, or any other edible sea creature. We tried jigging for other fish, but our handlines didn't come close to reaching the mighty depths of Wakeman. We were once again back to a life of crawling into bed hungry.

On day three we spotted what looked like a sandy clam beach on the distant shore, but after two hours of rowing we came to a clamless pebble beach. We slurped hot seaweed soup for dinner. The following day we set off with our bows and arrows to hunt ducks. Unfortunately, they were two miles away, on the other side of the sound. When we neared the flock, we found we couldn't float within 75 feet of the skittish diving ducks. Any closer and we saw only their feet pattering along the surface of the water and heard only the high-pitched whistle of their wings high overhead. We also failed to bring down any seagulls when we shot from the boat with our bows and arrows.

I used to wonder how a hawk could miss catching a single bird in a group of hundreds. Now I knew. The benefits of a flock are brilliant. My untrained eye found it impossible to concentrate on a single target in the midst of beating wings, distracting motion, and frantic calls of panicked birds in flight. I would never mock a bird of prey's hunting abilities again.

Our fruitless harvesting expeditions used more energy than we gained from seaweed soups. Like all the other waiting mammals, birds, and fish, we needed the spawning herring.

On day five we found herring "tracks." Miles away from camp, along a small section of beach, we discovered a patch of tiny, sparkling, clear eggs glued to seaweed and surrounding rocks, a fraction of what we had expected to see. Given that only one herring egg in 10,000 is expected to mature to a spawning adult, the species was obviously in trouble.

I knew my efforts would probably fail, but I was determined to give the herring any help I could. We collected loose bladderwrack bundles of eggs and tucked their anchoring stems under heavy rocks to prevent them from floating away or being washed ashore.

After gathering a small basketful of roe-covered seaweed to eat for dinner, we sat down on a large boulder and gazed across the sound at graceful white trumpeter swans. I wondered what the fate of the herring would be seven generations from now. Each tiny life faced survival challenges that far exceeded my own. The missing herring, vanished basking shark, struggling salmon, and depleted rock cod were heading to eternal silence. I gave thanks to the human angels around the world who were giving everything to save them.

I had sought the grandeur of the wilderness to escape modern society and the changing world, if only for a brief time. The herring taught me that environmental tragedies were happening everywhere, even in the places I believed were still wild and free. The pattern of blaming others for nature's crisis will continue until each of us feels a soulful connection to the wild world. With this profound understanding we will make informed decisions about how to co-exist with nature. Only then will we be able to make a positive difference for all life gracing our beautiful planet.

We sat in silence, leaning up against each other, contemplating our thoughts until a surprising gust of wind blew through our hair.

"We've gotta go now," Micah called out. I leapt off the rock. He was right.

"I can't believe how fast the wind picked up," I responded. "How could it go from flat calm to white-capped waves so quickly?"

We darted from rock to rock, retrieving our baskets and hats.

"Do you think we can make it?" I asked. "We have a long way to go."

Micah surveyed the whipping, frothy water. "I guess so. What do you think?"

"We should try. I don't want to spend the night here."

By the time we reached the halfway mark, waves were cresting into the bow of the boat. We were committed now. We took turns bailing. The steep mountainsides offered no protection; we had to make it to Corson Creek. We never talked when our lives were in danger. Instead, the wind howled in our ears.

The dolphins heard our silent pleas. They lessened our fears, slipping over the barrelling waves, happy to surf in the windstorm. Our fearless friends escorted us all the way back to our Corson Creek camp.

Finally safe and dry beside a warm fire, I picked up my gourd cup of soup, which contained bladderwrack seaweed dotted with herring roe, a wilted onion, alder catkins, and a sprinkle of Scout's last salmon jerky. I inhaled the steamy seaside aroma and smiled at the richness of my first slurp.

"Wow, I can't believe how good this is," I commented. Micah had already finished his small portion but it warmed him as well. Tucked inside our warm bags, we said a prayer for the herring, hoping we would wake to see the milky spawning waters on Day 6.

We didn't. We couldn't decide how long we should wait. Our energy levels were nearing those we'd experienced at Native Anchorage, and we needed to save the last shreds of our reserves for our huge row back to Booker Lagoon. Since we hadn't found anything in the sea, we dragged our feet up an old logging road in the hopes of spotting a grouse. Instead, we found ten bitter fireweed shoots that we peeled and ate for lunch. After another five-mile row back to camp, we flopped down on a soft patch of moss to soak up the energy of the late-afternoon sun.

Spring had not yet arrived; many animals were still hunkered down for the last days of winter, and I could see my breath during the day. But I sensed a new feeling in the air, an excited anticipation murmured in hushed tones, as if all of us forest critters were saying, "Thank God I made it through the winter."

A week passed. Perhaps the spawning was over. The herring rake appeared outdated. It hardly felt right to take any of the fish, even if they did come.

I saw Micah eating the skin off his gourd cup today. We had a good laugh. I didn't think we were that hungry but as I walked away I saw half a rosehip we had had for tea the first night lying on the ground. Without a second thought I picked up the soggy hip and ate it. Guess we are hungry. I'd enjoy a squirrel right about now, if there were any. Where the heck are the squirrels?

After two more days of grey, murky soup, we reluctantly bid our camp adieu. "Wakeman is the asshole of the world," Billy Proctor had told me. "If the world needed an enema, Wakeman Sound would get it." He had trapped and hunted for years in Wakeman's wild winters, where the ice froze around his boat and the wind whipped into gales within minutes. He knew the moodiness and frigidness of the sound and loved it as much as we did.

Once we were on our way, though, we couldn't wait to hear our squeaky door and see the familiar blue face of Young Jay greeting us at the steps. The greatest incentive to push through our fatigue was the vision of visiting Echo Bay's post office. We hoped to use the phone there to make a call home. We had been gone 381 days.

"HI, MOM. I'M ALIVE."

The most valuable thing any of us can do is find a way to say the things that can't be said.

—Susan Scott, *Fierce Conversations*

After more than 15 hours rowing from Wakeman Sound, we finally made it to Echo Bay. A blue and white speedboat headed straight for us. It was Billy Proctor.

We grabbed hold of his 16-foot Surfer with giant smiles.

"Ah, you made it," he laughed. Scout dashed under my seat to hide from the new voice.

"Yup, we're alive, barely," I said. "The row nearly killed us. We're frozen and super sore, but we saw some beautiful sights and laughed a lot. We're heading to the post office."

"Well, if you want, when you're finished, come on over for dinner," he said. "I'll be home in an hour or so. I'm going beachcombing for logs."

"Thanks, Billy. We'd love to." We could hardly wait.

❧

Approximately ten families lived in and around the tiny, isolated community of Echo Bay. We had made our first trip there from Booker Lagoon when we started out on our December deer hunt, two months earlier. Although tourists and other locals had given us a variety of nicknames—the Survivors, the Row Boaters, the Shit Ducks (from a distance we looked like seagulls floating on a log), the Pioneers, the Bush People—in Echo Bay we were known as "the kids."

Our new friends spoiled us rotten with delicious meals, goodies to take with us, sweets for me and coffee for Micah, and lots of laughter. Their encouraging words and generosity never ceased, even as we entered their homes with our stinky sleeping bags, smoky clothes, feral cat, and unusual attempts at gifts.

Billy nearly puked when we gave him some of our dried seaweed. He yelled out, "Jesus Christ, are you trying to poison me? God, that's horrible." We later tried offering a duck to our new friends, Al and Yvonne, in exchange for their kind hospitality, but they politely declined. I don't know why we were shocked by this; of course they didn't want a headless duck we had picked up floating on the water!

Visiting Echo Bay was like coming home for Christmas. We rowed straight to the post office to pick up the mail that was delivered by floatplane once a week. And then we went to the tiny convenience store.

Micah and I never craved much of anything living in Booker Lagoon. Our minds stopped longing for cookies or toilet paper because we knew we were never going to find any, but when we stood on the threshold of Echo Bay's little store, packaged food consumed our thoughts and conversations. We traded baskets and other crafts for confections (candy, ice cream, and other edibles we couldn't find in nature) and phone-call money.

Our stomachs hated us for our junk-food binges, but that never stopped the part of us that believed the pain was worth it.

Day 381
I think what spurred us back the last mile to Echo Bay from Wakeman was thinking of the ice cream we hoped to buy at the store. I'm not sure how I kept from throwing up, but I convinced myself I loved every mouthful. We ate the entire tub.

Despite our sweet tooths, the letters and phone calls were the best part of our Echo Bay visits. Our parents' thoughtful care packages and lengthy letters were our fuel. They made me smile and cry at the same time. To receive family news that was at least a month old sharpened my realization that we lived alone at the edge of the world.

We ripped open our packages as if we had never had a present before. We received packages of Jell-O, noodles, and hot chocolate; bags of gummy worms; cans of mandarin oranges; magazines; a new T-shirt; and lots of love. But it was the phone call home that I longed to make.

I paused before pressing the last digit of my mom's phone number. *Please don't be an answering machine.* Nothing was worse.

I had a hard time choking back the tears when I first said, "Hi, Mom. It's me."

Emotions flooded in when I heard my mother's voice say, "Hello, Miss Nikki. How are you? Are you safe?"

"I'm doing great, Mom. So is Micah. We're healthy and happy and loving every minute of our adventure. It's everything I've ever dreamed of."

Her voice crackled with as much emotion as mine. "I'm so happy for you, Nikki. And so proud. It sure is wonderful to hear from you."

After my first phone call home my mom told me she had finally realized the depth of who I was. She knew at times I was in danger, but at last she understood that if anything happened to me, she could find contentment knowing I had died while living my dream.

Both Micah and I did our best to refrain from writing or telling our parents about scary, life-threatening events. Conversations and letters were filled with beautiful imagery of our lives and wonderful updates about our families. My mom told me she loved my letters, stained yellow and reeking of campfire smoke, as much as I loved hers.

"I miss you so much, Mom," I nearly sobbed. "Give everyone a hug for me and a big hug to you. I never forget to light a candle on the full moon for you. It makes me feel a lot closer to you, knowing you're doing the same."

"I'm still using the candle you gave me before you left, Nikki. It's on the windowsill."

The inevitable "I don't want to say good-bye, Mom, but I better go now" always came sooner than we wanted. I knew the moment I pushed the end button, I would once again feel an enormous emptiness and disconnection from my family.

"I love you," my mom shakily said. Tears welled in my eyes.

"I love you more."

🌿

Our first night hanging out with Billy and his wife was like stepping into a dream. We ate deer stew, licked ice-cream cones, and listened to hilarious stories of rare characters of the coast. Billy was like the grandfather we always wanted.

"Wouldn't it be cool if you lived next door to Billy Proctor?" we would ask each other as we rowed away. "Think of all the things you would learn." We soaked up his stories and advice. We knew he looked out for us, as he did for everyone in his community. Some windy, lonely, cold nights I could feel the good thoughts being sent by our loving friends and family.

We had one rule about treats and care packages; nothing could return to Booker Lagoon. The six- to eight-hour row back to Booker after our modern food and candy binges was always the same. Bent over with intestinal cramps, I would complain, "I sure wish I had bought the orange. I really wanted an orange." The allure of a devitalized sugar buzz never let me buy an orange.

We made it to the post office nine times during our stay in Booker Lagoon, but no matter how fun our Echo Bay visits were, they never made me want to return to the life I once lived. I loved being wild.

LUXURY AT LAST

When a man has nothing, he may finally learn the value of all things.
—Alexander McKeag, a character in the TV movie *Centennial*

Becoming wild may not have fully changed my tendency to choose unhealthy food when it was available, but I definitely felt my body's cry to stop poisoning it when I returned to Booker Lagoon after an Echo Bay visit. Our first wild meal home always felt like I was once again honouring my body. On the other hand, I didn't necessarily take care of my body when I wanted to learn something new or get some work done. Too often I was an energizer bunny workaholic. One of the survival schools I attended taught me to multitask, which was not a useful attribute when I was trying to still my mind in nature. However, it did help me master some primitive skills. And it meant I always had at least five projects on the go at any given time.

Micah had a different style. He worked endlessly on one project at a time, sustaining his focus until completion, even if he had to start over more than once. He astounded me.

We both loved the challenge of figuring out how to make primitive tools and crafts. Not every project succeeded the first time, or even the second or third. Some never worked at all.

When we returned from our Wakeman Sound and Echo Bay trip, we spent some time at home in Booker Lagoon, working on things around the camp. I tried replicating a gigantic cedar branch "burden" basket, but it worked better as firewood. I spent countless hours carving, sanding, and oiling a gorgeous digging stick made of yew, only to hear a shoulder-slumping *crack* when I dug my first silverweed root. I also attempted to make a cedar flute, but my only instructional reference stated, "The author has made several, some of which will not make any tone whatsoever...It still looks great hanging on the wall." When I finished, I tucked my pretty, tuneless flute away in a back corner. On the evolutionary timeline, Micah and I were still pre-*Homo sapiens*. We had not progressed far enough to spend much time on decorative art projects.

Micah broke two bows in the finishing phases. It was like saving up to buy his dream car, only to crash it the first time he drove it. He spent days on eyeball-poking, sweaty-browed hikes to find yet another.perfect rare yew branch.

Both of us spent months trying to make oil containers and rope from bull kelp tubes. We had seen old photos of kelp coiled up in bentwood boxes, storing the highly prized eulachon grease, but found few clues to help solve the mystery of kelp bottle production. I wrote, "Doing our 100th experiment with kelp again! When will it end?" Eventually we discovered the lost secrets of kelp and made a bottle that held our cooking oil, but we never did solve the problem of its brittle-ness and could not get our bottles to coil up for packing without breaking.

Though we figured out how to make strong kelp rope, we couldn't find a knot that would keep the lengths of kelp from slipping apart once the rope dropped into the water, even though Micah was a human encyclopedia of knot tying. When a huge bundle of kelp rope accidentally burned up by the stove, we finally called the experiments off. Plenty of other projects were waiting.

One that did work was my primitive lantern. As the saying goes, "Necessity is the mother of invention." On a moonless night, creeping down our tar-black trail of salal jungle to the outhouse, I couldn't ignore the irrational fears my mind conjured up, and I was embarrassed when they sent me rushing back to the shack. I had spent hundreds of nights in the woods alone, sleeping under ferns, wandering blindfolded through the brush, and stalking animals close enough to touch them. People who knew me when I taught at WOLF Camp viewed me as a hardcore, primitive sur-vivalist, not someone who was afraid of the dark. But the darkness that shrouded the coastal forest felt wilder than any I had slept in before, as if nature gifted us with beauty during the day but withdrew it at night. Both of us felt it.

So even though I knew my night vision would be completely ruined by the artificial light, I sewed up a small, cylinder-shaped rawhide lantern, complete with an adjustable lid for rain. It held a single precious tea-light candle.

My lantern rules. It doesn't keep me from being spooked in the dark, but it kinda takes my mind off of it and gives me a false sense of security.

Our most arduous and laborious projects were steam-bending traditional bentwood boxes and pounding rolls of cedar bark for softened clothing.

The process of turning a washed-up cedar log into a functional water-proof box was beyond survival—achieving success verged on the miraculous.

We taught ourselves how to make the most of our projects through the painful process of trial and error. Our one successful bentwood box took nearly a month to make.

Making bentwood boxes also taught us about jealousy.

Micah and I silently competed with one another to learn new skills. Though we had embarked on this adventure understanding the advantage of two minds, our stubborn egos meant we didn't always appreciate and reap the benefits.

One afternoon I heard Micah let out an agonizing "Noooo!" I knew he had either broken his bentwood box or failed at his steaming experiment. I smiled and silently rejoiced. Then was horrified. Holy hell, I thought, how could I have felt happy at Micah's disaster? What an ass.

I realized jealousy ruled my life in many small and inconceivable ways. According to Murray Bodo, author of *The Way of St. Francis*, "The reason we don't become saints is not that we cannot overcome sin, but that we are unwilling to overcome shame...In overcoming shame...[we discover our] true self."

I shared my shame with Micah and he confessed he'd had a similar reaction to one of my broken projects. We couldn't believe the power our negative egos had over us. It was so easy to slip back into those old habits, to ignore our faults and fear-based thoughts, even when surrounded by the beauty of nature, living in such a pure way. We constantly shared the hard truths we were uncovering about ourselves, even our most shameful thoughts. With each apology, admission, and genuine compliment, my patterns changed, my ego shrank, and my spirit smiled with a brighter light.

I doubted the warmth of a cedar mini-skirt would convince me to toss away my jeans, but I had always dreamed of wearing a primitive outfit, so I spent weeks making it.

In contrast to the boxes, our primitive clothing verged on the absurd.

John Jewitt summed up coastal clothing perfectly in his memoir *The Adventures and Sufferings of John R. Jewitt, Captive of Maquinna*: "From my being obliged at this season of the year to change my accustomed clothing and to dress like the Natives, with only a piece of cloth of about two yards long thrown loosely around me, my European clothes having been for some time entirely worn out, I suffered more than I can express from cold."

Micah and I were accustomed to the damp, chilly climate, but not in the way the ancestors were. At 23 degrees Fahrenheit we could wash dishes in the ocean with bare hands without a wince of agony; we could sit on a frosty toilet seat without discomfort; but we couldn't walk barefoot to dig clams in the winter nor row for miles in a rainstorm with only cedar-bark mats tied around our waists. Jewitt was right. Shredded cedar-bark clothing failed to provide warmth, but I spent many agonizing hours making some anyway.

I measured myself for a skirt, while Micah envisioned a vest. During one three-week period we pounded rolls of seasoned cedar strips with a wooden beater for hours each day to make soft, flexible strands of bark. It was the one project we always worked on at the same time. I wrote, "I figured I may as well join in the loud banging rather than try to put up with it."

I decorated my skirt with a few beads and a leather waistband for added comfort, and was sure it would become a wardrobe favourite—until I put it on. The shortcut I took, using thicker strands of bark, made it a little stiff. In fact, it looked and felt like I was wearing a lampshade.

My next garment was a bearskin vest that made me look like Fred Flintstone. Then I sewed a brain-tanned buckskin tank top with cute spaghetti straps, a leather front pocket, and a beaded patch of two leaping dolphins. It turned out beautifully.

I completed the look with beaded moccasins, a stylish new cedar-bark baseball cap Micah had made for me, and my own line of primitive lingerie. Wearing all my clothes, with my bear-claw necklace hanging around my neck and cedarbark bracelet tied to my wrist, I had the ultimate primitive outfit.

❦

The concept of living freely in the moment was hard for us, considering the expectations we carried about how we should live in the wild. We felt limited and burdened by these demands, which dictated what we should do and how we should do it. Whether it was our pride, stubbornness, childhood dreams, or expectations set by ourselves or our peers, we found it difficult to decide to keep a few timesaving modern tools; to use warm, waterproof, comfortable modern clothing; and to live in a modern shelter.

First, we let go of the dream of building a mini cedar-planked bighouse. We had the shack; that was sufficient. Over time we chose to keep our knives, axe, saw, nylon rope, a few Rubbermaid bins, a shrimp and crab trap, and our pots and pans.

We tied 100 feet of cedar-bark rope onto 300 feet of nylon to prove to ourselves that our handmade cordage could haul up a shrimp trap. We boiled water and cooked our food with hot rocks enough times to know that method added hours of extra work to already busy days. We knew that using a stone axe would not change our already profound appreciation for modern tools. As we adapted, I found it felt good to live by what I was called to do, not by what I was expected to do.

Author Agatha Christie wrote, "I don't think necessity is the mother of invention. Invention…arises directly from idleness, possibly also from laziness. To save oneself trouble."

But we knew we weren't becoming lazy; we just wanted time to enjoy everything nature had to offer us. One stormy evening I was scrubbing dishes down on the beach with a handful of sand and was struck with a revolutionary idea: I needed to invent something that washed our dishes for us. I began dreaming up possible plans.

As I walked back to the shack with the clean dishes, I remembered humans had already invented my brilliant machine. It was called a dishwasher.

Our imaginations, force of will, hearts, and nature provided all we needed. Even though we modified our primitive goals, we still lived our dreams. In fact, by keeping some modern tools, our dreams became more than we ever imagined possible.

Day 424
Another beautiful day in paradise. How could I want to live any other way? It's so simple and real.

I could hardly believe I wrote the statement. When I embarked on my year in the wild, I was positive this lifestyle would not be a long-term future for me. The more I lived it, though, the more I loved it. I pondered all the possible roads my life could take after I left Booker Lagoon. What will I do after it is over? Where will I go? What do I *want* to do? Do I have to leave? Question after question popped into my mind, demanding answers. As much as I had felt the need to venture into the wild, I also knew I had to return to civilization, even though I didn't know why—and didn't want to think about it right now.

The first signs of spring were peeking up around us, and I still had a few months to fully enjoy my cavewoman existence before modern life consumed me. In the meantime, I would soak up the energy of spring's renewal, new growth, and hope as it burst forth.

I caressed the first swollen buds of berry bushes, greeted the first plantain leaves poking up in the rocks, and said goodbye to the last pair of bufflehead ducks departing for their nesting grounds.

A pulse of excitement rippled through us forest dwellers. Soon I'd be eating tangy salmonberries with the robins and fresh greens with the bears.

The wind feels wonderfully warm today. It's like a mid-summer breeze and the air is so sweet, smelling like a thousand flowers blowing on the wind. I had to sit on the rocks that much longer to enjoy all the tiny subtleties. Even the ocean smells incredibly rich and fresh today.

The sea lettuce grew fast and covered the tide pool at my secret place until it became a jungle of seaweed. It was almost impossible to see the array of life under the canopy of floating plants. However, this loss was soon compensated by a hundred other possibilities that satiated my desire to learn all I could about the natural world.

I sat on the lichen-covered rocks watching hundreds of shining gold and silver perch ripple the water as they darted in unison. They gathered in the shallow waters to give birth to their live young.

I heard the sound of something wet shaking near me. I knew it had to be Matsa, our neighbouring mink, and turned in time to see her with a shiny perch in her mouth. She hunted beside me for the rest of the afternoon, taking each fish up to her den. Then a female rufous hummingbird with her shimmering colours came to sit beside me. I heard the soft peep she made to a show-off male as he tried impressing her with a diving aerial move. I'm not sure if she was applauding him or telling him to get lost, but I leaned over anyway and whispered, "If you ask me, I think he's pretty darn handsome."

Our music had returned, and I no longer had to fill the void with my own humming. One morning I sat on an old cedar stump listening to a winter wren whisper pieces of his song, as if rehearsing for the day he would proudly sing it to the world. Even the seagulls were singing a lovely song I had never heard before.

Living with Young Jay was like taking a university seminar on corvid family behaviour. His personality and mannerisms intrigued and entertained me. His vocal repertoire was astounding.

I was leaning up against the shack, using a split cedar board as a backrest, sketching a plant in my journal, when I heard a curious birdsong. I caught Young Jay in the act of singing an uncharacteristic jaybird song. His new melody was a jumble of sweet notes, gentle gurgles, and soft squeaks.

"Ah ha. It *is* you singing!"

Startled, he flew up to a higher branch.

I reached into my pocket, retrieved a precious hazelnut, and called out, "Come on down, Young Jay. I'm sorry for scaring you."

He flew down a bit closer to examine my bribe, cocking his head to one side for a better look.

"It's okay, you can take it. It's your favourite."

Down he flew, flapping his wings as he steadied himself on my outstretched hand. My heart quivered at the touch of his long, thin toes upon my hand, while I admired his unique and intricate markings.

Young Jay was also an incredible mimic.

It's like he's softly mimicking the voices of other birds all at once, creating one song from all of theirs. I can hear the call notes of winter wrens, kinglets, chickadees, and even an eagle in his voice. Micah even heard him do a fart noise. I didn't have to guess where he learned that from, since Micah's "Rhea" is still in full force and I hadn't seen any yellowthroats around, who are the only other birds I know of who make such a noise.

Sometimes I sat at my secret spot to feel the fog float in around me. It tickled and poked at my bare legs like teeny, pin-sized fingers. I watched chestnut-backed chickadees take bits of sheep wool I had left hanging on nearby trees for their nests, and witnessed river otters mating and seals fighting for dominance. I tasted the season's first elderberry flowers, frying the creamy white clusters in batter.

I caught a glimpse of the sweet-tasting world of the hummingbird today while I sat on an unexplored island eating the sugary flower buds of a plant called scurvy grass.

Spring treasures were everywhere, and we explored every nook and cranny around us. The marine charts Tom Sewid had given to us on our first boat ride to the Broughtons begged us to visit new places. We missed hanging out with bears and figured many would be yawning and stretching their way down to Viner Sound for a smorgasbord of green goodies. We packed the boat, loaded Scout, and reached the photogenic estuary in about ten hours. The lush, grassy riverbanks pulsed with a vibrant green glow, and the shiny white undersides of silverweed glistened in the sun. Glossy black bears dotted the landscape.

After collecting miner's lettuce and nettles for lunch from a secret forest garden, we spent the first morning basking in the sun on the cool grass. I spied on a hummingbird who was gathering woolly brown casings off sword-fern fiddleheads for her nest, and a mink nearly ran over my foot.

Viner Sound at low tide is a mud-sucking monster. The shallow estuary tried its best to swallow us up when we underestimated the speed at which the water recedes and failed to get out of the mudflats in time. The knee-deep, gooey mud suctioned off our gumboots more than once as we slogged and pushed our boat into the water.

After rescuing Scout from a logjam she had escaped into, and after being chased by a bear, we decided it was time to move on. Safe, muddy, and relieved, we travelled to the charming Burdwood island group, a wildflower hotspot. I spied bright red Indian paintbrush decorating a defensive island used long ago by warriors. Dove-shaped red- and lemon-yellow-centred columbines waved amongst the grass. The islands were home to patches of yellow-faced monkey flowers, eagle nests, and deserted midden sites. We even found an ancient planked cedar tree.

After a week of exploring we picked up the oars for home. We ran into thousands of bluish white, bell-shaped moon jellies congregating in several places along the way. I could smell perfume lingering on the breeze. As we neared the Booker man, the setting sun gleamed off the heads of a pair of curious seals, while xawi (kah-wee), the common loon, yodelled his trilling, laughterlike call.

By far the greatest spring jewel we found was a place we eventually named Spa Bay. One afternoon we rowed over to an island we had not yet visited so we could document the plant and animal life. After snacking on a carpet of spoonwort flower buds, we continued our survey. When we reached the back side, we froze in our tracks.

"Do you see what I see?" Micah asked.

"I sure do."

We stared in rapt anticipation at the square, shallow, algae-filled hole in the rocks. Could this be the hot tub we had been looking for?

Micah stripped off his socks and shoes and waded into the slimy water, rolling up his sleeves to feel for the bottom. He looked up and smiled. "I think it's deep enough, Nik."

"Yes!" I exclaimed, jumping up and down with excitement and throwing my arms to the sky. I had spent 418 days dreaming of finding a suitable primitive hot tub. We agreed to come back early the next morning to further explore its potential. I could hardly sleep.

We spent most of the next day scooping out water; digging out sand; transplanting all the clams, limpets, and crabs; and cleaning the rock tub until it was smooth and algae-free. Together we stood back to examine this perfect rock rendition of an acrylic hot tub, with one glorious slanted side for reclined comfort. It seemed too good to be true.

The first two attempts failed. On try one the water remained lukewarm. During try two, small shore crabs that had moved back into the tub came out of hiding and pinched our legs and butts in the hot, itchy salt water. By our third attempt we had thought of everything. We scraped the tiniest sharp barnacles off the walls. We removed every crab. We hauled 35 buckets of fresh water from a nearby creek to eliminate our itches. Then it was time to heat the water.

We gathered over 30 stones, ranging in size from a soccer ball to a cantaloupe melon, stacked them in a pile nearly four feet tall, and chopped enough wood to cover the rock pile four times over. When we set the wood on fire, it reminded me of a teenager's Halloween fire, started with a can of diesel and too hot to stand nearby.

Then we rolled the red-hot rocks into the cold water of the tub, running for cover as each stone hit the water. They exploded with a thunderous *crack* and a huge, fountainlike spray of water before hissing and settling to the bottom of the tub. When the 31st stone settled, I stood back in amazement at what we had accomplished. The water sparkled with tiny bits of floating mica that had fallen off the cracked rocks. It was as if fairies had sprinkled it with pixie dust. I added sprigs of mint, then dipped my big toe into the pool. The temperature was perfect.

We slid into the steamy, hot, bubbling water and lay back against the soft cedar mats we had lined the tub with. We let out deep sighs of satisfaction. We sipped spruce tea from our gourd mugs and used folded leaf spoons to eat our first and only batch of chocolate-seaweed pudding, made from a recipe I gleaned from Jennifer Hahn's book *Spirited Waters*.

We had spent hours in *Gribley*, rowing around to find red, carrageenan-filled seaweed for the pudding. Micah volunteered for the agonizing job of dunking himself over the side of the boat, receiving repeated brain freezes, so he could fill our small pot with blades of bumpy Turkish towel and iridescent rainbow kelp that shimmered like shiny tissue paper. I boiled the seaweed in four cups of milk for 20 minutes to extract the carrageenan, removed the blades, and stirred in two packets of instant hot chocolate mix that had been sent to us in a care package from home (I'd smuggled the forbidden treat to Booker Lagoon and used months of willpower to save it for a special occasion, but it was worth it). Then I cooled the mixture in a slow-moving section of the creek with the pot lid on. The resulting pudding tasted as good as the hot fudge brownie delights I remembered back home, though I have yet to find anyone besides Micah who thinks it's that good.

Our evening of bliss continued. Two eagles soared overhead, silhouetted against a rosy pink sky. Black and orange varied thrushes whistled their long, melodic, single-note songs in the yew trees beside us. The heat waves from the fire turned a nearby white-shell beach into a wavy vision of ancient chieftain baths.

Near Village Island, I had seen a rounded depression in a cliff wall that I learned had been used in the past as a chief's bathtub. A red-ochre pictograph of *Baxbakwalanusiwae* (*Buk-buk-walla-newks-ee-way*), the first cannibal warrior, was painted beside it. Apparently the chief would bathe four times a day before potlatches, wars, and special ceremonies in order to prepare himself, praying to the Great Spirit for strength and guidance. I wondered if the hot tub in which I lazily floated had been used for such ceremonies when time was mist. I closed my eyes to dwell between the ancient days of long ago and the modern world from which I came.

When the temperature cooled, we climbed out and dried off by the dwindling fire. As we rowed home, electric-green phosphorescence lit our way. Streaking out from under the boat, the luminous sparks transformed schools of perch into ocean comets and shooting stars. Another wish had come true.

WHALE BREATH

I had long ago decided that anthropomorphism wasn't such a great sin. Indeed,
it is perhaps a good thing, for it allows a human to relate with an animal, to
see it as a fellow being and to be willing to share the world with it.
                        —R.D. Lawrence, *The Ghost Walker*

*P*foooohf. *Pfooohf.*
    "I hear whales!"

Our heads swivelled, trying to locate the orcas in Fife Sound. "Oh please be coming to us," I thought.

When the pod surfaced again, we dashed toward them, arms flailing in a wild frenzy as we splashed one another with our oars. It was soon obvious the family was farther away than they'd been when we started. We stopped and bobbed.

Shiny black dorsal fins rose and fell in the distance, fountains of mist dissipating in the air around them. I looked down at the bone-barbed hook and cedar-bark rope I held in my hand and thought of the Kwakwaka'wakw fisherman long ago who used the same kind of hook. I had been told that when a Kwakwaka'wakw fisher died, he was reborn as *max̲inux̲* (*mah-gee-nouk*), the killer whale, to learn about the underwater world in which he had hunted. Once he learned all he needed to know, his spirit was blown through the orca's blowhole to rise to the Everlasting Potlatch above.

We had spent weeks inventing and replicating different types of primitive fish hooks that would have been familiar to that fisherman—bone throat gorges, abalone flashers, trolling hooks, jigging hooks, stone hooks, and bentwood halibut hooks. We had seen them in books and copied them from museums and filled our cedar tackle box with an array of homemade hooks, stone sinkers, and shiny shell lures.

When we could no longer see any trace of the hunting whales, we rowed off to find our own fish. I held up my prized jigging lure. Thinking of all the hours

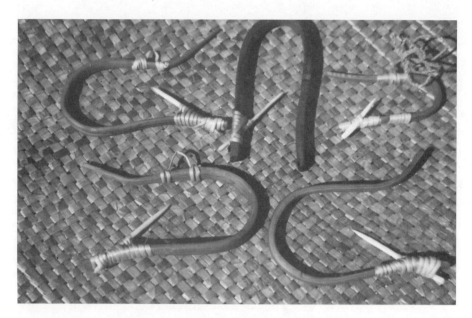

We carved the bear's bones into sharp barbs for our steam-bent halibut hooks. They looked like masterpieces, but unfortunately we never brought a fish to the surface with them.

I had spent pecking and sanding the stone jigger made me want to try another hook first. I didn't want to lose this one in a tug-of-war with the ocean floor.

In the few moments it took to tie a piece of clam to the hook, I fully understood the customs, prayers, and ceremonies of fishermen in the days of the dugout canoe. I no longer wondered why someone would spend days carving intricate designs on hooks in the hopes of incurring a spirit's help. For primitive hunters, anything could go wrong, and they could use all the help they could get. Modern man calls such beliefs "pagan" or "savage superstition," but it made sense to me now that I was living it.

I tied the stone hook to a coil of cedar-bark rope and knotted that rope to another few hundred feet of modern line. I relied on a lot more than luck to catch *tsaxu'* (*chah-koo*), the lingcod. I felt at the mercy of the sea, the earth, the air, the animals, the plants, and the Great Spirit around me.

I didn't have the confidence in my gear I did with a 100-pound test handline. My hook reached bottom and I started jerking the line up and down. I hoped the cedar root that held the bone barb in place hadn't loosened. I prayed the barb was sharp enough, tough enough, and long enough. I couldn't just tug and jerk on my line to yank the stone hook free from the bottom. I couldn't afford to lose the hook; I hadn't seen a similar rock in all my travels. Using primitive hooks turned an enjoyable day of fishing into a nerve-racking, anxious afternoon.

Hours went by without a single bite.

Billy Proctor remembers when his hook couldn't reach the bottom before a lingcod bit it. When he pulled it up, the water turned brown from all the larger lingcod following it. It was clear the days of the plentiful *tsaxu'* were gone.

We tried all our hooks, and at the end of slack tide one fish nibbled my stone lure. Then I caught beautiful British Columbia. My hook never saw sunlight again.

Large rollers started to form in Fife Sound as the dark sky enclosed us in a shroud of grey drizzle. "Monsoon June" was upon us. The warmth of our little shack beckoned us home, even without a fish. When we reached the gap into the lagoon, I stuffed my hands into my armpits to warm them up while we took a ride on the current.

The next morning, before fishing, I sat on the steps leading to the beach and listened to pollen-laden bees buzzing nearby.

> *I wonder what fashion styles are coming back in. I hope it's not the 80s! Strange thought, I guess, from someone who has been looking at this same navy blue V-neck sweater for over a year. A strange thought for someone who wears a coon-skin hat and lives in a place where pants tucked into rubber boots is the fashionable norm.*

I picked up the pieces I had assembled for the construction of yet another hook and hoped the fads in fishing lures would recirculate, just like trends in the fashion industry.

We spent days trying every style of hook, using every kind of bait imaginable, and we never caught a single fish. We had whole hooks bitten off, bait nibbled free, and bone barbs broken, but we were not able to land a fish.

The finished hooks looked like perfect replicas of those used in the old days, but their good looks seemed not enough to catch the halibut. One night I wrote, "It seemed like the ocean was empty today as we jigged and jigged among the seals and the sunbathing cormorants." Large black cormorants, wings outstretched, on floating logs or rocks vanishing in the tide, were a familiar sight. This black seabird, with its slender hook-tipped bill and long S-curved neck, was created for deeper diving than most birds. To reach such depths and sink their buoyant bodies, cormorants are equipped with solid bones and non-water-resistant feathers. After a morning of fishing they always needed some drying out.

The cedar-root lashing swelled in the water and held our barbs tight, while the abalone lures enticed many fish to bite our favourite style of hook.

"No worries, Micah. We'll get a fish," I kept saying. "When we truly need one, it'll jump right into the boat." Finally, one did.

Just as we were pulling in our cedar lines to give up, Micah spotted a female greenling following his hook to the surface. He jerked the line, hoping to set the hook in the fish, but it didn't work. Instead, she must have bitten onto the very end of the wood, for out of the water flew a wriggling fish, free of hook and line, which landed in the bottom of our boat with a loud slap. Our jaws dropped open.

After our greenling gift we had little trouble feeding ourselves with fresh fish on bone hooks. We finally determined that the best type of primitive hook was a small J-style hook carved out of yew wood with a single bone barb lashed to the side. We baited the hook with a cockle clam cut to look like a squid, and tied on a dangling, oval-shaped abalone shell for a flashing lure above.

Unfortunately, our primitive longlining did not produce the same results as jigging. We had to leave the hook in the water much longer than would have been necessary in the past, and a wooden hook, no matter how much tallow or beeswax is rubbed into it, will bend back open and release the fish. We tried to solve the problem but ran out of time.

We spent the last days of solitude spearfishing perch, searching for rock crabs, gazing at fishing eagles, and making clay pottery that we fired in an outdoor cooking pit.

🌿

With the arrival of summer tourists at Booker Lagoon, we had an opportunity to share our food. That, of course, was only when we found someone courageous enough to try it. We wanted to honestly know if our menu items were as tasty as we thought they were. The Wakeman Sound Seaweed Soup we had raved about wasn't so delicious when we weren't starving, and we worried all our gourmet meals might disappoint us when we returned to supermarkets. We had to learn the truth.

One night we rowed over to a nearby yacht to see if the inhabitants would like to sample our leftover dinner.

"Hello there," I called from the rowboat. "We have so much leftover fish head soup. We were wondering if you would like to try some."

Strange looks appeared on the couple's faces, as if we were asking them to suck the goop out of fish eyeballs. "Oh no, thank you, we've already eaten."

Rowing away, we burst out laughing. I said, "Wow, I bet the words 'fish head soup' sounded good. What was I thinking? We have to get our looks and wording down."

One woman didn't even come out of her boat; she just locked the doors and closed the blinds.

Eventually we became better at convincing people to give our food a try and found willing test subjects. To our delight, most people genuinely enjoyed the taste of our favourite menu items. All but the smoked clams.

❦

The hot days of blood-cracked lips and squinting eyes arrived. I started calling Micah "Snapper," as his fair skin turned crimson red from the burning reflections off the water. The wicked winds of the winter had changed faces. The mellower westerlies beckoned us to embark on another long boat trip, so we headed to Blackfish Sound.

In his book *Full Moon, Flood Tide*, Billy Proctor wrote, "The rowboat trollers started up around 1900 and the last one to come to Blackfish Sound was in 1944. I got my start as a rowboat troller in 1943 and I was the last one to fish in Blackfish Sound with a rowboat, as I moved to a power boat in 1948."

Like the rowboat trollers before us, we headed to Flower Island, still a hotspot for the red-fleshed sockeye, feisty coho, plentiful pink, and the Cadillac of all salmon, the spring.

This salmon migratory route also attracted whales. I desperately wanted a close encounter with an orca (which in the early days were known as "blackfish"). Several decades ago it would take more than an hour for the whales to pass by a single point of land, they were so abundant. When these huge pods travelled by Flower Island, they stretched from one side of the sound to the other. Though it's not like that anymore, Blackfish Sound is still a summer destination for whale-watchers along what is now known as the Orca Highway.

The first time I saw whales in the sound, we were the only boat. Bobbing on the still waters, I saw tall plumes of mist in the distance, and shiny black dorsal fins of all sizes. About 35 whales were coming our way.

When multiple families of orcas get together for social reunions, the gathering is called a super pod. It's a rare sight, and as this super pod funnelled past us, we saw giant males with six-foot-tall dorsal fins, young whales, mothers, and three tiny newborns, distinguishable by the grey saddle patches on their backs.

"*Gilakas'la, max̱'inux̱!*" I called out. "Hello, orca whales."

They talked back. We could hear their high-pitched voices and squeals all around the boat. Even their rhythmic breaths sounded like songs. I sat spellbound.

I didn't think I could feel more blessed until a mama orca brought her newborn right beside the boat. I could have reached down and touched them when they surfaced beside me. Their misty breath tickled my face. I saw the soft look in Mama's eye as she turned slightly to nudge her baby, proudly showing her off. I reached out my hand, then paused. I didn't want to spoil this magical moment of trust. I refrained from touching their glistening backs, rippling just under the surface of the water.

After swimming by us, the super pod fanned out again across the sound. Their voices drifted away until only small puffs of breath could be heard in the distance. I felt like I had just woken from a wonderful dream.

Though orcas usually receive most of the attention in the world of charismatic megafauna, I loved to watch the mighty humpbacks even more. As they travelled in Blackfish Sound, these gentle giants dove near our little boat often, usually diving deep on their third or fourth breath. We counted, then held our breath in anticipation as their gigantic tails appeared in slow motion out of the water. The distinctive markings on their flukes flashed in the sun, while rivulets of sparkling water dripped from the tail tips.

We celebrated midsummer's day with _Gwa'yam_ (*gwah-yum*), the humpback. Watching a 40-tonne whale the size of a bus leap completely out of the water before cannonballing back in is extraordinary. One particular whale heard my midsummer wish and breached fully out of the water beside us.

Humpbacks are baleen whales, filtering small plankton and krill from the water, so they swim in circles, blowing nets of bubbles to frighten and corral small schools of fish before scooping up the entire school in an exciting display of lunge-feeding at the water's surface.

We were all searching for fish. One day a large baleen minke (*mink-ee*) whale surfaced right beside the boat to feed on a small school of herring. Other balls of herring were forming in the sound thanks to the rhinoceros auklets who had rounded them up. We decided to join in and frantically rowed toward the boiling mass of water, entering the eye of the feeding frenzy as a squawking flurry of rhinoceros auklets, seagulls, and eagles plunged into the swirling, shiny

Twining hundreds of feet of cedar rope for our dip net finally paid off months later when I dipped up our first ball of herring.

ball of corralled fish. Hundreds of birds lifted off or dove under the water to move out of our way as our homemade dipnet swooped over the side of the boat. It pulled up full of sparkling, wriggling bodies. The cedar handle bowed with the weight. We had more herring than we wanted to eat.

Micah and I had come to the straits to catch salmon, so we took our place in the lineup of trolling boats along the renowned fishing shores of Swanson Island. We sat amongst the motorboats and high-tech gear with our woven sun hats, rowing and dragging cedar-bark rope behind our boat. Some folks trolled over to offer us fish that they assumed we desperately needed, while others stopped to give advice, wave, or simply stare.

"Hey, where's your boat?" a sailor yelled out.

"This is it."

A look of disbelief came over his face. "You're kidding, right?"

We laughed. "Nope, this is it!"

He turned to his wife and pointed at us as they sailed on by.

We both had to row to keep up a proper trolling speed, so we wrapped the ends of our line around our feet to feel the tug of a fish. A hundred-foot line of quarter-inch cedar rope that dragged a primitive bone hook and an abalone shell flasher was attached to my foot. Spun around Micah's was another length of rope dragging a hand-pounded, shiny spoon Billy Proctor had made for us—what he used to use when he was a rowboat troller. I felt like I was living in a black-and-white photograph.

With cheers and pointing fingers from fellow fishermen, we finally caught our first pink salmon, landing it in our cedar-bark dipnet.

Of all the creatures on the coast, none were more revered by the Kwakwaka'wakw people than the life-giving salmon. I felt an intrinsic connection to the beautiful sparkling fish known as "Swimmer."

After rowing to the nearest islet to clean the salmon and gather fresh onions, we scooped up Scout, hopped back into *Gribley*, covered the fish with kelp fronds to keep it cool, and set off for the familiar beach of Village Island, estimating we would reach it before twilight. We wanted to celebrate the first salmon of the season back where it all began.

Arriving at Village Island felt like coming home. When *Gribley* softly crunched ashore, Scout leapt off the bow and ran for cover in the blackberry thickets at the edge of the white-shell beach. It had been over a year. I wandered, touching familiar trees, bending back bushes to nibble on sweet salad greens, and resting beside my cherished wolf totem pole. We honoured our pink salmon, *hạnu'n (hah-noon)*. I placed it on a woven cedar mat, cutting it with both a flint-knapped obsidian blade and a sharpened slate knife that I had sanded and shafted onto yellow cedar handles.

I pulled the thin stem of a horseweed plant from my leather fire-kit pouch. The dry summer weather eased the creation of a hand-drill fire. I loved spinning the pithy stem between my hands until smoke billowed from the fireboard and a teeny coal glowed in the fine dust. It felt like I was twirling a hand-clasped prayer in motion. I blew on the tender spark of fire in my hands. *Swoosh*. The soft, shredded cedar bundle burst into flame.

Micah carved the *tlupsa'yu (gloop-sigh-you)*, or barbecue stick, and we cooked the salmon in the traditional way of the people of 'Mim'kwạmlis. We waited until the dripping fat turned into caramelized icicles that hung from the skin. The fish's tender flesh flaked off the primitive barbecue rack and melted in our mouths.

For dessert we roasted the tail on a stick until it was black and crispy. If I had eaten blackened mice, I could try anything.

I couldn't believe it. The fin was delicious. It tasted just like bacon. Micah fried up the salmon eggs, but were they ever disgusting. He claimed it would be just like eating scrambled eggs, but it wasn't. We obviously were not dining on bacon and eggs just yet.

After the feast I gathered all the bones together and placed them on the cedar mat with a single downy eagle feather. According to coastal tradition, the first salmon was honoured with a sacred ceremony. I walked down to the ocean shore and set the mat adrift with my prayers and gratitude. I wanted to honour the ancestors of the land and give thanks for all the lessons their skills had taught me. As I sat watching the mat drift off, I was once again reminded why ancient wisdom matters today.

The ancients believed that if salmon bones were not returned to the sea, the fish would return the following year with missing parts or would perhaps not return at all. The salmon are now on the verge of disappearing from the Broughton Archipelago, perhaps because we have failed to follow the ancestors' wisdom. It's not the act of returning the bones that will bring back the salmon. It's the respect and connection that comes with that act. If we hadn't lost our deep connection to the natural world, each of us would be able to make a difference as the voice for our wild world.

I watched the bones float away until twilight, when the darkening ocean and the mat vanished at their moment of unity.

We crawled into our sleeping bags next to the fire and stared up at the twinkling sky. That evening the old ways were not forgotten. My thoughts drifted back to the first time I had visited the ancient village. I had sat by the fallen totem with the young eagle as I told the ancestors my intentions. This night, I thanked them for all the teachings they had blessed me with on my adventure.

I spotted Aquila, the celestial eagle, mirroring my thoughts.

Scout nudged my face. I lifted up a corner of the covers and she crawled in to curl up beside me. I couldn't sleep. I watched shooting stars streak across the black sky until I couldn't hold my eyes open any longer. I must have made 25 wishes that night.

STALKING GRIZZLIES

Far away to the north and south the ends of the rainbows touch the sea. Four rainbow ends and no pots of gold, but treasure is mine nonetheless. Perhaps until now I have always looked for the wrong kind of coin.
                    —Steven Callahan, shipwreck survivor—76 days at sea

The day had come. We had to pack up our little cabin and say goodbye to the Broughton Archipelago. I felt unnerved, knowing I would soon return to my civilized home, a world I had lost touch with and could no longer relate to.

The days sped by in the last few weeks. I visited all of my favourite places one last time, shedding tears in each. These places had become like my childhood keepsakes: the ragged teddy bear. My first puppy's collar. The blue ribbon I won at my first horse show. A part of me refused to leave.

Day 543
I am sitting on my island for probably the last time. I remember watching the otter family for the first time, a bear that turned out to be a rock, the dolphins swimming in the distance, and all the other cherished moments I have had. I will miss leaning up against this tree, nibbling onions amongst the strawberry plants, listening to the long whistles of the thrushes, never having to worry if I need to get home or if I am going to be late for an appointment. A squirrel has just come by to eat on a nearby branch. I see the bunchberries are bright orange and ready to eat. Better go and enjoy them one last time and explore what still lies hidden, for I know there is always something.

We didn't want to end our journey with sad hearts for the place and lifestyle we had come to love, so we decided instead to celebrate the success of survival with the returning salmon. We chose the wildest place we knew: Bond Sound, home of the Ahta River, or Hada, as the Kwakwaka'wakw know it.

Bond Sound is the last pristine watershed left in the Broughton Archipelago, home to three animals we dearly wanted to see. Along the banks of the Ahta River, and in the untouched old-growth forest beside it, we hoped to spy on grizzlies, swim with salmon, and track the endangered wolverine, phantom of the wilderness.

Bond Sound is a survivor. It beat the odds. I prayed it would always stay wild and free. I hoped I would too.

We pinned our usual note to the outside of the cabin.

We are summer camping. Please do not take anything. This is all we are living with. If you need something please try to replace anything you take. Thank you.

When *Gribley* was packed up, Scout hopped in all by herself.

The weather smiled for us, the salmon bit our hooks, and after another excruciating back-aching, butt-blistering row, Bond Sound was in our sights. I had a feeling Ahta River was exactly the place I needed to visit.

What follows are my last ten days in the wild, just as I experienced them.

Day 1: Bond Sound

So here I sit, with an eagle feather dip-pen in hand, to journal our last big adventure. I feel like I am in the tropics. It must be the hottest day of the summer…

We found a beautiful little camp spot on a small island in the middle of the estuary. It looked like a safe space to sleep in grizzly country, until we realized any animal could easily walk ashore during low tide. It's a popular place. We found a bear-scratched tree, wolf scat, dinner leftovers from a mink, and the feather remnants of a seagull and a sharp-shinned hawk, all within 20 feet of our campsite. I think we might be sleeping in a cougar's lair too. There's a cougar scratching post and a perfect cat lounge beside our beds. Bond Sound is a tracker's dream vacation.

A nice sandy beach lay next to a small rocky outcrop, providing a perfect vantage point for both the sound and estuary. Scout hid in the tall grass beside us, amongst the purple-flowering asters. My skin pricked as if electrified, and I felt a flow of energy vibrating through my chest. We had found our utopia.

We just sat and watched an osprey family fishing at the head of the river. It was quite a welcoming. The youngsters sure didn't look as skilled as their parents yet, but they were practising their hovering, diving, and plunging techniques in between their loud begging calls from the trees beside us.

Day 2: The River

We survived the night sleeping in a cougar's lair. Biting insects harassed us instead! It feels like I'm living in a perfect dream, waking up to the sounds of cooing band-tailed pigeons and walking barefoot.

While eating breakfast biscuits with bear butter, we watched a pair of transient killer whales enter the sound.

Four distinct groups of orcas live off the coast of British Columbia: the southern residents, northern residents, offshore orcas, and transient killer whales. The pods of transient orcas are the wolves of the sea and feed primarily on seals, sea lions, porpoises, and other whales. This pair's sharklike dorsal fins sliced through the water toward us. They took nine breaths to reach the head of the sound, which is several miles long, then passed in front of the island and disappeared. We thought they might have stopped to rest in a small bay, so we rowed over to take a peek, hoping we wouldn't become brunch for a couple of hungry transient orcas. They were nowhere in sight. They had somehow held their breath all the way down Bond Sound and into Tribune Channel.

There are two major river systems in Bond Sound: the Ahta Valley River, which has been logged, and the Ahta River, which is still surrounded by an old-growth forest. The rivers are separated by a grassy estuary, several hundred feet long, that is filled with mint and flowers.

The Ahta Valley River meanders through grassy sedge flats adorned with the maroon seed heads of western dock plants, white-domed yarrow, and blooming purple asters. Micah paddled along the shores while I lounged in the back of the rowboat as if on a private gondola ride in Venice, smiling at the flittering butterflies that danced among the swaying flowers. The hot sun toasted me under my new cedar-brimmed sunhat.

We paddled over to the Ahta River, where we spotted the returning pink salmon swimming under our boat. The *hanu'n* had made it home. We slowly rowed up the cobblestone river as far as we could, under the canopy of moss-draped trees, passing riverbanks filled with flowering lilies of the valley and sandy shores pockmarked with bear tracks. The air smelled fresh.

We decided we couldn't do any fishing in such a place. These fish are the best of the best. They have returned to their natal stream after travelling thousands and thousands of miles. They have survived the perils of their lives and I think they deserve to spawn unharmed, for future generations. It's an awesome sight to see. One jumped right beside the boat as we left. I think I was just as happy to see them as they were for making it home. I feel I'm home too. We both made it.

Once salmon reach their spawning grounds, they stop eating altogether and live off their own flesh until the time and conditions are perfect for each pair to lay and fertilize their eggs. They need all the energy they have left to fulfill the miraculous cycle of their life before their bodies literally fall apart and die.

Day 3: The Drop Zone

I stopped worrying about sleeping in a cougar's hideout the morning I met the resident squirrel. A green spruce cone plummeted from 90 feet above.

Startled out of a peaceful sleep, I popped out of bed to find a Douglas squirrel scratching amongst the leaf litter by my head. I spooked him as much as he did me, as he darted up the side of the cougar's scratching post. He sat on a low branch with his tail flicking behind him, scolding me with his sharp, ear-piercing alarm call. After a couple of minutes of constant yelling, he ran up the tree out of sight, proceeding to pelt us with fresh spruce cones. With the first painful thud to the thigh, I yelled out, "Incoming!" Micah used the "cover up and hope for the best" tactic. I chose the "I'd rather see it coming" tactic, while Scout took the "I'm climbing up and taking him out" route. After ten minutes of dodging cone bombs, the one-sided war ended as the squirrel scurried off to continue his busy day of harvesting.

We sat in a fog bank most of the morning, tightly wrapped in a world of greys, silvers, and blues, listening to the soft breathing *pfoofs* of harbour porpoises nearby. After the fog melted we set off for the blueberry-covered alpine meadows above. I wanted to give thanks in a special place for all I had experienced and secretly hoped I would discover something else I needed to learn. Sitting on top of a mountain seemed like the perfect spot to share my gratitude with the earth and receive divine messages from the heavens.

We hid *Gribley* in the bushes along the Ahta River and followed ancient bear trails, nibbling purple salal berries and colossal red and blue huckleberries as we went.

> *I saw the most beautiful grizzly tracks today. The forest floor was thick with bright green sphagnum and step moss. Through it, we could see the perfect walking pattern of a grizzly bear. The trail had obviously been used over and over as each footprint was worn all the way down to the dirt. Walking in those tracks somehow made me feel like a big old grizzly bear myself. The fairy tale trail quickly turned into a torturous haunted forest of tangly berry thickets and thick salal jungle.*

Drops of sweat poured off my forehead when we finally burst through the brush and found ourselves at the top of a gorgeous waterfall surrounded by mighty boulders covered in lush moss. We had assumed the forest would open once we reached the old-growth trees, but it never did. Gigantic trees surrounded us, but the underbrush below was unrelenting. We could barely get close to the big trees in the head-high berry thicket. Our slow bushwhacking drained our cheery spirits. Exasperated, we took to the slippery rocks by the river's edge.

Underneath the thick forest canopy we didn't notice the change in weather, but when we reached the river, dark foreboding clouds filled the sky. I was determined not to feel a raindrop during our last week. Soon we came to a beautiful swimming hole at the base of a small waterfall. Ten minutes into our skinny dip, I felt a depressing drop of rain on my nose. In seconds I was standing under nature's showerhead.

We rushed under the cover of a gigantic cedar log near the river's edge and hunkered down, waiting for the rain to ease. It didn't. Scout was not impressed. Neither was I.

Day 4: Am I in Native Anchorage?

We sat in front of a smoky fire all day, trying to dry out our sopping wet sleeping bags and clothes, marvelling at the dusky grey dipper birds that bobbed up and down along the riverbed, gleaning insects from the rocks. Dippers love river rapids. We watched them wading along the shores, plunging into the frothy white-water, flying and walking under the clear water against the current. As I watched them navigate the rushing river I could barely walk across, it made me wonder why I was fighting my way up to the top of a mountain.

Stranded under a dripping log, squished between a jumble of rocks that jutted through hard-packed sand, I suddenly knew nature was doing her best to get me to stop, listen, and become more aware of the choices I had been making and the life lessons she was trying to teach me.

What could I possibly still be searching for? I asked myself. What do I think I will find up in the alpine that I can't find down below?

The dipper bird had perfected the art of flowing with the path of no resistance, while I was forcing myself to achieve a goal I finally realized wasn't necessary. The universe heard my thoughts wherever I was. I didn't need to climb a mountain to become closer to the earth or the divine. I had a feeling the universe and all its knowing was inside me all along and my fighting to find it was only pushing me farther away from the truth. I felt the contrast between my plans and nature's message more acutely than usual.

The dipper bird taught me about contentment. When I was truly content in myself, my heart ceased its painful longing to dwell somewhere other than where I was. I hoped returning to the rush of modern life would not cause me to forget all I had learned from my wilderness quest.

Scout jumped off my lap, jolting me from my thoughts. I noticed a tiny mountain ash, ripe with berries, across the river. I remembered the sound of its voice asking me long ago, "Do you know my name?" We had come full circle together and I now knew who I was. The whispering tree had greeted me upon my arrival in Native Anchorage, and it was now bidding me farewell in Bond Sound. Or perhaps it was beckoning me to stay.

Day 5: Rain on the River

It was another wet and cold night. All the goose down in my sleeping bag has balled up into a lumpy wet mess, so instead I slept in only two layers of nylon. At least I have Scout; she is a great heating pad, at least for my neck.

The rain finally eased. Micah and I realized we didn't need to climb to the alpine meadows. We knew life's beauty no matter where we were.

I turned to Micah. "I would rather wade down the middle of this river than hike back the way we came."

"I fully agree."

Off we trudged down the river.

The sky flooded us with pelting rain five minutes into the hike. The drops were the size of blueberries. The sound was deafening. It ignited misery in both my cat and my survival companion. Scout would not stop crying, while Micah uncharacteristically started grumbling about the river being shitty and the forest being crappy.

It was time to tease. We started laughing again, and the perilous hike developed into something we were forced to love.

Scout did not find humour in any of it. She gave up following us like a dog after our third river crossing, disappearing into the rocks. No amount of coaxing would bring her out. Micah belly-crawled into the small cave, but all he could reach was her tail.

Out came a muddy, skinny, frazzled cat. She looked like she had just come out of a bathtub. I had to carry her the rest of the day as she yowled and squirmed in my arms, clawing for my head as I balanced precariously upon the algae-covered rocks in waist-deep pools, struggling against the raging current.

Our route along the river eventually became too hazardous to continue. We opted to scramble up the steep, boulder-strewn bank, climbing into serious bear country. We were in no position to fight off a perturbed or hungry grizzly, so our little companion had to stop crying. I held her mouth shut a couple of times and she finally gave in and accepted her pitiful state, riding quietly on top of my backpack, grooming herself all the way down the mountain.

When we reached the familiar banks of the estuary, we found ourselves on the wrong side of the river at high tide. We would have to swim across to our boat. Though we both had dreamed of swimming with salmon, that dream hadn't involved wearing rain gear, shoes, and backpacks, not to mention carrying a kitty on our heads.

Just as we stepped into the river, the sun beamed through the clouds. Steam rose off the wet plants as millions of crystal droplets sparkled. In that moment of Ahta magic, a small school of pink salmon swam by our legs. I knew I was meant to find myself standing in that moment of grace.

I passed Scout over to Micah. We hoped his height might save him from having to swim across the channel. He sank up to his chest, with Scout perched high above his head, sitting on his backpack and contentedly wiping her face with her paw.

I took a deep breath and slowly exhaled as I waded into the river. I gasped when the water level reached my chest. I knew my next step would plunge me under, so I cinched up my backpack and kicked out my feet so I was floating. The weight of my clothes pulled me down, but it took only a few floundering frog kicks with my legs to reach bottom again.

When I reached the sandy bank, Scout climbed aboard my backpack. We sized up the next channel. Like a mirage, a boat of fly fishermen came into view at the river's mouth. We turned to each other to confirm that we both saw it.

Before I had left, my dear friend Jeanne taught me a skill I'd always wanted to learn: how to whistle like a guy at a football game. I remembered standing in front of a mirror, learning how to shape my mouth and position my fingers. She told me, "You never know when you'll need a loud whistle." She was right. I needed one now.

Tired of hiking down a raging river in a torrential downpour, my kitty opted to ride on the top of my backpack.

With our thumbs up like hitchhikers, waist deep in the river, I formed a circle with my thumb and middle finger, curled back my tongue, and, with lips tight around the tips of my fingers, I let out a piercing *Shee-ah-shweet*!

My whistling lessons had paid off. One of the fly fishermen pointed our way.

When they pulled up beside us, the looks on their faces were priceless. Water ran out of my sleeves as I reached up to pull Scout off my backpack and sloshed to their boat to lift her aboard. She clawed her way over the side of the boat as the fishermen shook their heads.

We couldn't believe our good luck, while they couldn't believe our story. They dropped us off at our rowboat, which, due to the extreme high tide, was only accessible by wading through knee-deep water.

When we emerged from the bush with *Gribley*, we heard an unfamiliar voice. "Are you Nikki and Micah?"

We turned around to find two kayakers paddling toward us. In a state of disbelief we just stood there, dripping from head to foot.

In unison we replied, "Yup."

News of a young couple with a kitty-cat rowing around the Broughtons had travelled from boat to boat that summer.

The female kayaker pulled out her camera. "Do you mind if we take your picture?"

We laughed. "Of course not. Go right ahead."

Many months later we received the photo addressed:

To the kids rowing around with a cat
Echo Bay, B.C.

Once back at our little island, we stripped naked and hung ourselves out to dry alongside our clothes.

Day 6: The Grass Flats

The tall, flowing grass flats are beautiful. They are full of blooming yarrow, purple aster, field mint, plantain, silverweed, crab apple, dogwood, and a variety of blue-green grasses that I am going to harvest for basketry material. Some seagulls showed up on the rocks while we ventured off for a while and pooped on my pants and T-shirt drying in the sun. They'll be wet another day.

The sky's golden orb caused a severe case of laziness. We lounged all day in its hot rays like basking sea lions and spotted a rarely seen elephant seal bobbing in the water like an old stump.

Day 7: Grizzly Bears

We woke up at dawn's twilight so we could stalk the grizzlies today. I can't believe I had to sleep in Micah's smelly sleeping bag again. It somehow felt like I was sleeping in his underwear! I hope my bag is dry today, even though it isn't looking that appealing anymore either.

We picked our way across the mouth of the Ahta Valley River, rock by rock, until we reached the dewy, grassy estuary. We quietly parted the tall blades of grass, inhaling the refreshing scent of wild field mint as we tiptoed toward the sandy river flats. We spotted grizzly tracks and hurried to find a safe place to hide as the sun's first rays peeked over the mountaintops. The grizzlies would be up for breakfast.

We settled into our hiding spot. The edge of my field of view was filled with detailed shapes and shadows of leaves and needles. Sunlight dappled the forest. Spray from a nearby logjam sparkled in the distance. The river spit and gurgled while I sat waiting for grizzlies.

I had no idea what I should do if a thousand-pound bear walked up and sniffed my shoe dangling three feet above the ground. I shuddered with excitement. Every animal that had stopped to sniff me before had never shown any aggression as long as I stayed perfectly still and unafraid. I would treat the grizzly bear just as I would a squirrel. I let go of my rational mind's scenarios and drifted into a place of timelessness.

The minute my wanting thoughts stopped and I embraced the contentment that Bond Sound was offering to teach me, I caught a movement out of the corner of my eye. *Gala* (*gay-lah*), the grizzly bear, walked onto the river bar.

She was a long-legged young bear with a tawny golden coat. We guessed her age at about three or four years. She stopped at the edge of the riverbank to sniff the air, looking up and down the river, but never knew we were there. She wandered up the sandy bar a few more paces, urinated, and then crossed over to shallower water.

The bear, Micah, and I all noticed the salmon leap from the water in the deep pool beside her. Without hesitation she quickly turned in its direction, jumping up and down in one spot with her front paws in excitement, trying to spook the salmon. When her attempts failed she continued on her way, sauntering up the riverbank out of sight, her wet coat sparkling in the sun.

After a quick shift in position when the bear was long out of sight, we tried relaxing into another long wait.

It's tough sitting still in a tree stump with a guy who fidgets all the time. I have no idea how many times I turned slowly around with a confused look on my face, silently saying, What are you doing making noise? Are you crazy or something? We're sitting waiting for grizzly bears, remember?

Then a smile would slowly creep upon our faces, trying not to giggle in disbelief. A few minutes later he would start stripping bark off a broken twig, fidget with a leaf, or tap his fingers.

Being still is about melting into your surroundings. It's not vacuous staring. That creates boredom. It's about shifting from a mundane mindset to one of wonderment. Enjoyable stillness comes from expanding one's awareness and finding excitement and interest in even the smallest happenings.

I watched a kingfisher catch a small fish below us and then fly up to a branch beside me to eat it. I watched salmon swimming in the deeper pools and relished the rays of sun that occasionally reached parts of my body. I patiently waited for big brown bears.

Out of the bushes one stepped. The same young bear had reappeared, ambling down the river toward us. My heart raced, not from fear, but from exhilaration. She walked within ten steps of us and climbed onto a small log that jutted over a deep pool. I could see her every detail: the individual hairs clumped together from splashing in the river; her shiny, damp, twitching nose; her fuzzy amber ears.

She raised her head, stretched her neck, and wriggled her nose to absorb the faint scents dancing in the breeze. The light wind whispered a message only her nose could understand. I had developed a finely tuned nose by human standards, but as I took a deep slow breath and wiggled my nose like she did, I knew that I would never experience the world she could.

Bears have an incredible sense of smell. With the right wind they can smell a human coming over a mile away and have been known to smell rotting carrion ten miles away. Though she never saw us, she smelled humans and slowly retreated back into the forest. I hoped she would never get accustomed to the smell of a human. Though Billy Proctor and others in the Echo Bay community had saved the forest from logging, the Ahta Valley was still open for trophy hunting, and soon hunters would be coming for their prized hides.

While we were thrilled by our encounter with the golden bear, our precise dream was to see a monstrously big bear. Judging by the size of the tracks we had seen, the Ahta River had some big boys fishing along its banks. We wanted the *National Geographic* experience. We wanted to see a big grizzly fishing in the river, and we wanted him to walk within 20 steps of us. Humans can be greedy.

We waited. And he came.

A big, round grizzly bear stepped onto the river bar and lumbered toward us. We didn't dare move for fear of spooking him.

Then, to interrupt our blissful dream, a series of "Hello bears, hello bears" came echoing loudly through the peaceful forest. A human was coming, a man afraid of grizzlies.

When he came within whispering distance of our stump, I put a finger to my lips and whispered, "Shh, please. We're trying to see bears."

The man nearly jumped out of his skin. We motioned him to come over, invited him into our hiding spot, and rearranged our positions to make room for him on another root. He climbed in and sat for a couple of uncomfortable, antsy minutes.

The peaceful energy of the place was gone.

Within a couple of minutes he asked us if we wanted to follow him to a spawning pool to count salmon. We climbed out of our hiding spot and followed him up the riverbank.

We came to the top of a mossy outcrop surrounded by huckleberry bushes that overlooked a small pool about ten feet below. A thousand salmon milled about in the dormant section of the river. Big purple striped chum and hump-backed pinks fanned their powerful tails to face upstream.

We stood in silent awe at the picturesque scene until the sounds of heavy-footed humans jolted us. The fly-fishing company we had hitched a ride with two days earlier was bringing new guests. I didn't know what to say or how to feel the moment I saw them trudging over bear tracks in hip-waders, carrying rods on their shoulders and coolers in their hands.

"Hey, do you mind if we fish here?" the guide asked us.

I joked, "If I said yes, would you not?"

I guess it wasn't an appropriate joke at the time. The man who had brought us to the spawning pool was not as open to fishing as we were. He said, in a rather harsh tone, "The fish do."

Micah and I slumped.

Though I may not have agreed with fishing the salmon the way they were, I didn't feel that ruining the fishing group's experience by barking statistics or shouting my personal views of catch-and-release fishing would change their methods or values. Perhaps they were also living their dreams.

When the fishers returned to their boat, we greeted them, hoping we hadn't offended them earlier. They invited us aboard for lunch. We could hardly contain our excitement when we saw the food being served. We scarfed down a plateful of potato salad and fruit, four chocolate bars, two cans of pop, and four homemade chocolate-chip cookies. Then we traded a bone salmon hook for a package of smoked salmon and two oranges.

A fisherman examined it. "When I look at that hook, I know you are *real* fishermen."

They asked us why we didn't fish the river, since we were the ones surviving off the land.

"I don't feel right about it," I responded. "I don't really know the impact I may be causing. I can't be sure hooking these fish and releasing them is not hurting them, not affecting the fate of their future. I see these fish as the best of the best, and I think they deserve to spawn in peace."

A client said, "When I caught my first fish I felt so small." She told us we were an inspiration to her.

We were glad to share the things we had learned with others. Teaching, to me, is not about infringing on others' beliefs but about being aware enough to know what is right to say in the moment.

The next afternoon we noticed the guide didn't bring his fishing rod when he accompanied his new guests to the river. We asked him why.

"Well, I thought about what you said and maybe you're right," he said. "Maybe we are hurting them. I don't know either."

Day 8: The Last Wish

We woke before dawn. We wanted to get to the salmon pool before the bears. Stalking through the brush during the twilight hours of morning created mixed feelings of apprehension, eager anticipation, and paranoia. Luckily we never bumped into a grizzly in the dark.

We squished together on our bellies along the bank of the salmon pool and waited. We waited and waited. Hours later I finally whispered to Micah, "Dude, I'm losing it." His look told me he felt the same. That's when I saw the big guy coming up the river. I nudged Micah to slowly look in my direction.

The bear was a giant. He clambered up onto a log that stretched across the river. He scooped his gigantic paw into the water, trying to snag a salmon. The dark chocolate grizzly walked back and forth along the log, scoping out his situation. He eventually gave up and walked out onto the gravel bar.

He was magnificent.

He stopped ten paces away to examine the fish huddled together in the safest, deepest part of the pool. He didn't plunge in. Instead, he continued to lumber up the river. When he reached a smaller pool of fish he jumped in, bounding and splashing in the sparkling shallow water. His massive body leapt up and down as he chased the darting fish back and forth. Unsuccessful in his attempts, he sauntered out of the water, gave a big shake, climbed the bank, and disappeared into the vibrant green forest. I took my first deep breath in hours. My wish had unfolded exactly as I envisioned it.

We shook too, massaging our cramped and tingling limbs. We snacked on plump huckleberries while walking to the river bar to track. I called Micah over to check out what I first thought was a bear cub's footprint.

"What do you think this is?"

He knelt down for a better look and said, "It can't be. Is it?"

We had nearly forgotten our last wish. Luckily the Ahta had not.

Nay-gley, the wolverine, had walked by early in the morning. Without stopping, he turned his head sharply to the left when a salmon splashed in the river beside him and then continued his slow walk up the river bank. The most elusive animal of the forest had left its story in the sand. I blinked back a tear.

Today I feel that the world is as it should be.

Day 9: Peace for the Ahta

Today we woke ready to see the river again. I felt like I had to sit and make up new dreams before I left. Everything I wanted to experience had come to pass. In that moment of realization, I decided to let the Ahta have a day of peace without humans.

I rowed over to a small woodland stream to collect our drinking water. I parted the dogwood and cedars along the shore and hiked a short distance upstream to a small, clear pool. As I knelt down on its bank and cupped my hands to drink the golden water I had come to prefer, I knew I would miss it all. Somehow the vision of turning on a tap held no excitement for me anymore. I loved splashing cool, sweet-smelling stream water on my face and looking up to see the forest around me.

This. This was living. This was real. Maybe I will always need this life because I now know what I had once forgotten.

Day 10: Rowing Home

The last day of this adventure is really here. I'm not sure if I am rowing back to what feels like home or to what is only my family. Home seems to be under this cougar-scratched cedar tree in Bond Sound. The flocks of V-shaped honkers are flying south again. It's time for me to fly home too.

We each must seek what is sacred and meaningful to us. And when we find this thing we are compelled to do, we must live it to its fullest, never knowing where it will lead us.

On our final day listening to the familiar, rhythmic sounds of our oars, we travelled with a full, arching rainbow behind us.

It was September 1, 2005. The two peaks of prophetic Thunderbird Mountain peered over the low-lying islands behind us. I remembered Tom Sewid explaining the mountain's prophecy 19 months earlier, on our first water-taxi ride: "You will have a tough time ahead, with many hardships, but it will be successful." The mountain's prediction had come true.

We spent our last wild night rowing by the light of a bright moon and slept on a tiny, unfamiliar island amongst a tangle of salal brush. The barred owl came to join us. I thought of Moonwalker, my barred owl friend at my first secret place.

I prayed I could live my truths in the world when I returned home.

When the breeze blew out my tiny candle, I finished writing my last sentence in the dark: "Well my candle is finished and so am I."

What's your dream?

RETURNING FROM EDEN

"In the moment that I strike you and smite you," the Friendly Soul replied, "in the moment that I do the worst to you that you could possible imagine—in that very moment..."
"Yes?" the Little Soul interrupted. "Yes...?"
"Remember Who I Really Am."

—Neale Donald Walsch, *The Little Soul and the Sun*

First night back to civilization. I'm lying on my mother's carpeted floor, next to the sliding glass door that I need to leave open for "fresh air." My feet ache from walking on concrete sidewalks and my eyes sting from the perfumes and harsh acrid smells of the city. My intestines hurt from all the strange food my body is dealing with and I have to light candles in the bathroom because I have yet to adjust to the bright, fluorescent lighting. I feel tired from all the noise and frenzy of movement that I can't help but notice. There was a time when I longed for an acute awareness and now I find myself needing to turn it down. I feel as if I am walking around in some kind of modern daze and I can't help but feel that I am no longer truly living. I've returned to the "real world," yet my heart says I've left it.

Richard Steele, writing about the famed survivor Alexander Selkirk (the model for Robinson Crusoe), noted, "The man frequently bewailed his return to the world, which could not, he said, with all its enjoyments, restore to him the tranquility of his solitude." That's how I felt too.

Adjusting to modern life was a painful, difficult process. I found it harder to survive in the modern world than in the world I had found at Booker Lagoon. I felt anxious simply watching the crowds of people buzzing around, trying to find purpose in the madness. I had forgotten the sensations of riding in a car, sitting on the Skytrain, and zipping up elevators.

Everything was overwhelming and exciting at the same time. I remember lining up in a Subway restaurant, utterly bewildered by the menu. I stood dumbfounded at the counter, my mind unable to discern what I wanted or the proper procedure for getting it. My senses took in everything at once, overloading my system.

One of the first things I wanted to do was go to the movies. As I stood in the aisle, trying to decide where to sit, I immediately realized a movie-theatre experience should be eliminated from anyone's "Top 10 Things to Do When Reintegrating into City Life."

My senses nearly burst. I thought my ears were going to pop. I had to cover them with my hands to dampen the deafening sounds. I could hear every person chewing popcorn. I accidentally eavesdropped on whispered conversations. I had to look away from the screen every few minutes to rest my eyes from the brightness and flashing movements. I don't even remember the name of the movie. When I walked back to the car, my friend had to pull me to safety as I stepped off the curb into oncoming traffic, oblivious to pedestrian protocols that were once engrained in my psyche.

I then went grocery shopping. Walking through the automatic doors of a supermarket was like visiting another planet. I wandered aimlessly up and down the aisles, flabbergasted by the variety of fancy food packages and the numerous choices available for a single product. After drifting around for ten minutes, I glanced at my shopping basket to discover it was still empty. I went to the produce section. Everything else looked too weird, too colourful, and too manufactured to eat.

I could pack a tremendous amount of modern food into my belly. I could eat a whole bag of cookies the moment I ripped open the package, but I never felt truly full or wholly satisfied after a meal, as I did with wild food. As well, city life revolved around eating—it was a form of entertainment. I felt bombarded by the socially accepted custom of stuffing my face, so I started eating all the time, even when I wasn't hungry. I gained nearly a pound a day when I first returned. Although city food was fun, I missed my stir-fries. In Booker Lagoon I had always called modern food "real food," but now I know it's not.

I felt rushed, even though I didn't have a busy schedule. I saw that modern living was designed for efficiency and speed. I knew what real peacefulness felt like, but it was hard to maintain that peace when I was living amidst the chaos and pulse of the city.

The novelty of pampering myself at a day spa, buying new clothes, wearing gem-studded jewellery, eating at my favourite Thai restaurant, ordering pizza, soaking in bubble baths with scented oils, and all the other big-city treats quickly wore off. Entertainment could be found at every corner, but I felt a strange boredom, as if something was missing. Television lulled me into a state of apathy, and I spent hours watching cartoons and survival reality shows. I no longer pondered or wandered. I missed sitting on a rock in the wilderness. I even missed my ritual of bathing with a pot, though that didn't stop me from having at least three showers a day upon my return. I even ate my breakfast in the shower. I washed my hands incessantly—I think that was because I stopped wiping them on my pants. I loved the feeling of hot water gushing from the tap and soapy suds in the dishwashing water. I began wasting an unbelievable amount of water.

I noticed my reflection everywhere. In mirrors, glass doors, and store windows. I saw how easy it was to become self-conscious of appearances, and I found it hard to be myself in a society where I was inundated by expectations of how to look, act, and live. I found myself immersed in a world that constantly argued against goodness and overwhelmed me with negativity. By becoming wild I was free to be me. Back in town, the heartbeat of the wilderness and my true self pulsed more and more dimly as the days went on.

Seventh Day in Town
The problem I struggle with today is now I know what it truly feels like to be free, to feel total contentment with my life. I know what happiness really is and I struggle to find it in mainstream society. I'm not exactly sure where I belong now. I haven't found the balance between the worlds for me just yet.

I see the world entirely differently now. When I drive or walk down the street, I'll catch myself spotting delicious patches of dandelion or eyeing the dock growing against cement walls. What were once desirable life goals feel like a waste of valuable time.

I recognize the price we pay for our modern lives. I now decide which conveniences are worth working for. The more we want, the longer and harder we have to work. Consequently, we have less time than ever to spend with our families and to pursue that which we passionately love. I lived a year and a half with nothing, and for the first time had everything.

🌿

At our going-away party, my mom told me that she didn't think I would be coming home. She was right. I didn't stay in town. Within three weeks I moved back to the Broughton.

I couldn't leave the place where I felt truly at home.

Roger, our friend who had helped us move to and from Booker Lagoon, offered me a job caretaking his fishing lodge in Blackfish Sound. For two years I looked after the property from the end of September to the beginning of May, accompanied only by Scout and Roger's cat Max. I had my own little cabin on the property. I brought out my books and a few other belongings I hadn't sold before my survival journey and moved in. Roger taught me how to fix just about everything that could possibly break down in a house powered by generators and 12-volt batteries. He brought out a whiteboard and scribbled diagrams on scrap pieces of paper to explain the workings of engines, capacitors, or electrical wiring.

"Nikki, if you're going to live out here, you have to know how to fix things," he told me. "You've got to take care of yourself, and I don't mean like surviving in Booker Lagoon."

He was right. Roger gave me the foundation and confidence to live in the bush with powerboats and modern amenities. I became Swanson Island's plumber, electrician, boat mechanic, and satellite technician.

❦

I am now living several other dreams with my dog, Cricket. I've finally finished building a log cabin in Echo Bay. While the walls went up I lived in a tiny shed next to a mountain ash in Billy Proctor's yard.

Billy has become the grandpa I've always wanted. He's taught me the skills of a hand logger, log salvager, and commercial fisherman. He's opened his home to me and continues to teach me new things every day.

I always say, "Hey Billy, I've been thinkin'…."

His big smile wrinkles his face as he shakes his head. "Oh boy." He's become my dearest friend.

"You're going to build something nice, aren't you?" Billy asked me when we walked my property boundary and stood staring out at a gorgeous panoramic view.

I laughed. "Of course, don't worry. It won't look like the Booker Lagoon shack." I didn't envision it looking as nice as it does, though. Most days I think it's too luxurious, even with the bearskin rug and primitive gear displayed. Becoming wild instilled in me a lack of attachment to possessions. I know I can leave it all behind, grab my knife, and set off for the real world.

I still cook on a woodstove, use the same cast-iron frying pan I did in Booker Lagoon, and harvest much of my food from the wild. However, I now preserve a lot of my food with a canner, use a washing machine to clean my clothes, and soak in divine showers every day, which are heated from my woodstove with coils of copper wound around the stove pipe. I still light my home mostly by candle-light, but I can turn on a lamp whenever I want—it runs off a 12-volt battery and is recharged by my four-kilowatt generator. I'm uptown in the wilds. I think I've finally found a balance between yesteryear and modern times.

I've even become a gardener and tour-guide operator. I started my own busi-ness, Echo Bay EcoVentures. I specialize in unique, custom-tailored adventures for all ages and fitness levels. It gives visitors a chance to experience the life of a coastal survivalist without the hardships, while learning the secrets of the natural world and visiting the hidden treasures of the Broughton Archipelago. It is my hope all who visit will return home with *atlakam* (*at-le-kim*), the treasures from the forest.

I have access to everything now, even here in Echo Bay. I'm in contact with my family via satellite, I speed around in my own motorboat, which I named *The Cadillac Fish*. I watch movies on my computer and listen to music by way of 12-volt batteries, though I still have no idea what day or time it is.

Micah moved in with me for several months during my first winter caretaking the fishing lodge. I will always have a special love for him, but I felt I needed to walk my own path, and with many tears he started a new life back east, in the city, where he has remained ever since. He wrote:

> *It's been nine years since Nikki and I stepped onto Village Island. It was one of the most amazing feelings I have ever had. A lifetime of dreams and years of preparation led to that moment, and it was only the beginning. I wish I could share with you the peace I felt on a February day in Booker Lagoon, when the sun broke the clouds and I had nothing to do but watch raindrops glisten on trees. But then, maybe everyone has their own Booker Lagoon. I sure hope so.*

> *When people ask me why I came back, I tell them I went to the woods because I didn't want to be a part of something I didn't believe in and that I came back when I realized I was a part of it whether I wanted to be or not. I couldn't watch idly as even the most beautiful places were destroyed for ink on paper. I've spent the years since returning trying to integrate back into society, but more importantly, trying to bring back what I learned and integrate that as well. It's been difficult. I have had to admit that I am virtually powerless*

*against the tenacity of the forces that drive us to destroy what we value most.
But I have found new hope in the people I have met along the way, people like
Nikki and me all over the world who have felt the tide of love and compassion
rising from within and all around us. I think about what the future could
be now, and less about the past. I find comfort in what I discovered out there,
though I probably knew it somewhere all along: that love has had fear out-
flanked since the beginning of time; it's just waiting for us all to call upon it.*

*Nikki taught me as much as anyone I have ever met. Even in those moments
when it felt like I was in a three-legged race with a cougar, I couldn't help but
be awed by her passion, and grateful for the chance to match strides with her.
Her courage and enthusiasm inspire me to this day. My dear friend, thanks
for the memories.*

With my adoption of a blue heeler puppy, Scout decided to move in with my
mom, leaving the wilderness behind forever. She loves her town life, with comfy
couches, cardboard boxes to play in, catnip toys to drool on, and all the treats
she can eat, and she much prefers hanging out with the local raccoons in North
Vancouver to the lurking cougars in Echo Bay. Though I miss wandering the forest with my little friend, she deserves the life she is now living.

The two most common questions I have been asked since my return are *Would you
do it again?* and *Could you have done it without Micah?* Absolutely. I think about
new, solo survival expeditions all the time. Micah was a stronger rower, could
carry heavier loads, and could chop wood faster, but he also had to consume more
calories. We had a perfect blend of strengths and weaknesses.

But although there were many times I wanted to survive alone, I'm glad it
didn't happen. Having a soul-friend to share such a journey was a blessing. I'm
glad my guardian angels helped set it all in motion.

I've learned that survival has little to do with one's physical capabilities. It's
more about the strength of our minds and our willingness to listen to our hearts,
whether in the wilderness or city. Micah and I didn't need each other for survival;
we had proved that to ourselves long before we met. We needed each other to
light our darkness. Our lives had come together to help us raise each other to a

After returning home, I adopted a blue heeler pup. My not-so-feral cat chose a plush city retirement over continued wilderness living.

higher spiritual place. Without him I would not have become the person I am today. Micah and I were meant to survive in the wilderness together. It is still a comfort for each of us to know the other is out there, living with our unique understanding of the world.

For years, I struggled to regain the true happiness and freedom I had felt living my wild ways. I had begun to think I'd never find it again, even living in the remote community of Echo Bay.

Then, in the winter of 2011, I had a traumatic experience and nearly died. It mimicked in many ways my dream with *Dzunukwa,* only this time my attacker was human. A barred owl's hoot saved my life, magically interrupting the attack and giving me a moment to escape. Although I survived, a short time later the hunt for me continued. This caused me to plummet into a darkness filled with

As a child I was mesmerized by the image of a wolf totem pole that I had seen in a guide book. It was a thrill to find the actual pole at Village Island.

fear and paranoia. I couldn't find my way out until, in a moment of calm grace, I was able to seek help. Two beautiful new human friends helped lead me back to who I am. Donn Smith's I AM Energy Program allowed me to rediscover my internal perfection, hidden beneath the toxic patterns I stored inside, thereby erasing my fears and limitations. What was once lost has now been found and more.

Nature reflects both dark and light aspects of the world. Each side offers us an opportunity to learn and grow. Both are blessings. Owls have swooped down on me, rattlesnakes have coiled to strike, a bear charged me, a humpback whale tipped my boat, and a mother elk snorted in my face, but frightening encounters will never keep me from city streets nor wild places. For each teddy-bear-hugging experience, I've encountered more than a hundred moments of pure bliss. A butterfly-filled oasis welcomed me in the desert, a deer sniffed my nose, thoughtful and timely gifts arrive from friends, a coyote trotted over my arm, a rufous hummingbird sat on my head, and two wolves walked over my legs.

Life is no longer complicated. It's based on my decisions to embrace Love or Fear. I choose to live in a state of unconditional, non-judgmental love, for perfect "goodness" is love. And when I shine as bright as I can, it gives permission for others to do the same.

I've since realized our journey is not about changing into the person we want to become; it's about letting go of all we are not. The saints and masters of the ages continue to remind us that we are all perfect beings of goodness. We create our own unique journeys of learning as we walk our path to divine wholeness. When we choose to live as our true selves, nothing is unattainable. In seeking "oneness with nature," I forgot we are also one with each other, and one with the universe.

With gratitude, I have now risen to an even higher place in my life. Once again my spirit feels the exaltation of being fully alive. I don't need Booker Lagoon anymore to feel true happiness and freedom. It's right inside me.

❦

I distinctly remember flipping through a guide book to British Columbia and finding a small photo of a wolf totem pole when I was ten years old. I promised myself I would one day see it in real life. I recently came across an old photograph of my favourite wolf totem pole at Village Island. It was the exact photo I had seen as a child.

THE UNIVERSE NEVER FORGETS OUR DREAMS

Remembering Jean Craighead George, author of *My Side of the Mountain*

My mother always tells me, "You never know what you do or say that will affect or change another."

When I returned from my survival trek, I wrote Jean Craighead George a thank-you letter. I told her of my adventures and the inspiration I received from her story of Sam Gribley.

She was thrilled to hear the two of us had lived the dream and wrote back, saying, "Now I can tell all the children who write me that someone has done it and so can they."

In 2012, shortly after Ms. George died, I received a card full of images from her award-winning books, including Sam's falcon Frightful, from her children. It read: "We found a wonderful CD and letter from you. Mom kept it on her desk. I thought you might like to know."

Wherever you are flying now, thank you, Ms. George.

ACKNOWLEDGEMENTS

My dream of survival would not have come true without the inspiration I received from the true survivors I've read about, the masters who have walked the earth, and all my furry, winged, green, and upright walking teachers leading me deeper into the natural world.

I give thanks to Chris Chisholm of Wolf Camp and all the instructors and students who touched my life there. Tom Brown and the Tracker School, Jon Young and the Wilderness Awareness School, Joel Hardin and his team at Professional Tracking Services, Frank and Karen Sherwood of Earthwalk Northwest, Anna Jefferson and the Lummi Indian College, Wes Gietz of Windwalker, Ray Rietze of Old Turtle, and all the other teachers who inspired and shared their knowledge with both Micah and I.

To the friends, tourists, and community of Echo Bay, we send big hugs to you all for treating us like family when we missed ours so much. Thank you Roger Laton, Tom Sewid, and of course, Billy Proctor who not only enriched our lives but who continues to set a beautiful example for me to follow in becoming a true friend. BP, you're the best!

I send much love to Micah's and my family, godparents, and friends, who have supported, accepted, inspired, challenged, loved, and set me free along my journey. Thanks for your patience and understanding when I disappear from contact. And to my little kitty who is no doubt curled up on a new pink bed looking out the sliding glass door I opened long ago to hear a talking tree. I miss you Scout.

CURIOUS RECIPES
AND POTIONS

Fungi Tapioca
Serves 2

1 large handful toothed jelly fungus
4 tbsp powdered milk
2 cups water

Cut clear fungus into tiny pieces. Stir powdered milk into pot of water. Add fungus and gently warm mixture over dying embers of a small fire. Serve warm. Garnish with a sprig of mint.

Chocolate-Seaweed Pudding
1 cup Turkish Towel or Rainbow Kelp
4 cups milk
2 packets of hot chocolate

Boil a large handful of seaweed in a covered pot with milk for 20 minutes. Remove blades. Stir in hot chocolate mix. Cool pudding in a slow-moving area of creek with the lid on.

Prawns and Rose Kelp Bottles
Serves 2

4 large kelp bulbs
20 prawns
1 cup of cooked rice
6 wild onions
3 palmfuls of de-seeded rosehips
4 tbsp rosehip syrup

Soak kelp bulbs for a day and a half, continually changing the fresh water. Boil water. Once roaring, drop prawns into pot and cook no more than 2 minutes.

Immediately place in cold water to stop further cooking.

Combine cooked rice, peeled prawns, onions, and rosehips. Stuff bulbs half full with mixture, then drizzle rosehip syrup inside bulb and continue filling rice mixture to top of bulb. Wrap bulb in green grass, fern fronds, or kelp blades and then cover with an inch of malleable clay. Bake in coals for 30 minutes to 1 hour, turning frequently. Serve when tender.

Nourishing and Tightening Face Mask
For 2

2 heaping handfuls of the largest gel-filled tips of bladderwrack seaweed (do not pull entire plant from its holdfast or it will kill the plant)
1½ cups of water

Pop tips with fingers and place in pot.
Add water.
Lightly boil seaweed for 5 minutes covered.
Remove lid and mash seaweed with a rock or wooden spoon. Continue simmering for several more minutes until mixture is gooey and light green in colour. Cool till mask can be handled.

Application: Rub gel onto face and leave on for 10 minutes. Rinse with warm water and pat dry.

Divine Body Rinse

15 cups of water
1 large handful of dried nettles
4 handfuls of crushed spruce tips
3 handfuls of cedar tips
2 handfuls of wild roses and several stems

In a large pot simmer nettles, spruce, cedar, and rose stems for 15 minutes. Add roses. Simmer 5 more minutes. Cool to desired temperature. Strain.

Application: Add to a bath water or use as a final shower rinse.

Nikki van Schyndel graduated from the Dominion Herbal College in British Columbia. She has studied with, and taught under some of North America's leading survivalists, trackers and primitive artisans. Nikki shares her love of storytelling and secrets of the natural world with guests of Echo Bay EcoVentures, her custom-tailored wilderness tour operation. She has gone from wild woman to forest dweller, now living in a log cabin that she built in the remote community of Echo Bay. Nikki continues to have unimaginable intimate encounters with the wildlife that captures our hearts and feeds our fears.